Praise for *Octavia Boulevard*

Yvonne Daley's *Octavia Boulevard*, for my money, ranks right up there with *Angela's Ashes* and *Eat, Pray, Love*. From Chinatown to Haight-Ashbury, Daley brings San Francisco to life in literature as no one has since the Beat Poets. Best of all is the marvelous apartment house on Octavia Boulevard, the "microcosm" and "small village" where Daley lived for several years with Wisdom Man, Stretch, Noel, Robin, Ann, Alexandra and a host of other unforgettable friends and neighbors, all of whom poured out their good hearts to this splendid writer. In the end, *Octavia Boulevard* is a story about community, family, friendship, and, in all its wondrous forms, love. -- Howard Frank Mosher, *Disappearances, Walking to Gatlinburg, North Country*.

Yvonne Daley is the only writer in America who could have drawn such an illuminating portrait of San Francisco in the Awful Age of Bush. She is the sharp-eyed and patient listener who's caught the soul of this remarkable city and its most resilient citizens. What Daley tracks in these pages is how and why America began dreaming of Obama long before it knew who he was. *Octavia Boulevard* may break your heart, but it also offers some street-smart hope. -- David Huddle, *The Story of a Million Years, La Tour Dreams of the Wolf Girl, Tenorman, Glory Days*.

Octavia Boulevard is a microcosm of San Francisco, San Francisco a paradigm of cities. *Octavia Boulevard* offers a reader experience of the plenitude and disorder that is humanity's creation (*ex nihilo*, in its own image) of the urban planet with its joyous and disturbing interpenetration of pains and pleasures trying to fill the endlessly unfulfillable gut of human hungers. -- Tom Smith, *Spending the Light, Jack's Beans: A Five-Year Diary, A Very Good Boy*.

OCTAVIA BOULEVARD

To Natacha, here's to independence

A Memoir of

Excess, Friendship & Homelessness

In America's Most Self-Indulgent City

Yvonne Daley

YVONNE DALEY

Verdant Books

Rutland, Vermont & San Francisco

Octavia Boulevard

A Memoir of Excess, Friendship & Homelessness
In America's Most Self-Indulgent City

©2011 Yvonne Daley
ISBN Number 978-0-615-43933-4

Front cover, photo and design: Rebecca Kmiec
Back cover, design: Debbi Wraga; photo: Chuck Clarino
Inside photos: Chuck Clarino and Yvonne Daley
Author photo: Ron Powers

Also by Yvonne Daley

An Independent Man, co-authored with Senator James Jeffords

Vermont Writers: A State of Mind

NORTHSHIRE BOOKSTORE

Building Community, One Book at a Time
This book was printed by the Northshire Bookstore, a family-owned, independent bookstore in Manchester Ctr., Vermont, since 1976. We are committed to excellence in bookselling. The Northshire Bookstore's mission is to serve as a resource for information, ideas, and entertainment while honoring the needs of customers, staff, and community.

Printed in the United States of America
using an Espresso Book Machine
from On Demand Books

To Jul & Mary
who brought us together
To Gordon
who knew our dirt
To Ann & Alexandra
who made us family
To Jack
who cleaned our streets
To Robin
who had a good heart
To Wisdom Man & Silent Guy & Jay
who made my mornings
To Stretch
who kept me humble
To Daniel
who kept me sane
To Chuck
who understood

Foreword

A million years ago, I was a girl walking somewhere on Boston's Beacon Hill, Charles Street maybe. Actually, it was 1966, which only seems like a million years ago. My girlfriends and I had rented a railroad apartment on the corner of Myrtle and Joy. This was just a few months after my boyfriend was killed in the Vietnam War and I was still in that place after a close death when everything is laden with significance. Furtively, Bob Dylan's voice infiltrated my sorrow, intoning "Hey, Mister Tambourine Man, play a song for me." His song had become a kind of mantra that summer, laced as it was with its improbable mix of weary fatalism and blind trust in what we so naively called the universe. Despite the war, despite the deaths, or perhaps because of war and death, I clung to a precious drop of hope for the future, a speck of trust. That's why I opened the door to the building from which Dylan's voice leaked like wind spilling from a jar, walked into a stranger's apartment, sat cross-legged in front of his stereo until the end of the song, and later that day or the next made plans to head west in search of Mister Tambourine Man and the dream he was peddling.

Patrick and Susan, who were connected back then and therefore would know, said there actually was a Tambourine Man who'd inspired Dylan's song. He appeared in countless locations that year, playing a flute, telling stories of the road and the kindness of strangers. Or so the story went; everyone had a version. Who was he? The wanderer. The Pied Piper. The vagabond. What was he selling? Freedom. Love. Where was he? The rumors abounded but as far as any of us were concerned the place of enchantment, the point of possibility, the home of reinvention was San Francisco.

I followed him there after that summer in Boston or followed the myth he embodied, chasing my own vague traces of skipping reels of rhyme, one among thousands heading west in search of something we couldn't quite articulate, some form of grace that might protect us, not just from having to fight in a foreign country but from a way of life that, among so many other wrong-headed ideas, justified the sacrifice of young people in the name of democracy and honored money over most everything else. We wanted something more out of life, a cause beyond the causes of our parents. Not capital or country, but the cause of the human, the planet, the universe. Or so we said.

Life brought me back east quickly enough, but forty years later I returned to that magical city, a middle-aged woman seeking again some intangible dream in San Francisco. It had something to do with the state of the world in the Bush years – America in trouble; the prison count; war in other people's countries, those old familiar themes, but different now because I felt my generation had failed as much as our parents', maybe more so. We had been so eager to shatter the prudent world they had constructed from the ruins of their war, so keen to alter the politics of the kitchen, the dynamics of suburbia, the rules of the bedroom, to give peace a chance. We were quite good at that, at demolishing our parents' version of propriety, at conjuring catchy phrases. We thought we could do better. Had we?

What better place to ask that question, to look for Mister Tambourine Man, than San Francisco, where every day progressive politics bumped up against capitalism, that old enemy now so generously embraced; where you could still hear the songs of the lost and of the found, the damned and the hopeful. I added my tune to the mix, left a good job in the country and, using the skills of the journalism profession I'd honed in the intervening years, began cataloguing what I found in San Francisco. Here it is, a journalist's journal: the underbelly, the sublime, hopeful and heartless, flawed as its creator and recorder, my story, our story, that is.

PART ONE
2003-2004

No, said the Hobo, No more tales of time;
Don't ask me now to wash away the grime;
I can't come in 'cause it's too high a climb,
And he walked away from my fleeting house.
                    Tim Buckley, "Morning Glory"

I'd wasted a week looking at potential apartments and eliminating them. Too expensive, too dirty, too small, too lecherous a landlord, with several falling into more than one category, such as that last offering, advertised as having a "quintessential San Francisco view," which it did when you sat on the toilet. Otherwise, its "turn of the century" amenities included a narrow, three-story staircase, an antediluvian kitchen and no closets. A steal at $1950 a month. Still, thirty-three potential tenants applied in the time it took me to get in and out.

The last place on my list held promise. It was located just off Market Street, San Francisco's real main street, and within walking distance of the Castro, the Mission, Haight-Ashbury, Hayes Valley and the Civic Center, some of the city's most entertaining neighborhoods. It was also close to public transportation, a plus as I sure couldn't afford to live in San Francisco *and* own a car. I was early for my appointment, and hungry, so when I spied a little Italian place on Castro Street I decided to pass the time over coffee and a sandwich. As I was maneuvering through tables filled with tattooed young men in muscle-shirts and real estate agents in Wilkes-Bashford suits murmuring about body waxes and Bukowski's poems over their lattes and lunch-hour merlots, a woman reached out a hand.

"Did you know her?" she asked, pointing to the Angela Davis for Vice President button attached to the strap of my backpack. The woman was middle-aged with earnest brown eyes and long white hair, hanging like silken drapes on either side of her face, a fashion reminiscent of the Sixties. Back then, white girls had the drapes; black girls had the Afro. I wanted a 'fro, but my hair, it couldn't do it. Angela Davis, now, she had an important Afro.

I didn't say any of that of course, standing there with tray in hand, but rather mumbled something about finding the old campaign pin in my closet when I was packing for San Francisco. Then I offered the sentence that caused the rest of this tale to happen, "Maybe it reminded me of the time when people did something with their beliefs."

"What do you do with your beliefs?" she asked without hesitation.

Before I had to actually respond, the woman's husband emerged from the men's room and she pointed out my pin to him. The man was gray of hair and pale of skin, tall with rough hands and long, muscular arms encased in a well-worn T-shirt, giving the impression he might work as a day laborer. He quickly pulled their table next to mine and took over the conversation, launching into a rambling soliloquy about Angela Davis as if he'd written a thesis about her between jobs and had been awaiting the opportunity to present his theories on her significance.

It was delightfully odd. One moment I was thinking how ridiculously expensive living in San Francisco was going to be and the next I was chatting it up with perfect strangers and the subject of our discussion was Angela Davis, a well-known commodity as a radical member of the Black Panthers back in the day but someone I hadn't thought much about until her campaign pin appeared in the back of the closet of my Vermont home. I'd just chuckled when I found it there and without much thought pinned it onto the backpack I'd also unearthed from the closet's depths. In the years since I had bought/found/been given the pin – I had no recall whatsoever – Angela Davis had pretty much disappeared from the common lexicon. Not from the mental glossary of the man at the next table, however.

"Did you know Angela Davis was the daughter of an auto mechanic and school teacher from Birmingham?" he asked, focusing metal blue eyes on me. He spoke quite formally and with a particular inflection, pausing often to chew his food. "Angela Davis represents the American dream – living as a political and social radical, listed on the FBI's most wanted list, winning her freedom …" Long pause. Chewing and more chewing on his grilled eggplant on focaccia before resuming, "… running as the Communist party's candidate for vice president and getting an honorary degree from Moscow University. And now …" Another pause, more chewing. "Now I think she works as a college professor or at least she did last I checked." The man's Adam's apple yo-yoed for a couple of seconds before he finished the thought. "A radical, of course, no one I would support but living proof the American Dream is alive and well."

"Alive and well? You must be dreaming," I snorted. Then, regretting my ill manners, added, "I don't know how she sees it but wasn't Angela Davis one of the few of those Panthers to get out alive? What were their demands? Land, Bread, Housing, Education, Clothing, Justice, Peace – the American dream, right?"

The man had taken out rather large, black-framed glasses to read the menu and peered over them scornfully. "Oh, you must be one of those fans of affirmative action," he said. "Affirmative action certainly served a purpose. But race is no longer an issue in America. Gender is no longer an issue in America." He roughed the hair on his upper arms, swallowed deeply while I waited for him to finish his thought. "At least not here in San Francisco. Here, you're better off to be a member of some minority or a woman, better yet gay or lesbian *and* black."

I'd like to believe the man was right, that anyone could make it on the power of hard work and determination, the old Horatio Alger idea, regardless of race or gender. However, I had concluded long before that success in life – not material success but rather satisfaction or at least a sense of accomplishment – required talent and determination and hard work, for sure, but also luck and circumstance and so many other factors both within and outside each person's control that success was pretty much a crap shoot. I wanted to argue for the downtrodden, the unlucky, the disenfranchised, screwed from the start due to the color of their skin, place of birth or gender identification, screwed despite talent and determination.

I was tempted to introduce myself, to point out that Angela Davis's middle name was my first name, Yvonne, and that she had taught at San Francisco State University where I was now a professor, which was why I'd been delighted to find her campaign pin, and to ask where his interest came from. But I needed to get to my appointment so I simply laughed and let him have the final word.

Still, as I stepped into the sunlight of San Francisco's Castro District, a place where people had permanently altered society's rules, I had to laugh. I sure wouldn't have had a conversation like that with an absolute stranger in Rutland, Vermont. Yes, Rutland. That was the unfortunate name of the Vermont city I had just left and would return to during the months between semesters. I was about to begin the latest chapter in the bi-coastal life that I'd forged a few years previously after working as a journalist in Vermont for twenty years and raising my kids there. Rutland, Vermont, and San Francisco, California. Quite a contrast I thought as I trudged down Market Street and turned up Octavia toward the apartment for rent.

$

I found the front gate leading to the rental unit propped open, stepped inside tentatively and peered down a long hallway. I was about to ring the bell, when the white-haired woman from the Castro restaurant, the wife of the loquacious man with whom I'd just debated what one might consider the big questions of the age, opened a door at the end of the hall and squinted back at me. Mary and I shared a good laugh about our serendipitous meeting. Her husband, he of the big hands and long pauses, was named Jul. (You pronounced it Yule, as in the log.) He was off getting supplies, she explained, undoubtedly having provocative conversations in hardware stores, plumbing suppliers or wherever he might be. "He gets waylaid easily," she said.

From the outside, the building had looked less than promising. Layers of fusty gray paint obscured its Victorian lineage and a row of ficus trees on the far edge of the sidewalk had grown so unruly that their top branches covered the third and fourth-story windows. One side of the street was lined with similar buildings, handsome relics showing decades of neglect, while a rusty, broken-down fence surrounded a wide expanse of clumpy soil, weeds and debris on the other side of the street. Mary explained that the rubble was left over from the demolition of a double-decker elevated freeway that had long cloaked the neighborhood in shadow. The freeway had been damaged in the Loma Prieta earthquake in 1989, fourteen years before my arrival, but the buildings had survived with little to no damage.

The ad on craigslist said the apartment house was built in 1904, meaning it had also survived the great San Francisco earthquake and fires of 1906. Indeed, Octavia Street marks the fire line where buildings were leveled to stop that inferno from raging through the city.

The coved ceilings in what I was already considering my apartment were ten feet high; ornate medallions held handsome art deco light fixtures that Jul had hunted down and installed. The floors were oak accented with black walnut chevrons. The bathroom had a claw-foot tub, the original, as was the marble sink, tile walls and Majolica floor, all in remarkable condition. The apartment had been freshly painted in calm, creamy colors. It was lovely. It was big. The rent was $1750 a month, the outside amount I could afford and ridiculously expensive by Vermont standards or standards that apply to most anywhere else in the country, but reasonable for a two-bedroom apartment in San Francisco. I rationalized the cost by the fact that I could do everything I needed on foot or on Muni, the city's transportation system of busses, trains and trolleys.

The apartment was also attractive to other prospective tenants, however, dot-com couples who arrived armed with their credit reports and resumes. I hung around as the interlopers made their personal sales pitches. I listened as Mary told each there could be lead paint in the building; that there could be asbestos residue in the basement; that there would be disruption out front while the city built something she referred to as Octavia Boulevard, a replacement for the damaged elevated freeway. The construction would take at least a year, she warned, but when it was completed a Parisian-style boulevard, a showplace of American ingenuity, would replace the old street and freeway. Unbeknownst to me, entrepreneurs were grabbing up available properties in the neighborhood in anticipation of this being the next hot spot in San Francisco. It was precisely that promise that had led Jul to buy the building and that had lured the throng of would-be tenants.

I need not have worried. "Wait till I tell Jul the woman with the Angela Davis pin showed up to rent the apartment," Mary said. "He'll love that." She knew better than to rent to anyone without Jul's approval. It being a Saturday, I would have to wait until Monday for Jul to complete a credit and reference check. An hour later, however, after I had canvassed the neighborhood, meandering toward Hayes Valley and avoiding the men sprawled asleep at the corner of Haight Street, my cell phone rang. It was Jul back from his errands. "I'll just check your references and get back to you in a day or two," he promised.

Several hours later, as I was making my way on the Muni N-line across the city to my niece Bonnie's home in the Sunset District, Jul called again. He'd looked me up on Google. He'd read some of my news stories. Would I talk to him later about the piece I'd written about Chief Justice Renquist and the covenant on his Vermont property? And Solzhenitsyn? Had I really met the great Russian author? While I was thinking about the extent of his Google search and what that suggested about the man, he said he'd also confirmed that I was a legitimate university professor. I wouldn't need a credit report, my history impressing him more than it should have.

After I signed the lease, Jul and I had our second heated discussion. When I subsequently referred to it as an argument, he corrected me. Jul didn't argue. He had "discussions." It had begun with my lament about the homeless men I'd encountered in the neighborhood. We were eating at Pasta Pomodoro in the

Castro. "Don't expect me to be sympathetic about the vagrants and the drug addicts in this city," he said coolly over his beer, served in a room temperature glass, the way he liked it, having sent a frosted glass back. "Politically, I consider myself a greater-good libertarian, a radical centrist. Social mechanisms that work intelligently should be utilized only as long as they do what they were intended to do, not followed blindly without constant review of their usefulness. This city runs on a deficit, has a chronic homeless problem and ridiculously high rents because of wrong-headed legislation that seemed humane and moral at the time but, as often as not, only made problems worse. I'm a temporary liberal. While this war is on, I'm doing all I can to get Bush out of the White House."

The conversation quickly segued to presidential primary candidate Howard Dean. "You covered Dean when he was Vermont governor, Yvonne," he said, creeping me out a little. How extensive had his Internet search been, anyhow?

"Dean and I, we are simpatico," he said with pride. "Under Dean, Vermont had a balanced budget eleven times. Dean lowered state income taxes twice and signed the first civil-union law in the country. We operate similarly."

I realized there was a reason I had been chosen over the other prospective tenants. Jul and Mary, I suspected, were people collectors. Having me in their building might provide ample opportunity for weighty "discussions." I had already observed that Jul liked to ask for your esteemed opinion about something and then argue against whatever you professed. It might be a form of mental calisthenics for him. His Adam's apple was muscular like his arms. When he held forth, he'd take a big swallow, jut out his chin, and let it bobble up and down while you waited for him to finish his thought. It was the distinctive way he articulated u's that had made me think he was European. He pronounced them like double o's as in the word goon. Somehow Jul arranged for the sentences he culled from his brain to include as many words with the letter u in them as possible. Either that or I had never noticed how many words contain a u. Or double e's. He said the word been the British way, as if it were the word bean. I oonderstand you've bean living on the opposite coast, he might have said, as we sipped wine and ate pasta and sautéed spinach, a Jul favorite.

As I was to learn, Jul had an opinion about most everything and, if it turned out that you knew a bit more than he did on a certain subject, he'd be sure to make up for that in a day or two, devouring books, websites and DVDs on the subject until he considered himself something of an expert and then he would engage you in a discussion that would provide ample opportunity for him to opine. He liked that word. I wondered how he did all this and managed to care for a twelve-unit building and, as I learned within days of meeting him, launch humorous get-rich schemes, drive his motorcycles around the country, study economics, politics and health, and torment Mary with constant suggestions about diet and exercise. I was just beginning to understand all this as I sipped the wine he ordered that night – not the pinot noir I'd suggested, but something more robust, more to Jul's liking, even though I was the only one drinking wine – and deliberated with him the responsibilities of a civilized society, deinstitutionalization, the causes of addiction and a bunch of other subjects that clearly I knew little about. But I would. My education was about to begin, there on Octavia Boulevard.

Actually, the name Octavia Boulevard was just a pleasant term that Jul and Mary, the redevelopers, the City Hall mucky-mucks and the real estate agents used optimistically when referring to the planned refashioning of Octavia Street. City residents and supervisors had debated how to manage cross-city traffic for more than a decade after the Loma Prieta earthquake, finally deciding to replace the double-decker freeway along the four blocks of Octavia Street that ran from Market to Hayes, passing my building, with a four-lane Parisian style boulevard for through traffic, bordered by narrow, one-way streets for local traffic. The architectural drawing of the boulevard on the city's website showed a grove of palm trees and traffic island on one end and a public green at the other, with mini-parks lined with trees between each lane. For now, however, the street I lived on was plain old Octavia Street, a place that hadn't had much luck other than surviving the two earthquakes.

Myth had the street named for Octavia, the female form of the Roman Octavius, which means "the eighth," because it was the eighth street back from Divisadero, a former dividing line between the city and the undeveloped land beyond. More likely, it was named for Octavia Gough, the sister of a city alderman who had helped establish traffic routes and name new streets in the 1850s and '60s. Even then, San Francisco was a city of neighborhoods, but for some reason the lower end of Octavia where I lived and the surrounding blocks had never coalesced into a distinctive district. In my first few days there I literally walked in a circular pattern from one nearby neighborhood to another, gaining a superficial understanding of each one's idiosyncratic character. Walking south to Market then turning west, I'd quickly come to the Castro, once an Irish enclave but since the late 1960s home to San Francisco's gay community, showily announced with an immense rainbow flag that unfurled above Market Street a dozen or so blocks from my apartment. I loved the swish and roll, the strut of the Castro. Sex was always in the Castro air, not to mention equal doses of kitsch and tastefulness. One trip to Cliff's Hardware gave kitchen gadgets new meaning and the young sweeties who advertised for Hot Cookie bakery did so in very brief briefs, no matter the weather.

South of my neighborhood, a fifteen-minute walk led to the Mission, the city's sunniest district. After shivering through Vermont's six-month winters for years, the Mission was candy to my senses. Its streets were lined with taco stands and fruit and vegetable stalls with all their accompanying smells, mostly delectable, although the sidewalks were filthy. Dollar stores sold candles in clear glass holders decorated with images of Michael the Archangel, Our Lady of Guadalupe and Anima Sola while women sold homemade tacos on the sidewalk, cheap and delicious, authentic. In the midst of all this Latin food and culture, I would sample one after another exotically flavored delicacy at Bombay Ice Creamery – rose petal, fig, saffron pistachio – before settling on one scoop of cardamom and one of coconut.

Four blocks north from the apartment building, Octavia Ts into Hayes Street, the main artery of a neighborhood called Hayes Valley. Hayes Street was lined with chichi stores displaying over-priced designer clothing, eyeglasses, underwear and shoes, but it contained unpretentious elements as well. One afternoon, I chatted with two homeless men who routinely hung a tin can from a fishing pole for donations. They were stationed near Marlena's nightclub, where the Sunday evening drag show featured Marlena herself, a city icon known as Empress XXV, the reigning queen of Hayes Valley, singing show tunes and wearing her various wigs, jewels and other extravagances on the bar's corner stage. Jul brought me to see her as part of my education in all things San Francisco a few nights after my arrival, but I found myself outside talking again to the homeless duo, whose stories of life before and after the freeway came down made me realize how dicey my neighborhood had been in its not-so-distant past. Even recently, the men had become local heroes after they interrupted three car break-ins in one weekend. For weeks, their cups and cans overflowed.

Street artists roamed the city at night, leaving their messages on sidewalks, like this one, which I passed on my first thorough canvassing of the neighborhood.

One block uphill from my house, the lower Haight was a confusing blend of blocky public housing buildings and glorious Victorian mansions broken up into apartments. Beyond, further up the hill, was the real Haight-Ashbury, birthplace of the counter-culture. I was saving that for later.

Facing east, I could literally stand on my doorstep and see the gilded dome of San Francisco's City Hall in the nearby Civic Center. The way there, unfortunately, was a no-man's land of boarded-up buildings, struggling businesses and single-residence hotels surrounding over-priced restaurants, condos for the wealthy, and lots of wine bars. Civic Center Plaza should have been the city's showplace, not only because Mayor Willie Brown had spent millions fixing up City Hall, gilding its domed roof at a cost of $64 million a few years previously, but also because the area encompassed an opera house, symphony hall, the city's main library and the UN Plaza where the documents creating the United Nations had been signed in 1945. Despite these elements, addicts and other unfortunate souls traded drugs and diseases there, hassling tourists on their way to the ballet and ignored by the government wonks on their way to and from work.

And I was plunked down right in the middle of it all.

I awoke to the sound of "Swing Low Sweet Chariot" streaming through the half-open bedroom window. The music was coming from the Baptist Church next door, a beautiful old building with a neon sign along its side that pulsed B-A-P-T-I-S-T, red and blue, red and blue, all night long. A white neon crucifix was affixed to the church's golden dome. Altogether, a study in mixed metaphors.

A large, trapezoidal building painted turquoise and magenta enveloped the corners of Market, Waller and Octavia streets, just below the church. It was the headquarters for the Lesbian Gay Bisexual Transgender Community Center. The previous night as I'd struggled past the building, laden down by the necessities of the larder, my attention had been drawn to a karate class underway behind the LGBT center's floor-to-ceiling windows. Teenagers practiced karate chops while I read the signs in the center's windows, offerings such as, "Young? Queer? Hang Out Here."

A Bible meeting had just broken up and I crossed Waller and made my way through a crowd of black families in church finery, an ancient white man clutching his Bible reverentially, and a trio of women with Patty LaBelle hairdos looking warily at two homeless men who sat on the furthest steps, a bit put out that their sidewalk had been invaded by the church-goers. The men had arrayed wine bottles on the sidewalk and parked a grocery cart burdened with sleeping bags and empty bottles a few yards away. As I passed, one of the men leapt to his feet and tipped a non-existent hat. "Evening," he said, "The neighborhood's really jumping tonight."

The image of the men on the sidewalk came back to me whole as I lay in my bed with the sounds of Sunday morning church music and parishioners greeting one another filling my bedroom. I couldn't help but think of all these lives unfolding within a few yards of a single city property, the children practicing their karate at the Lesbian Gay Bisexual Transgender Community Center, the homeless men perched on the church steps, the Baptist parishioners spilling onto the sidewalk fresh from their Bible meeting. I belonged to none of these worlds that surrounded me. And yet, as I padded off to the bathroom for the morning ritual before venturing out to the street, I felt deeply that I would find some part of myself there, that Octavia Street or Boulevard, whatever they would call it, would someday feel like home.

It didn't take long for Gordon and me to bump skulls. He would open the front and basement doors to our apartment building so the wind that blustered down Octavia Street swept a typhoon of dust devils into our building. Up in the hothouse of Gordon's apartment on the third floor, fresh air was welcome as money; where I lived at the end of the first-floor hall, it was a mechanism for bringing the swag of the city into my apartment. Gordon believed in airing out the entire building regularly, something he'd been doing for the thirty or more years that he had lived there. And so, he would prop the doors open and I'd shut them. He'd re-open them. I'd close them. And so on.

Gordon also had a thing about his whites, especially his undies; he washed them once in bleach water, more bleach than water, or at least it smelled that way, chlorine smacking you in the face as you walked into the building. He'd wash them again with fresh water and detergent. He had other unusual laundry habits, habits that exhibited themselves in diligent monitoring of the dryers, fussiness over the proper hanging of shirts and pants and, even on days when he did no laundry, a careful wiping down of appliances and frequent washing of the laundry room floor.

Gordon had seen dozens of tenants come and go. Their bad habits had certainly impacted his welfare many times, which was why I brought up the trash bags I kept finding on the landing leading to the basement. Since Gordon had been so fastidious with the laundry room, I hoped he'd speak to whoever left their trash on the landing. Instead, Gordon informed me that the trash came from Mae West, the eighty-something-year-old blind woman who lived on the second floor, and that she was doing as much as she could to get it that far.

"That's her real name?" I asked.

"She's the building's project," he said, ignoring my question.

Garbage equals bugs and one reason I'd rented in this building was the apartment's cleanliness. Of course, when you rent in a multi-unit building located in one of the sketchier parts of town, you have no control over the cleanliness, or lack thereof, of others. "I bring Mae's trash to the basement as soon as I see it,"

Gordon said. "You can bring it down before I get to it if it bothers you so much. That would be nice."

It would be nice, I supposed, to help an old blind lady but couldn't we put a receptacle there for her trash?

Gordon's voice suggested I had no commonsense whatsoever. "Do that and Jul will know we let Mae leave her trash there and he'll put an end to that." His pale skin had a sheen of scrubbed cleanliness. He was folding sheets into uniform rectangles, so crisp they could have been fresh from the box. Maybe he'd like to do my laundry. Responding to my unspoken fancy, Gordon laughed and said, "Just like the Bible says, cleanliness is next to godliness."

"Right," I said. "That's why I don't want bags of trash left on the staircase."

"Now, you aren't gonna be like those other tenants who move in here and try to run the place, change how we been doing things here for years, are you? You're not one of those kind of people, are you?"

The most dramatic impact on my neighborhood since the earthquake of 1906 was one that had been imposed on cities across the country, beginning in the 1950s, in the name of progress and homage to America's obsession with the car. In the mid-1950s, the first spur of a double-decker freeway was built as part of a more extensive plan for looping traffic around downtown San Francisco. Called the Central Freeway, this elevated freeway cut an ugly wedge through the city's southern neighborhoods then crossed Market Street and traversed overhead down Octavia past my building. From there, the freeway met on and off ramps at Fell and Oak streets, which led to and from Golden Gate Park.

That freeway had cast its shadow on the homes along the four blocks of Octavia for more than thirty years. Exhaust fumes and road trash rained down from above while an assemblage of the city's underlife did business beneath the freeway's metal girders: pimps and their men and women; drug dealers and those who used drugs; vagrants and those who served the needs of the vagrants. Yanni, who ran the dry-cleaner shop around the corner, knew a man who'd parked his car on Octavia one night while he slept it off in a friend's apartment and woke to find the frame and not much else remaining. "He was lucky," Yanni said. "If he'd slept in that car, he might not have woken up at all."

The Central Freeway was one in a network of superhighways intended for San Francisco, similar to projects that had annihilated whole neighborhoods in New York and Los Angeles. In San Francisco, freeway proponents planned more than a half-dozen highways that would have crosshatched the city, sliced through the Haight and Golden Gate Park, tunneled under Russian Hill, and blocked the city's stunning waterfront from view. This being San Francisco, however, a group of citizens who called themselves the Freeway Revolutionaries organized rallies and neighborhood meetings to fight these various proposals. In 1959, they presented the city supervisors with a petition protesting the freeway plans signed by more than 30,000 residents. The supervisors ultimately heard their protests and cancelled the bulk of these proposals even though that meant turning down millions in federal and state funding. Their success came too late for portions of freeways already built – the one along Octavia and another along the waterfront.

All that changed at 5:04 the night of Oct. 17, 1989 while two-thirds of the TV-watching public was tuned to the World Series played by two Bay Area teams, the Oakland A's and the San Francisco Giants. An earthquake measuring 6.9 on the Richter scale shook the city for fifteen seconds. Those double-decker freeways and ramps heaved and buckled. Both the Embarcadero and Central freeways needed sections repaired. The first to go was the Embarcadero along San Francisco Bay, removed between 1990 and 1993. The wide multi-lane roadway that replaced it now wends gracefully along the waterfront, providing a stunning view of the Bay Bridge and the Oakland hills beyond. Removal of the Embarcadero freeway led to the restoration of the Ferry Building, construction of AT&T Park and the budding of the Mission Bay neighborhood. And with its removal as their model, the Freeway Revolutionaries brought their energies to bear on the proposal to rebuild the Central Freeway where it sat partially demolished along Octavia. After three ballot measures, in 1997, 1998 and 1999, city voters overwhelmingly backed the idea of a boulevard modeled after the thoroughfares of Paris, rather than rebuilding the double-decker freeway and its ramps. The Freeway Revolutionaries were too late to stop the reconstruction of the Central Freeway south of Market, although their efforts made that project's impact on neighborhoods less damaging. That project would begin soon, culminating with a single-deck ramp that would dump traffic onto Market Street at Octavia, just three blocks from my building.

But that was a different story. Mine would encompass another moment of history. The city of San Francisco, as it had so many times before, was about to go against the flow once again by building a radically different sort of roadway, the first of its kind in a major American city in more than forty years. But as with much of what occurred in San Francisco, the project contained a heavy dose of the practical and the unconventional. The plan called for more than four hundred trees to be planted in median strips along the boulevard's four blocks to shield residential and commercial buildings from noise and exhaust. Short benches perfect for a quick rest but not long enough to actually recline upon would be situated along the boulevard. And just for fun, kaleidoscopes designed by an artist and inscribed with haikus were to be installed at major intersections along the boulevard for pedestrians' entertainment. I could only imagine describing all this back in Vermont: San Francisco at its best and most self-indulgent. Jul said the construction was scheduled to begin in a year, but a year is a year. Anything can happen. After all, 1959, the year the Freeway Revolutionaries convinced the city to rethink its freeway construction projects, was also the year that Alan Ginsberg had published his poem, *Lysergic Acid*.

Ann lived above me in number 6. Among the reasons Jul had chosen her as a tenant were these: she was fluent in Russian, she played classical piano, and her father had served as the shrink for half the murderers in recent California history, or something like that, I could never get the story quite right. Jul figured that combo could only ensure interesting conversations. I would have chosen her for other reasons. Ann was nice, really nice, and funny. And generous. And warm. I knew from the moment I met her we would be friends. Her politics were right. She was totally unapologetic about her love of trash food and trash TV. She wasn't concerned about letting anyone see her in her green and blue plaid fleece robe, which didn't quite cover all of her. Ann had the most gorgeous Vietnamese daughter, about 15 months old when I met them. Alexandra's crescent-shaped eyes were so dark you could see yourself in them. Her skin reminded me of amber maple syrup, of burnished wood, of caramel sauce. In the evenings, as we traded histories and watched whatever Ann had on the TV, one of us would say of

Alexandra, "She's all cheek," meaning everything about her was plump and rolled and perfect.

Here was their short story: After attempting to adopt a baby from China, Ann had given up and traveled twice to Vietnam, where the authorities were less strict than the Chinese about foreign adoptions by single parents. On her second trip to Vietnam, Ann brought the baby, then four months old, home to San Francisco. She knew nothing of Alexandra's parents. Ann had been married briefly; she didn't talk about the ex-husband other than to say the marriage was a disaster. I admired that she had wanted a family, didn't get one out of the marriage, and decided to just make her own.

Of course, as a single mother living in San Francisco, Ann had to juggle a bunch of jobs. Among them was her work raising money for non-profits, one after another goodwill cause. She wrote grants for nuns who took in recovering prostitutes and she managed the affairs of a bitchy millionaire who clothed low-income women while treating her own staff like shit. Each project made for fascinating conversation and opened up my understanding of the city's underpinning of social agencies and non-profits and do-good organizations. Jul would say it was the existence of those agencies that attracted so many vagrants to San Francisco. Ann, with her liberal education and democratic upbringing, would argue that it didn't matter where the needy came from, that if there were a need someone should attend to it.

This extended to her own needs. As a single mother, she expected the other adults in her life, including the people living in our building, to be part of Alexandra's rearing. As unapologetic as she was about her love of trash food and trash TV, Ann felt no embarrassment asking for help carrying groceries and a toddler upstairs, soliciting babysitting from the more reliable residents of the building, or expecting us to treat Alexandra as one of our own. Of course, we willingly obliged.

Ann had a speaking habit almost as singular as Jul's. She elongated the last syllable of the last word in almost every sentence she spoke and her voice went up a key, as if she were asking a question. Oddly enough, it was a speech pattern that I associated with both New York and the Valley Girls of the San Fernando Valley. It's one of my most unlikable traits, being annoyed by other people's quirks of speech and accents when I hadn't shed my Boston accent (even though I haven't lived there in decades) or my tendency to interrupt, out-argue, gloat or preach. Ann with her big heart liked me anyhow.

Ann knocked on my door just days after I moved in, bearing two lattes and store-bought cookies, which we promptly devoured. The baby was shy and sweet, better than cookies. We sat her on the couch, silent and watching as I heard the story of how Ann had come to be a mother and I told her about my brood of children and husband back home, how I had arranged my bicoastal life. I told her how I spent my summers and winter break ensconced in my Vermont life with my husband Chuck, that I had four kids and six grandchildren, who all lived close by, that he worked as a sportswriter in Vermont most of the year, but would travel to San Francisco for months at a time when money and schedule allowed. She was the first person I'd met who didn't think my decision to live more than half the year away from my husband and family was nuts or selfish. She understood that love does not mean ownership.

"I need a dog," I confided to Ann that first day. It wasn't that I minded being alone. After raising my big family, I liked the quiet and order of my single life. And, as anyone long married could relate, a little distance can be a good thing. But when bad things happened or the news was particularly depressing, when the war deaths piled up or the man splayed across the sidewalk looked like he too might be dead, when the Cascade Mountains were on fire or someone spat on you on the bus, a dog would offer some relief. Besides, it would be nice to be welcomed home by something other than the correspondents on National Public Radio.

I didn't have such a need for comfort before that 9/11 morning when Chuck phoned and said to turn on the TV. At moments like that, when human frailty and strength were challenged, when the human propensity for monstrous acts was overwhelming, when solutions seemed impossible, you needed to be with the really important people in your life. I was living in Palo Alto then, about forty miles from San Francisco, in a sweet apartment near Stanford University and commuting into the southern end of San Francisco where San Francisco State University is located. Toward the end of the school year, I was awarded the next year off from teaching to work on a book about Vermont's literary history. Rather than pay rent or sublet, I gave up my Stanford apartment and returned to Vermont for the year. I also decided that I would live in San Francisco upon my return to the West Coast, to immerse myself in the city rather than be only peripherally connected to it and the subjects that I taught.

When my research was completed, Chuck and I rented a lovely villa owned by a colleague in Provence for a few months. The house was in the town of Carcès, an adorable village in the Var. Our habit there was to spend the morning writing over coffee and pastries, and then pass the afternoon exploring the mountaintop villages located a short drive from our temporary home. The threat of war was in the air and we marched in several demonstrations with others who thought there were better responses to 9/11 than more killing. We were in Aix-en-Provence the day the Iraq war began. Chuck was in a busy bar paying the bill while I waited outside when a local fellow grabbed him and yelled in broken English, "Bush, bomb." Chuck thought the man was saying, "Bush, bum," so he just nodded in agreement and chuckled, but the man's insistence made him turn his gaze to the TV above the bar. Chuck was glad he had worn his peace socks that day. He pulled his pants up to show the man the universal symbol for peace stitched along the top of the stocking and, in his broken French, tried to tell the men in the bar about the Americans who did not support the war. Still, he felt the man's disapproval.

After that, we stayed closer to home. We ate in at night, then drank absinthe and cried while we watched the war unfold on CNN Europe. That was when I fell in love with little dogs. Instead of rambling far and wide as we had before the war, we would walk into town in the afternoon to sit at a café where they didn't hold our nationality against us, drink espresso and play with a little gray and white dog named Daniel. He was a cockapoo, small and adorable. Daniel would see me coming and his little tail would wing around like a whirly-gig; he'd climb over the wobbly café tables to clamber into my lap and lick my face. I can't explain how much comfort I took from him singling me out.

Now, living in San Francisco, I wanted a little Daniel of my own for comfort. Day after day when Ann and I met in the hall or one of us stopped by to visit, as we commiserated about life in general and Bush in particular, the price of food or the upcoming street construction, I'd report on my Internet search for the right dog, small and cuddly.

"I need a dog," I'd say.

"You should have a dog," Ann would say.

"I want one as cute as that little Daniel from Carcès," I'd say.

"You should have one that cute," she'd say.

And I'd peruse craigslist for puppies for sale and study the various websites where they described canine breeds. After a while, I started noticing Maltese dogs with puppy cuts. In the dog shows, you always see the Maltese with amazingly long white coats, the hair on their heads tied up into ribbon-festooned ponytails, definitely not something that would work with my lifestyle. But with the puppy cut, short and punky, a Maltese was about the cutest little critter I'd ever seen. They averaged between four and seven pounds, perfect for my bicoastal life. I perused the Maltese websites. I learned what loyal companions they were, playful into their old age, smart and easy to train. And they didn't shed or smell.

"I want a Maltese," I'd whine to Ann. "But they're so expensive and hard to find. I'll never get one."

"You should have one," Ann would say.

"But I can't afford one."

"Why not?" she'd say. "It's only money. And if you get one, Alexandra will have a puppy to play with without me having to feed it or take it to the bathroom." And the way she said bathroom, with that nasal elongation and the almost-question in the last word, made the thought of a puppy a little less appealing.

Wednesday night was free supper night at the Baptist Church next door. I rounded the corner at Market and there they'd be, the customers, smoking and conversing in small groups, or sitting, head in hand from exhaustion or dismay, or passed out against the building. It was a jolt, the first time I saw them as I returned home from work at the university, so many people in need. One man toked on a crack pipe in the diminishing daylight. Just feet away, a pitiful old woman huddled in layered sweaters while an equally frail man paced the street, trying to stay warm in his tattered clothing. There was only one other woman in the group of about fifteen people waiting for a free meal. She was tattooed from neck to wrists and probably elsewhere, in places I couldn't see. She sat with a group of pierced and equally tattooed guys, all in tattered jeans and big boots. The thought struck me that they were too young to be in line for free dinner, to be begging for money on a street corner, children really. They had a pit bull that looked hungry. When I stopped to talk to them, to ask where they were from, they said they weren't homeless. "We're travelers," the woman said. "Home is everywhere."

The homeless men who had claimed the church steps on previous nights were nowhere to be seen. The smell of something good, pot roast and vegetables maybe, wafted from under the church door. As if on cue, the young tramps and wastrels, the old woman and the guy with the crack pipe got to their feet to stand in an orderly line along the church exterior.

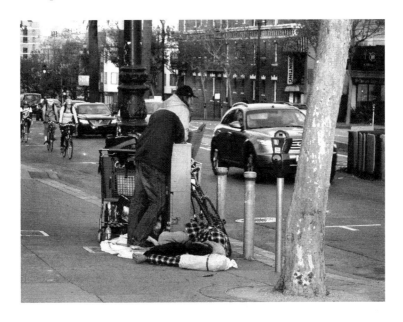

One man watches over a bike and shopping cart full of possessions while another sleeps on Market Street a few blocks from Octavia.

Travelers, now that was a unique way of putting it I thought until I learned there was a culture of young people who referred to themselves with that term; they moved about the country, living on hand-outs, the modern form of hobo. I had done much the same as a young woman, even after I had children, roaming the country in a VW van, traipsing from one commune or friend's home to another, eating at hippie gatherings and cooking over campfires. There were months when we lived on food stamps, an institutionalized form of handout, but I think of myself as industrious in those years, no burden on society. I admit I once told a border guard that I was a child of the universe; I was that green. Still, around those months of wandering, were many more months of domesticity, often with others in my rather extended family, during which I sewed our clothing, grew vegetables and preserved them, ran a food coop, tended goats and chickens, and with other parents co-taught an utterly disastrous "free" school. If we had been labeled travelers, we would have thought the term poetic. It suited as well as the word hippie. In various amalgamations, a group of us had traveled and lived together in Goshen, Vermont; Evergreen, Colorado; Boston; West Palm Beach, Florida; and both Coarsegold and San Francisco, California. We never had much money but no one I knew begged on the street. Did that make us better than the kids lined up with the more seasoned street people?

That night, as I tramped the sidewalk I shared with the people lined up for free dinner at the Baptist Church, I felt a mix of shame and gratitude. I didn't have a lot of sympathy for the travelers, but I couldn't help but wonder about the others. How many of the homeless and poor awaiting a free dinner had failed to reap a modicum of such good fortune as I?

Thousands of pounds of organic vegetables, fruits and nuts, meat and fish, herbs, eggs, mushrooms, olive oils and vinegars, wine and honey, flowers, orchid plants – so much bounty – were displayed in mind-boggling perfection across the broad parking lot at the Ferry Building on San Francisco's stunning waterfront. You could feed the city on what wouldn't be sold that day. One of me said it was obscene, the cost, the abundance. The other of me, the one who always won in those situations, didn't even look at the prices as I bought baby shitake mushrooms and omega-3 eggs, flawless hearts of romaine, chops from lambs raised on organic grass and, as the picture-of-health young woman selling them said, "treated humanely from birth to your table."

I quickly developed an addiction to Primavera's Mexican breakfast of chilaquiles verdes – chilaquiles or tortilla chips, drenched in chile poblano-tomatillo sauce, with creama Mexicana, onion and cotija cheese, scrambled free-range local eggs, refried beans and avocado. $9.50 and worth every penny. I ate this creation at a table overlooking the bay. The Ferry Building's clock tower loomed high behind me; the Bay Bridge was a beautiful thing from this distance – it's nicknamed The

Silver Dream — and the Oakland hills were a verdant backdrop on the horizon. Then, there was the choosing: these Brussels sprouts over that Savoy cabbage, these heirloom tomatoes over those Romas, these artichokes, raspberries, grapes, leeks and basil over equally gorgeous offerings at another stand. I bought goat cheese from Point Reyes and chartreuse olive oil pressed by the Sciabica family from trees the Franciscans brought to California from Spain hundreds of years ago.

There were two stages to the pleasure. The first was the actual shopping, comparing the produce from stand to stand, placing the selections in my red pushcart. The second stage would be the unpacking at home: the discovery that I'd bought, along with everything I remembered, a bag of key limes, a bundle of oddly shaped citrus fruit that looked like a flange of fingers and smelled of lemon, and two Asian pears.

Stumbling onto the Muni F-line with my load, however, I found that guilt awaited in the form of an elderly man immersed in a kind of emaciated stupor as he sprawled across the front seats of the bus. The beautiful people had been on the dock where the ferries come in and out with their handsome passengers, and the bridge to the East Bay had looked lovely and safe despite accepted knowledge to the contrary, high above paddling sea gulls and a diving western grebe. The beautiful people had been there at the Ferry Building with their beautiful babies and their beautiful dogs and their beautiful straw baskets for carrying their beautiful purchases. They had licked their beautiful gelato and feasted at the beautiful caviar bar. They'd bought all they needed and more, then placed their bounty in their beautiful cars or, like me, lugged it back to their beautiful homes. The emaciated man on the bus was not beautiful. He had been sleeping in his clothes; that was easy to tell. And he had wet himself. He looked ill. He might have been close to dying but he was invisible to my fellow riders and I, too, maneuvered around his sleeping form, careful not to arouse him.

I was attempting to get in the door of the apartment building with my load from the market, part of me still with the old man on the F train, while an elegantly dressed black woman was trying to get out the front door. She wore an impeccable white suit, low heels, a fuchsia scarf draped artfully around her shoulders. She used a gold-knobbed cane to block my entrance. Behind me, the wind whipped trash down Octavia Street.

"Who's that?" she shouted. "I don't know you."

"Not yet," I replied, introducing myself as the new number 3.

"Oh, I heard of you. Noel told me about you." She opened the gate enough for me to climb onto the landing where she obviously intended to hold court. Mae West stepped closer and placed a hand on my cheek as if to see me through her fingertips.

"Noel who?" I stepped away from her touch.

"You haven't met Noel yet, girl? Well, he seen you. Told me all about you three whole days ago. He said you were a fine-looking specimen."

"Specimen?" I laughed. "Well, somehow I've missed him, which sounds too bad given the compliment. But I'm just a middle-aged woman getting by, nothing special like you."

"Middle age gets to look pretty good after eighty," she said, laughing back.

"I've heard of you, too, Mae. And I'm delighted to finally meet you." I didn't mention the trash bags left on the landing. "Where are you off to, looking so lovely on this glorious day?"

She liked that. She brought her hand to the stylish wig upon her head, pursed then rubbed her lips together to make sure her lipstick was smooth. Then she grimaced, pulling her lips back to expose Chicklet-perfect dentures.

"Look," she commanded. "Do I have lipstick on my teeth?"

I did as ordered.

"No," I said. "Really. You look superb. Where are you going?"

"Oh, I'm off to see my Yahweh, my Yashua, my lord and master. I worship on the true Sabbath, Saturday. You know that's where the word comes from, don't you, honey child? Sundown Friday until the three stars arise on Saturday evening. The Sabbath."

Mae West's eyes were behind dark wraparound glasses but I felt their force upon my face as she continued. "I have your voice now and I think I have your steps too. So I'll know you now. And I've definitely got your smell. You use that vanilla lotion, is that what it is, and something else. Magnolia? Oh, that's priceless. You come visit me any time you like. I like chocolates and raspberry turnovers, if you're ever in the mood to entertain an old blind lady."

When a car pulled up, she announced that her Jewesses were there to fetch her. I was sure that was the phrase she used, "My Jewesses." I watched her navigate the front stairs without the use of the cane and watched her shoo away the young black beauties who spilled from the car and came rushing to her aide – or tried to, as she clambered into the back seat as deftly as a young person with sight. I suspected that reasons other than age and blindness and three flights of stairs explained why Mae didn't take her trash to the dumpster. I didn't think it was because she couldn't see. Indeed, I wasn't convinced she couldn't see. It didn't matter. From now on, Mae and her trash would be my projects too.

Moments later, unpacking the surplus in my own rooms, I discovered that I'd brought the old man home with me too. His face, puffy, pale, a few days' growth of whiskers. That smell. I regretted not leaving some of my bounty with him.

You start getting into the real Haight-Ashbury with all its seedy burnt-out hippies, wannabe waifs and gawking tourists after you cross Masonic. That's where I saw a guy with the biggest, dreadest mound of hair I'd ever seen, something surely living in there, ratty in the grossest meaning of the word, all patchouli oiled and rastaferianed up, speed-talking, you know, man, right on, duding it up with some other guy, thinner than a bamboo shoot, beady-eyed and smoking a big fat joint of skunky dope right on the sidewalk. Soon enough, the two men were surrounded by a couple of homeboys wearing baggy diaper pants above their skateboards and an old fat guy with one of those hombre goatees over triple chins. The old fat guy stepped into the circle of pot smokers and took possession of the joint. He must have had reefer lungs above his porpoise-shaped belly because he inhaled that whole smelly joint in one big, audible suck while the other guys just stared, bug-eyed, watching their free high fill someone else's bagpipe. It was a hilarious performance and, when the group finally noticed me gawking at the scene, there was an awkward moment before they started laughing. Seconds later, I was laughing too, right there on the sidewalk, laughing with the porpoise-belly guy and the rest.

It was easy to understand lesbian love on this day. It was hot so the young women were showing a lot of skin – the front porch, the whole piazza almost, displayed in multiple viewings. And pierced navels. And tattoos. And achingly angular hip bones. I wondered how many tossed cookies kept them so thin. As I strolled down Haight Street, I couldn't help but wonder why the young women were so pretty while the young men, well, quite frankly, most of them looked like leftovers from a rained-out beach party or refugees who'd bought their clothes at a not-new shop that specialized in big men's clothing. Gay guys show off their bodies, as well they should, at least those with pumped-up pecs and tight asses. Meanwhile, the straight men were so ensconced in layers, in gangsta pants and baggy everything, that you could barely imagine their physiques. I wondered what all this said about our culture, about our sexual roles and Madison Avenue meets prison life. But, because the sense imagery was so powerful, I quickly moved on to other observations, like the art stenciled on the sidewalks near Fillmore and Haight.

Stencils, both political and personal, decorated the sidewalks all through the Haight-Ashbury/Fillmore neighborhood a few blocks from my apartment building.

As a Vermonter, I have a particular affection for Ben & Jerry's Homemade Ice Cream, even though those old hippies Ben Cohen and Jerry Greenfield no longer own the company, but rather the multinational company Unilever, which also, oddly, owns Proctor & Gamble. One of the most famous – or infamous – Ben & Jerry's ice cream shops is situated on the equally famous corner of Haight and

Ashbury, a beacon for hippies both old and wannabe alike, not to mention tourists and just regular people needing a fix of Cherry Garcia. Most days, kids from Marin, an upscale county north of San Francisco, lounged outside the ice cream shop, barefoot and filthy, expensive jeans frayed to fringe where they dragged dirty on the sidewalk. The first day I went there, the kids were begging money as rubbernecking sightseers licked their Wavy Gravy and Chunky Monkey ice cream. Two urchins in tatters sat together on the curb, playing twin guitars collaged with so many stickers that the paper could have been holding the instruments together. One girl, she looked twelve, thirteen at the most, had a knitting needle stuck through her nostrils.

A block away, the Socialist bookstore Bound Together was jam-packed with revolutionary, fanatical, off-the-wall and totally entertaining books, T-shirts and posters, absolutely heretical stuff about that idiot Bush and his future-wrecking war. One T-shirt emblazoned with fighter planes and bombs and the words "Bringing You Democracy" hung near another with two panels on its front – the first panel, showing a woman pulling down her little undies, was labeled "the good bush," while the other panel, the one labeled "the bad bush," pictured W himself, looking as moronic as ever. A collective of Socialists who didn't take pay ran the store. One of them, a going-on-sixty guy with braids almost down to his knees (so strange, he looked like a walking mountain range) seemed to know everything there was to know about left of left and humored me as I asked stupid questions. Frankly, I wouldn't have been as nice to me.

As I stepped into the sunlight from the store's cool darkness with the radical diatribe of the Socialists in my brain, I noted how deftly the Sixties had been co-opted in the form of mandalas, incense, John Lennon glasses, peace signs, crystals, hash pipes, tie-dyed T-shirts, Indian print skirts and lava lamps, packed into store-front windows and spilling from doorways. Consumerism prevailed here in the birthplace of the counterculture. I did have to laugh at the baby T-shirt that read, "My parents got stoned in Haight-Ashbury and all I got was this lousy T-shirt."

But fuck it. It was too wonderful with the fog gone and couples holding hands to think about corporate America. Men held hands. Women walked arm and arm. Even men and women hugged and kissed, locked together. They all made me miss my own true love, 3,000 miles away in Vermont.

In the restaurant where I got my afternoon coffee, two burn-outs, probably no more than fifty years old but already depleted, ate in excruciatingly slow motion at a long wooden table set for communal dining, No one joined them, which was just as well. I had watched their entrance, their unintentional tragedy played out amongst a dozen or more patrons who didn't give them a second glance while I couldn't muster an ounce of dispassion as the woman directed the man, her husband, her companion, her brother, hard to say, through the motions necessary for him to balance the three slices of pizza he had carried into the restaurant. He was balancing the pizza precariously on one outstretched hand because the other hand was clutching a nearly bursting blue plastic bag.

The bag bore a county hospital logo and he gripped it like it contained all the valuables in the world. He somehow managed to get himself seated without dropping the pyramid of pizza or spilling the contents of his straining bag. His beard, grizzled gray and black, hid most of his face. Dark, wraparound glasses like Mae's and a baseball cap concealed the rest. While he maneuvered through the door and the maze of tables and chairs, his female companion wobbled on tiptoes beside him, arms and fingers outstretched, as if to catch any detritus that might spill from him. Mewling noises leaked from her mouth. When he was finally settled into a chair, she tucked a napkin into the nape of his shirt like a bib. She sat across from him, tucked her own crinkly hair into the back of her shirt, and deliberately delivered a mound of sprouts and shredded carrots into her mouth.

At some point, without a word exchanged, the woman stood and returned to the counter to procure a glass of ice, which she silently placed before her companion. He rooted around in his blue plastic bag, eventually pulling out a liter soda bottle from which he poured voluminous amounts of liquid onto the ice. When he raised the glass to his lips, his hands shook something awful. The pretty girls behind the counter, too young yet to have identified their own addictions or, if they had, to be suffering from them, stared and giggled, never saying a thing about the fact that he had brought outside food and drink into the restaurant. And, as far as I could tell, other than them, I was the only one fascinated by this sad play.

Later, on the walk home from the Haight, I watched a couple really going at it on the sweeping lawn of Buena Vista Park. She was humping him, fast at first, then slowly and ever more slowly, her dark hair falling onto his face as his hands reached up and touched her bottom, just the two moons of it peeking out from under her sweater. He touched her ever so gently. The bank below them was planted with penstemon and lobelia, sensuous purples and pinks, and the white, white of calla lilies, their holiness radiant in the pure, clean air. The couple kissed, absolutely silently. The smell of Thai food perfumed the air. There were no cops anywhere to be seen. It was that kind of moment on a hot and sunny afternoon, a Sunday, in San Francisco.

The first time I saw Noel, he was dressed in a suit much too natty for our building and had a striking Latina on his arm. She might have been twenty years younger than him; it was hard to tell. Noel's silk suit, black of course, was accompanied by a skinny black tie, pink silk hanky in the pocket, the crease in his pants perfect, a handsome cap on his head. The woman wore a black cocktail dress, red and black high-heeled shoes, one of those little fur stoles draped around her shoulders. She smelled of something luscious.

"Lor--dy," he sang, laying cataracts on me as we nearly bumped into one another in the doorway.

"You number 3?" He gave me a blatant once-over. "You sure are a sight better lookin' than those two Nancy boys used to live in number 3. Oh, that Jul, I see he has a sharp eye on him. He's so white, some folk might call him a blandlord. But he can pick the ladies, I see that now."

Then he let out a laugh that was so genuinely warm and happy with the world. Blandlord, how long had he been fashioning that term for Jul? Still, I felt for the woman, so beautiful with her eyes downcast as Noel threw the compliments my way.

"You two are gorgeous," I said, and meant it. "Where have you been, out for a night on the town?"

"Oh, we've been at the club dancing," Noel said as if we all spent the evenings clubbing in our fancy clothing, then he started singing "Star Dust" and took his lovely companion's hand and led her up the stairs to his apartment.

"Is that yours?" a curly-haired man asked an Asian man in the seat across the aisle on the Muni train. Curly pointed to a tour book of San Francisco that someone had left behind. The Asian man said no. Actually, he didn't say anything but something about the way he turned even further toward the window indicated a negative response. Curly picked the book up and slipped casually into the seat beside the Asian man. Curly was dressed neatly in a short-sleeved white shirt tucked high into shiny black pants above white socks and black tie shoes, that combination of black and white that always looks so nerdy.

"English my second language. I speak Farsi," Curly said. "You speak Farsi?"

"What's Farsi?" Asian asked without turning. It was dark in the bus and the flaps of his cap hid half his face. He might have been Chinese; I couldn't tell for sure.

"My language. Farsi. A language. Persian," Curly said, articulating each word as if he were speaking to a foreigner. His pronunciation was close to perfect. He thumbed through the tour book while Asian ever so subtly turned further away.

"You speak Farsi?" Curly asked again.

"No," Asian's voice was flat, barely audible. "What's Farsi?"

"My language. I student. Study business administration. Six years, I go to school. You?"

"I work."

"I American citizen. Last year, pass test. Study hard. You?"

"I work."

"I here twelve years, come from my country, just speak Farsi."

"What's Farsi?"

By now, everyone on the bus was listening to this conversation. Most of the passengers tried to look as if they weren't listening; others wore a slight smirk, entertained by Curly's candor, his self-pride, his optimism despite the failure at communication, his glee in the photos of San Francisco he was perusing in the tour book on his lap. He kept trying to show them to the Asian guy.

"Farsi. My language. Persian."

"What's Persian?"

"From Iran, my country. I come her twelve years ago."

"Iran? The place where the terrorists live?" Asian asked, finally turning to his seatmate.

"No, no. No terrorists. Just a few crazies. In my country, most people poor. Too busy just live. I American citizen now. You?"

"Iran. You're from Iran?"

"Yes, yes. Twelve year I come here. Just speak Farsi."

"What's Farsi?"

"My language. You speak Farsi? Is beautiful language," Curly said as he stood, clutching his tour book, preparing to get off at the next stop. He held the book up for Asian and all the rest of us to see.

"San Francisco," he said rather grandly. "Beautiful, your country."

I was mulling over this conversation between an Iranian immigrant and a person I surmised to be a native San Franciscan, the immigrant lauding America, perhaps proving Jul's argument that anyone could make it in this country with hard work and determination; the native fellow, an Asian whose ancestors might have migrated here a century ago to work on the railroad or in the mines, mouthing stereotypes about yet another foreign group destined for discrimination, as I stumbled off the bus and headed past the Safeway grocery store and the Redemption Center toward home. I walked by it several times a day,

The Redemption Center draws the homeless and the poor to the corner of Market and Duboce. They show up early in the morning with their shopping carts filled with recyclable bottles, sometimes dragging two or three carts tied together, each one overflowing, jangling, and smelling of stale beer. These are the working homeless and poor who make cash money pawing through dumpsters and barrels, collecting returnable bottles to redeem for a few dollars.

Now, it was night. The Redemption Center was closed and the fog had spread its chilly mantle over the city, but Hudson Bay Blanket Man still lay in front of the center's main gate. I didn't know his name. Indeed, each time I had seen the man, as I had that morning, he had been cocooned into a Hudson Bay blanket outside the Redemption Center's entranceway, the blanket's white wool and signature red, green and yellow stripes providing its limited shelter on the streets of San Francisco. That morning, I'd been struck by how the people had stepped over and wheeled around the sleeping man's humped shape so as not to disturb him. How many hours ago had that been, I wondered, trying to recall the shape of his body and blanket that morning. Had he moved? Was he alive? Mostly I wondered what it would take to lay on the ground, to sleep while the city moved on around you.

Then I remembered Curly and Asian and their conversation on the bus.

Beautiful country, indeed.

Ann was using the top of her baby grand piano as a serving table for hors d'oeuvres, which consisted of Pringles and Chex mix, but the wine was good. Wendy had brought it. Wendy was Ann's childhood friend. She wore a black leotard and pink tutu over Capri-length leopard-spotted tights, lace-trimmed socks and pink high-top sneakers. She had arranged her hair in two short ponytails pulled tight near the top of her head like a Mouseketeer. Her breath reeked of cigarettes. Jul was picking the peanuts out of the Chex mix and waxing poetic about Burning Man, the big desert party he and Mary had just attended. Burning Man is a festival and "temporary community" held Labor Day week in Black Rock Desert, 120 miles north of Reno, Nevada. Tens of thousands of people have traveled there each year since 1990 to "test themselves against unpredictable nature," as the Burning Man website put it. Jul called the gathering Burning Person. He was evolved, or goofing, hard telling. The burners camped in tents or elaborate installations or packed into what they referred to as "mutant vehicles," meaning milk trucks or buses or any other mode of transportation transformed into a temporary shelter, and spent the week setting things on fire, screwing around, looking at other participants' creations, sharing drugs, sex and philosophy, and otherwise acting out their visions or obsessions or fantasies of utopia.

Of course the Burners saw the event as far more symbolic and meaningful than I just described and, since I've never been to Burning Man and hope never to go – the idea of being stuck in the desert for the better part of a week with thousands of people, many of them naked and high on ecstasy, didn't attract me – I concede I don't know what I'm talking about but I sure heard a lot about it during my first weeks in San Francisco. Jul began urging me to accompany him and Mary there ten minutes after I met them. My impression was that nearly everyone who went to Burning Man was so blown away by the experience, and usually in a positive way, that they wanted to talk everyone they knew into experiencing it for themselves, I said no thank you to his invitation.

Ann, who would not be caught dead at Burning Man either, was having this party because Wendy had just attended her first Burn. Since Jul and Mary were veterans, she figured their stories would provide us with a little entertainment. So far, I'd learned that Jul had collected sturdy pieces of driftwood for months before the most recent Burning Person to use as ridgepoles for a festooned castle he and

Mary created in the sand out of tarps and reams of material from India, then outfitted the structure with air mattresses and candles. In previous years, Jul and Mary had joined a group of friends who created their own theme park organized around a different motif each year – the pirate's den, the warlock's warren, the hedonist's harem – which they erected on the playa close to other celebrants. But that year, they had erected their camp nearly a mile from the main site. Jul felt the new location allowed them to be part of the event but protected from the constant blare of music and human noise, the never-ending drumming, the thrum of generators that ran all night long, powering utopia.

While Jul was describing all this and chastising Mary whenever she deemed to interrupt and offer her version of Burning Man, Wendy was telling her stories of trial and tribulation. The two were having parallel conversations about Burning Man that went like this:

Wendy: We rented an RV that sleeps thirteen, at least that's what they said, but the six of us were all over one another. And that wind. It took me two hours to put my make-up on and do my hair. Soon as I stepped out of the trailer, that wind would whip it up. But the lightshow, now that was something worth seeing.

Jul: I rode around the encampment once every day. There's nothing like a bike ride on hard-packed sand with a bracing wind behind you. And what a way to see everyone's art installations. There you are on your bike, motoring on your own power, as you pass one after another amazing aspect of creation.

Wendy: And the sand. I tell you, it gets into places you didn't know sand could. If it weren't for the sand, and the wind, it would have been perfect. Well, it was perfect. Well, almost perfect. You know you can't ever have complete perfection. Well, maybe you can. Sometimes I look in the mirror and say, Oh, Wendy, you are perfect. But, that wind, it wasn't an ally to perfection.

Jul: We camped in the outer limits. It's much better out there (He said the word out like oot, that annunciation of his reappearing magically) away from the crowd. We had access to the village of Burning Man, but we faced the great expanse of desert so that we had the community to our back and the desert, both inhospitable and oddly inviting, to our front. You could say the same about the community of people who attend Burning Man, that it is both inhospitable and inviting. But I tend to think of it in a positive way.

Wendy: You have to bring the right outfits to Burning Man. You might walk around in your littlest bikini or, well, nothing at all in the daytime. Mind you, I brought plenty of sun block. But at night you need a down jacket. That camper now, we didn't think of that. All the gear you'd need to survive six days in the desert and not enough blankets or sleeping bags. But that's the price you pay to keep the fire burning in your heart and soul. Oh, did you hear that? I made a pun or whatever you call it, a play on words. Keep the fire burning in your soul at Burning Man. They should have that as a motto.

I had essentially tuned them out and was watching Alexandra who was watching all of us intently, her eyes roaming from one person to another, when I heard my name mentioned. "You will definitely have to come next year, Yvonne," Jul was saying. "You'd love it. No money's exchanged. Everything's on the barter system. The only things you can buy with American money are coffee and ice. You can come with us and live in our camp."

"Jul, if you think I am ever going to voluntarily spend four or five days or a week in the middle of the desert with a bunch of people I probably wouldn't like, with my skin, the driest in the entire country and the easiest to sunburn, then you are truly crazy," I said. "But, really …" and here's where I made my mistake, asking a question that would just prolong the discussion, "I don't get it. What's it for, what's Burning Man accomplish?"

"Accomplish?" Wendy blinked her eyes, incredulous over my stupidity. "Accomplish? It accomplishes a good time. What do you mean, what does it accomplish? It's for getting a good buzz or a good fuck or seeing a good show. It's about getting away from money and the city and society's stupid rules. It's about artistic expression, about non-conformity, creating a new world."

"In an RV?" I asked. I couldn't help it. Here we were, knee deep in the war in Iraq, Bush fucking up the environment and talking about drilling in Alaska, an election process mired in hype and bad journalism, and these two thought they were making the world better by riding a bicycle around in the dessert and dressing up in baby-doll clothing to watch the Burning Man light show. (Actually, I wouldn't mind seeing the light show but not at the cost of a week in the desert with a bunch of naked people.) I do have a tendency to preach and I'd started now. "What do you think we could do with all that energy if we aimed it at defeating Bush or getting the truth out about the war or solving the energy problem?" I asked. "By the way, what did you do, Wendy, run the RV all night, haul a generator into the desert so you could commune with nature?"

Ann was staring at me with her mouth open. Here, she'd invited me to a dinner party to meet her friend Wendy and hear all about Burning Man and I was being rude. I shut up, ate some Pringles and listened as Jul tried again to explain how Burning Man was about survival, about testing yourself against the elements, about sharing and gifting, about creative expression outside the bounds of conformity.

"Jul, I lived on a commune," I said. "I raised goats. I've seen enough naked people. I don't need it."

"It's impossible to explain. You have to experience it. It's art, music, self-expression and nudity and geek culture and human spiritual adventure, rolled into one. Surely, you're not against any of those things. Don't be so East Coast. Don't be so sure you won't love it."

"But, Jul," I said, "the big event of the week is the burn, right? Fifty thousand people watch a big wood and steel structure shaped like a man go up in flames. Let's burn ourselves together and pollute the desert while we're at it. Pyromaniacs Anonymous."

"You're too literal," Jul said. "You'll have to see it. I'm going to kidnap you next year. Drug you. You'll thank me later."

Elise, the young barista behind the counter at the Laguna Sidewalk Café where I'd taken to having my coffee on mornings when I didn't teach, wore her blue hair spiked on top and half shaved in back. She had a tattoo caricature of herself on her bicep and wore a rather large silver hoop between her nostrils. And she definitely liked rock, head-banging punk rants that she filled the café with way too early in the morning. She was solid in a way that made you take notice. Over my morning coffees, she told me her story. She was a wrestler in her former life in New York until her back gave out and she moved west. Now she was a Roller Derby chick who could throw an opponent over the boards with the best of them.

After I rolled my eyes over the person in front of me in the coffee line who had taken ten minutes to decide whether to order a straight soy latte or a decaffeinated soy caramel macchiato, and had included everyone in line in her deliberations, Elise bestowed this compliment upon me: "We're both from the East. You understand. I'd like to put up a sign: 'Keep your self-indulgence to yourself.'"

Elise made a great non-fat latte, double shot, which had become my morning drink of privilege. On that morning, I wanted to add a cartoon of Bush and the Pope to the Wall of Shame, which was above the cream and sugar and coffee lids. The Wall of Shame was covered with anti-Bush propaganda, good for a fresh laugh almost every day. My offering: The Pope, ancient and bent, holding his head in distress at one end of a long table as Bush, at the other end, explained to his Holiness, "It said Abomination so I bombed a nation."

"It's the best," Elise said, handing me a tack. "Give it prominence. Even the Pope knows Bush is a buffoon."

What I liked best about the Laguna Sidewalk Café was the crooked sidewalk outside the building with its tipsy tables and chairs where you could sit and watch the morning commerce of walkers and drivers, the buses and cars and bicyclists all somehow avoiding collision despite their drivers' many fine attempts, the monks crisscrossing from the Zen center, which was kitty-corner to the café, and the people walking their dogs and stopping in for coffee and conversation. In less than two weeks, I'd become a regular.

After posting my cartoon, I pulled my chair up to the sidewalk table where the other regulars had gathered. At the center of our circle, a slim, red-faced blond fellow usually held court. He had introduced himself as the director of the Wisdom School and told me his name, but when I told Chuck about him on the phone I called him Wisdom Man and half-forgot his real name. A Wisdom School? Now that was something I wanted to learn more about.

Wisdom Man's greeting was always, "Hail, there, fellow Earth dweller," and he'd send me off with the line, "May the farce be with you." In between the salutation and the goof on *Star Wars*, Wisdom Man regaled those who gathered on the sidewalk with lessons and discussions he'd had with his students, odd takes on local and national politics, erudite segues into Greek philosophy, the Latin root of words, and prognostications on the end of the world. He followed the Gnostic creed, sermonizing that salvation came through personal experience rather than by accepting what others told us to believe. Mornings often began with him pontificating about the divinity of the human, an opinion I wasn't sure I shared. When I expressed my reservations on the subject, Wisdom Man said it was because my soul, like all human souls, was trapped in a flawed and material world created by an imperfect god.

When he wasn't going on in this regard, he used any chance he got to castigate Republicans, academicians and organized religion, with Catholics and the religious right garnering his most vitriolic criticisms and witticisms. I've always had a disdain for street preachers and prognosticators but I was fascinated by the way he delivered his broad-ranging lessons to whoever happened to join him. Among those who gathered at Wisdom Man's table was a former Vermonter named Tom who had come to the neighborhood to visit his son months previously. Every few days he announced his imminent departure for Paris or Vermont but the next morning, there he would be in the rumpled clothing he had slept in the night before. He introduced himself grandly one day, assuming I'd have heard of him somewhere in my travels around Vermont. Tom and his estranged wife had run some sort of new age business that featured Celtic harps and meditation therapy. No wonder he felt comfortable in San Francisco.

Another regular was an old political activist who took it upon himself to keep me abreast of upcoming demonstrations, labor strikes and pickets, peace marches, radical talks and uprisings. After Tom invited me to join their group on the second or third morning I'd sat outside the Laguna Sidewalk Café, the old politico stood and formally introduced himself like this: "Hi, my name's Ted and I am a recovering alcoholic, a failed husband, a lifelong hustler and a chronic demonstrator." Ted looked ancient although he was only in his late 60s. "I've got cancer, cirrhosis of the liver, cataracts, an addled brain and false teeth that don't fit anymore. But when I think of what that idiot in the White House has done with our democracy, I swear it gives me the strength to carry on. I read the paper in the morning and it's like some sort of mental Viagra. I'll fight that bastard until they put me in the ground," Ted said as he lit one cigarette off another.

Some mornings we were joined by a young and pathetically thin street artist who was often burdened with items he picked up on his walks. His name was Jay. As we consumed our coffee and solved the problems of the universe, Jay would rearrange the items he had culled from the river of detritus perpetually available in San Francisco's alleys and dumpsters or cast upon the sidewalk – bicycle rims, vinyl records, dead plants, broken mirrors, tent poles, headless statues, the offerings were endless – into an impromptu creation. One morning shortly after I started hanging out at the café, Jay constructed a kind of mechanism from the discarded undercarriage of a grocery cart, a giant detergent box, a poster of Marilyn Manson, a partially deflated birthday balloon and some slats he arranged in a circle and attached to the back of the box like a propeller. He mounted the detergent box and makeshift propeller over the cart's wheels and tied Marilyn Manson's visage onto the front with the string from the deflated balloon, which floated wanly above the assemblage. He pushed the whole thing around the sidewalk with his foot and said, "I think I'll call it 'Chore Girl. Art by Distraction.'"

I didn't know the name of the other man who sat on the outskirt of our circle, drinking coffee and rolling one after another cigarette while the four of us complained about the asses of evil and the Dumbocrats who seemed intent on losing the presidential election once again. He sat with us but didn't speak. When he finished one rolled cigarette, he would snuff it out on the bottom of his work boot and put the butt in his left-hand pocket for future use. The right-hand pocket held his tobacco pouch and rolling papers. He wore a black beret over scruffy gray-brown hair and frameless glasses. His gaze was almost always directed at the street ahead rather than toward anyone in particular, but you could tell he was listening to the conversation. In my head and my phone calls and emails to Chuck, which had become a running dialogue of my city life, I called him Silent Guy.

The men were often in mid-conversation on one of the themes that Wisdom Man introduced each morning when I arrived. Somehow he would wind his esoteric Gnostic or historic references into the news of the day so that we might begin discussing the war in Iraq or the polarity of the electorate and Wisdom Man would tell us that our notions on how to stop war or improve conditions anywhere in the world would be futile until all religions promoted true respect for women and recognized that the true divine trinity was the father, the mother and the son, not all male like the Catholics and Protestants like to preach.

"What so many so-called religions have in common is fear of women," he said one morning. "Small men fear the power of women to give birth, to bring life into the world. The religions of the world are based on that fear; so are wars."

"Honey child, you in there?"

I crawled from bed and peered through the peek hole in my door. Mae West stood outside in a silver bathrobe, her beautiful black face framed by a matching turban. Bam, bam went her cane. "Wake up, honey child, I need you."

"Hold on, Mae. I have to get some clothes on."

"How come, baby doll? You know I cain't see you." Her laughter echoed in the empty hallway.

"Listen, I cain't get that old stove of mine to work," she said when I finally opened the door. "Come up and help me, won't you, honey child? I cain't raise no one up at Gordon's."

Mae West lived on the second floor next to Ann. It was a Saturday and Mae was anxious to get ready before her Jewesses arrived. The details of that church or temple of hers were as hard to nail down as the particulars of Wisdom Man's school. From the meager bits of information she had provided, her church sounded like a cross between Seventh Day Adventist, African Revival and some ancient Hebrew sect. Jul called it Hebrew Voodoo.

Mae kept candles lit in her apartment 24/7, a discovery that made me rather nervous, given that she was blind. "See, I put the candles in a pan of water," she pointed out when I ever so politely asked about the safety of the candles the first time I visited with the obligatory chocolates and raspberry turnovers. "I put the candles in pots of water so if I knock them over, I'll knock over the water too, or if an earthquake knocks them over, the water will put out any fire. I keep the candles lit so the angels will find me, to greet Yahweh, to shed a little light into this world of darkness. These are the preachings of my beautiful teacher and pastor Elizabeth Chambers and the Hebrew Cultural Center. Gordon, he's always after me about those candles but no harm will come from them."

Up the stairs we went in the darkened hallway, Mae sure-footed, using the cane more as scepter than steadier. Once at her door, she took out a jumble of keys and began unlocking a phalanx of locks, fingering each key then inserting it in the proper keyhole without hesitation. She locked the door behind us. I had already reverted to my Vermont ways, often leaving my front door unlocked or my back door open, especially when I was somewhere in the building. Mae had lived in our building for many years, moving there after her husband died. We had sat in her dingy living room, the pastries I'd brought resting between us on the twill couch while she talked of life on Octavia before the earthquake, when the pimps and prostitutes patrolled the dark places under the freeway structure.

"Everyone back then toted a gun," she said. I loved her use of the word toted. "Not me, of course. But there was a gun dealer right on the corner. You children living here now haven't a clue what it was like."

Unlike my newly painted apartment, Mae's flat hadn't been painted in decades; the walls and windowsills wore a uniform beige. The rooms had an eerie quality to them, each with its soft candle glow, all else in near darkness, the furniture pushed hard against the walls, devoid of decoration or lined with stacked boxes.

I tackled the stove; its pilot light had obviously gone out. Mae fretted as I tried to light it, worrying about gas explosions and asphyxiation. Matches and more matches later, it was apparent the stove was broken. PG&E would send someone to fix it but not for hours unless it was an emergency. As I talked to the dispatcher, Mae fussed about noisily, mumbling about her Sabbath. I lied and said I smelled gas so they would send someone out right away. Downstairs, I boiled water, made Mae tea with honey and a piece of raisin bread with cream cheese. Upstairs, she had arranged a lovely red suit on her bed alongside a matching hat, bag and shoes.

"Mae, how did you know those reds would match so well? Half the sighted people I know can't get their reds right."

"I know my clothes," she said, then lowered her voice. "I've got them organized in my closet but sometimes when I'm gone, someone comes in here and borrows my things. They's fat. I know because the waists are stretched out and they don't fit me right. And whoever it is don't even put them back where they belong."

"Mae," I said, stifling a laugh. "I don't think anyone's stealing your clothes, wearing them and bringing them back. Besides, how would they get through those locks? Maybe you're losing weight."

"Don't tell me, honey child. I know. I know things you don't. Don't think I'm scared. When my time comes, Yahweh Eloheem, consonants without the vowels, will fold me in his arms. And don't you worry about no fire, neither. I know why you asked about them candles. Gordon gives me the same grief. Just 'cuz I'm blind don't make me stupid. I tell you, someone's been wearing my clothes. Now, make sure you come up here and help me when that PG&E fellow shows up."

Although the lower end of Octavia had never coalesced into a neighborhood with a distinct identity, non-essential but telling elements of San Francisco history had unfolded all around my street. Chris Pirsig, the son of Robert Pirsig, who authored *Zen and the Art of Motorcycle Maintenance*, was murdered near the corner of Haight and Octavia, a block from my house, in 1979. Chris had lived at the Zen Center across from the Laguna Sidewalk Café. Robert Pirsig's book was a metaphysical account of a summer motorcycle trip with Chris at eleven years old. The house next door to mine overlooked the corner where he'd been stabbed and left to die. One of my older students had lived in that house the same year with an ever-changing throng of punks, gays, writers, actors, musicians and wannabes of various sorts who used the building as their staging ground for performances, trysts, trial balloons and the various dramas that unfolded in the Harvey Milk years when homosexuals were just learning to thrust their political power and worship at the church of camp.

On the other corner, the gay community center where I'd watched youngsters practice karate was once known as the Carmel Fallon Building. According to historian Tim Kelly writing in the *Castro Star*, Carmel Fallon was the granddaughter of General Joaquin Ysidro Castro from whom the Castro District took its name. She built the trapezoidal building after she found husband Thomas Fallon, the Army commander who conquered San Jose for the United States in 1846, consorting with the family maid. The story goes that she beat the two of them with an iron poker, divorced him, then moved with her six children to San Francisco where she became a rarity in nineteenth-century America, an independent business woman. Those grateful kids fought so long over the building after her death that the structure, like my apartment building, escaped the damaging effects of renovation. The building was at the center of gay and lesbian culture throughout the 1980s. Muralist John Wullbrandt had his studio there and in a delightful history of the building in the *Castro Star* he wrote that it was not unusual for "counseling sessions on stress management, sex, or financial stability to be taking place in one part of the house, a play reading or rehearsing of lines in another while sets were being prepared out on the roof of the 1808 Club or on the sidewalk on Waller Street."

By the time I'd moved there, that sidewalk had become a flophouse of sorts where small clusters of homeless people took up residence in ever-changing groups. Sometimes they made a kind of hobo camp from found furniture and mattresses. Other times, they'd sit on the back steps of the gay community center and pass the pipe. The tall, thin cop on hire at the center moved them along if they got rowdy or when black-tie events were held there. Otherwise, for however long they wanted, the men called the street home. There were homeless women in the city but other than two couples that often bedded down on opposite corners of Market Street, our sidewalk residents were primarily male.

The Carmel Fallon Building and my building, then known as the Lorenzo Apartments, were among the only buildings on this street when the Baptist Church was built in 1909, the seventh structure parishioners had built in the city. Michael Johnston prepared a history for the church's one hundred and fiftieth anniversary in 1999 in which he compared conditions in 1906, the year of the earthquake, to contemporary ones. "People are still living in tents," he wrote. "Disease continues to take its toll. The destruction of morals is still beyond description. Every day people die alone and uncared for."

People like Stretch. Stretch lived across the street from the LGBT Center. He slept in a little alcove where the Baptist Church's elevator had been installed. He was quite tall, obviously, and as slim as Karen Carpenter. She starved herself; he was just starving. His feet were probably size eighteen; his work boots extended forward from his jeans like paddles, an image accentuated by the rigid way he walked, especially when he was stiff from sleeping on concrete. If the weather were warm, Stretch would strip down to his pants and boots as he hauled his shopping cart full of recyclables, sometimes two carts tied together with a rope, down Market Street and back to his alcove in the church wall. It was painful to see the accordion of his ribs as he trudged his regular route to the Redemption Center, but Stretch rarely seemed angry or downhearted when I came upon him and stopped to chat.

Jack told me Stretch's name. Jack was my hero. He worked as the custodian at the Baptist Church, but the word custodian failed to embody all the tasks Jack performed so beatifically each day. Each morning, he swept the corner of Octavia and Waller, shoveling dog and human shit along with discarded paper plates from the church's free supper, and the general refuse that blew down the sidewalk. There seemed to be two groups who sought the church's secular services: those who came for a free meal, hung around for an hour or so after dinner, and then moved on; and those who slept in several small alcoves along the side of the church building. I never saw the night dwellers in line for food, not even Stretch who was the most regular of the overnight crew.

Those alcoves served as makeshift "apartments" where the homeless could bed down on their cardboard or plastic tarps or curl up under a mound of dirty clothing and blankets, and stay relatively dry. Stretch had been sleeping there off and on for seven years.

When I asked Jack how he so jovially cleaned up the accumulation of sleeping bags and blankets, clothing and half-eaten food, he just smiled and said, "I'm doing God's work." He didn't judge as I so often did. I couldn't help but think if I had nothing, or nearly nothing, I would hold on to everything I had. Maybe that was why I was not homeless; I hold on. As my husband often said when I dreamed aloud of being an itinerant teacher or just a vagabond writer, traveling from place to place in a VW van, reliving the hippie dream, my own version of *Travels with Charlie*, it would be damn hard to travel around the countryside with the mounds of plants, books, CDs, dishes and clothing I have accumulated in both my homes.

The homeless seemed to have two attitudes toward material possessions. Maybe half of the people who slept outside the church or elsewhere in the neighborhood rolled out of their sidewalk beds each morning and simply left, leaving behind sleeping bags, clothing, the mess from what they had eaten the night before, their cigarette butts and needles and sometimes their excrement. The others appeared to discard nothing but rather seemed to hold on to every worthless scrap of trash, plastic bag and miscellany they had scavenged from trash barrels and dumpsters or salvaged from their former lives. For both groups, the shopping cart served as suitcase, storage room, transportation and even bed. I saw a guy sleeping in two shopping carts tied together back to back to make a kind of elevated metal room on wheels, lined with old clothes and blankets that he had somehow managed to climb into. He had jammed the carts against the side of a building so he wouldn't roll away. I wished I could have been there when he got out of the contrivance to see how he did it.

Stretch fell into the second category. He guarded his carts carefully. They held few possessions but rather were often full of recyclable bottles that he turned in for cash at the Redemption Center on Market Street. The Redemption Center was located next to the big Safeway grocery in a small shopping area with a Starbuck's and Jamba Juice. The store's sign, red letters against a white background announcing SAFEWAY, was so large it served as a landmark in the neighborhood. Tucked into the Safeway's parking lot and the Duboce Alley, the Redemption Center was a cramped, stinky maze of containers, loud with the sound of smashing glass, of metal, of shouting. It was run by a nonprofit organization that offered jobs to people who were trying to get back into the workforce. The recyclers lined up by the dozens early in the day, broken men and women, a few derelicts still sporting their youth, a few couples, but mostly single men, dragging their shopping carts filled with bottles.

The U.S. Mint loomed above the Redemption Center, a huge cement fortress complete with moat and high chain-link fence topped with concertina wire. From its commanding position above Market Street, it looked like a stronghold. The symbolism of all this was so remarkable I found it hard to imagine that it had happened by chance, that the homeless people and the poor slogged down Market Street each day, a parade of them and their bursting shopping carts, and lined up at a place called the Redemption Center, which was located between a huge sign advertising SAFEWAY and the U.S. Mint.

The U.S. Treasury Department's website said that, while the San Francisco Mint "does not currently produce circulating coins, it is the exclusive manufacturer of regular proof and silver proof coin sets that set the standard for numismatic excellence with their brilliant artistry, fine craftsmanship and enduring quality."

The U.S. Mint on Market Street in San Francisco looms over the Redemption Center.

People line up outside the Redemption Center, located in the Duboce Alley beneath the U.S. Mint.

Seven years on the street. I kept thinking about that. Seven years of sleeping on cement in all kinds of weather. I wanted to know Stretch's story but he was a man of few words. This is what I'd learned in my first weeks of living next door to him. Stretch had traveled to San Francisco from Ohio in 1996. He'd had no regular job since he arrived but often worked odd jobs for cash. He expressed no goals or regrets other than the demands of the day, which were governed by the weather. He was so good-natured, however, and cleaned up after himself so well each morning that Jack looked out for him. The other homeless people came and went; Stretch resided outside the Baptist Church. I never saw him drunk or stoned, nor had I seen evidence of those activities around his bed.

Rather, his life looked relatively normal and structured. After working the streets all day and running errands for the neighborhood merchants, he came home late at night, erected his barricade of bottle-laden grocery carts, ate a Twinkie or bag of chips, lay down and went to sleep. When I came upon him lacing up his boots or unfolding his length from the cold cement, he always said good morning and gave the weather report and news of the night in the most cheerful voice, as if we were neighbors passing on the street, as in fact we were.

"Break-in last night," he said one morning. "I chased them away. You got a car?"

"No," I said, "can't afford one."

"Better off. Just something for the junkies to break into. Gonna be a nice day; fog's already lifting." And indeed it was.

Wisdom Man drank voluminous amounts of black coffee from tall, clear glasses and updated us each day on what the people in his "network," which I took to mean his students, had been discussing, although where his Wisdom School met had not yet been revealed.

"You know what happened with one of our students the other day?" he would ask, apropos of nothing, and then he'd be off. Wisdom Man's discussions about Socrates or Plato, the unification of Germany or the Vatican, Druid rites or mother worship spilled from him as non-sequiturs. He saw himself as a modern-day Socrates, presenting dialogues and allowing the rest of us to comment on occasion. One day his monologue went something like this. I'd captured it in an email home to Chuck: "The military and the religious fanatics have been listening in on our network and I was dying to give them something juicy to chew on, something that would put a serious kink in their knickers. This student of mine, quite brilliant, I must say, he had intuited that they were eavesdropping on us as well. Without letting on that he knew they were listening, he sent this missive to me, 'I wonder if the religious right knows their world is the creation of 'evildoers' who want to trap their souls in their physical bodies. Religious conservatives may view their Christology as the final answer, but that's a vain assertion. Truth trumps deception.'

"It was inspired," Wisdom Man continued. "You could almost hear the military guys and the religious wing nuts choking on the other end."

Ted, Tom, Jay and I had checked out of the diatribe after the words "religious fanatics," knowing Wisdom Man's rant would continue for a while. But that last line of his, the words "truth trumps deception," brought me back. Jul had expressed a corollary to that sentiment the day I met him, something about ideology making a person stupid.

By then, Wisdom Man had gotten himself so worked up with his own cleverness and that of his student that he had to take off his Austrian hunting jacket. The jacket was his most valued article of clothing. He had purchased it mountain climbing in Austria. He liked to point out the epaulets, the three inside pockets, nicely lined, and the handsome staghorn buttons. He arranged it neatly on the chair back.

"Quality," he said. "Not even Arnold has one this nice."

The Arnold he referred to was Schwarzenegger, he of the broad shoulders and Austrian heritage, a favorite source of derision there at the Laguna Sidewalk Café.

Under the jacket, Wisdom Man wore a T-shirt that read "Aesthetics" in the script and colors (Midas gold, wedding-gown white and Kelley green) of the Oakland Athletics. It was glossy clean. Wisdom Man didn't appear to have a lot of clothing but he was meticulous with what he did own. I was sure each piece expressed an aspect of his personality or philosophy.

"The other end of what?" I asked, taking advantage of his pause to bring the conversation back to the Wisdom School. "The military was listening in on the other end of what? A phone, a live computer hookup? Where were you when all this was happening?"

Teaching, I had discovered, was a pretty good gig but you did have to go to class a couple of days a week. It didn't seem like Wisdom Man actually worked, or worked much. He was always there, sitting at his table outside the café when I wandered by. And, if the military were actually listening in on his conversation with a student, I was curious as to how they were doing the snooping.

"No, no. No telephone. No computer. No classroom," Wisdom Man answered. "We're beyond that. We were on our network."

"What do you mean, 'our network'? Do you use something *like* a computer to communicate? A cell phone or some electronic connection, a virtual walkie-talkie?"

It seemed so utterly San Francisco, the idea of a Wisdom School existing alongside all the other unusual learning centers and classes offered here in this city on the nation's edge, ones dedicated, just for example, to holistic health and karmic healing, Tantric sex, Bodhisattva enlightenment, vegan cooking and safe bestiality. But the idea of a school somehow operating on a network not fueled by some tool of technology, now that was even better.

Wisdom Man took a deep breath and exhaled slowly, sipped coffee, cleared his throat. I was thinking he was seeking the right words to explain his school and its workings when he said a bit smugly, "Our communications are based on energy. Everything is electric at some basic level but not in the way you're thinking. This is advanced stuff. Neural. I'll explain it to you some day when we have a lot of time. You'll need to have a little physics."

"I hope you mean a very little," I said. Physics isn't my strong point. "But tell me, this school of yours, is it solely for Gnostics? You seem to promote the idea that knowledge and experience rather than faith lead to salvation. That sounds like Gnostic teaching to me. But you've got this other line of inquiry as well, one that supports rather leftwing ideas such as the equal distribution of wealth and privilege, not to mention Feminism. Gnosticism meets the feminine left, now that's rich. I might want in. How do you get into this school you run, anyhow?"

Jay seemed to come awake. "You want to join the Gnostics? That *is* rich. I would have taken you for an *ag*nostic, Yvonne."

I was stunned that Jay even knew my name, never mind that he had a perception of me as being *any* kind of person.

"Personally, I can appreciate the Gnostic view that the soul's salvation depends on experience rather than ideology dictated by religious hucksters," Jay said. "From what I understand of it, and that's not much, Gnosticism is very cool. And so irrefutable. I mean, think of it: how can one person judge the value of any other person's experience? But I was thinking that the Gnostic view of knowledge also seems rather self-defeating."

Jay seemed to be almost talking to himself but then he leaned forward and folded his hands on the table so deliberately that he drew our attention to him. "Isn't all knowledge mysterious?" he asked, directing his words toward Wisdom Man, who looked far from pleased with Jay's appropriation of the podium. "Tell me, how do we *know* anything?"

And with that, I left for the university. How indeed do we know anything at all?

I'd almost finished reading *Budding Prospects*, TC Boyle's novel about a slipshod, three hundred acre pot farm in Mendocino County set in the late-1960s. One of the main characters was an odd fellow named Vogelsang; he'd funded the enterprise but didn't bother to tell the unfortunate fellows he hired to run the pot farm that the land had come cheap because its previous owner had been busted for selling marijuana, thus increasing its chances of being watched by the Drug Enforcement Agency. Jul gave the book to me, and then casually dropped the news that Vogelsang might have been loosely modeled after him. I was, of course, amused that my landlord would inform me of his semi-criminal past, albeit a fictionalized one, then supply me with a novel that might resemble the seedy tale. Fiction or not, Boyle could have been thinking of Jul when he described Vogelsang as speaking "as he always did, with a peculiar mechanical diction, each word distinct and unslurred, as if he were a linguistics professor moderating a panel discussion on the future of language." Jul must have loved that. He often asked me for grammar lessons then would debate the proper use of who and whom and whether or not the semicolon served any purpose. He took offense when I asked where his peculiar accent came from. "I have no accent," he said. "I just pronounce words their proper way. You ought to talk. What do you speak, Yvonics?" Clever, clever.

Suffice it to say that Jul was not your typical landlord. He stopped over on a regular basis to discuss his latest reading projects and events in the news. While there, he would inquire about my progress on the Boyle novel. Each time, I felt obliged to ask if he had remained friends with Boyle after the book was published.

"Oh, yes, best of friends. We'll get together when he's next in town," Jul promised. I'd certainly have liked that as I was intrigued with TC Boyle as much as I was curious about his relationship with Jul. Frankly, if Vogelsang had been modeled after me, I might not have appreciated the author who created him. Nor, and this was more to the point, would I have gone about handing out the book to new acquaintances with the pride that Jul projected. Boyle, however, could have been thinking of Jul when he described Vogelsang "as characteristically brisk and nervous in the way of a feral cat attuned to the faintest movements, the tiniest scratchings. He smelled of rain and something else too, something musky and primal. It took me a minute before I realized what it was: he reeked of sex."

I had noticed that after a day of work and an hour's run, accompanied by the proper amount of boasting, Jul did smell a bit ripe but I wouldn't have associated the smell with sex. To me, it was just old-fashioned pit. Nonetheless, as the plot unfolded and the hapless fools Vogelsang employed to grow his pot failed abysmally at almost every step of the way, I couldn't help but pity them. Jul could not understand how I could sympathize with the losers while disliking Vogelsang, who was paying them to dig trenches in the endlessly pouring rain, sit around for mindless hours in a remote patch of wilderness with absolute nutcases for neighbors, and worry themselves into nervous breakdowns about an impending bust. It was irrelevant, Jul insisted, that Vogelsang bought the land at a federal auction and kept that information about its history to himself until the others were mired deep in the venture.

"Vogelsang risked everything, put up the money, hired the growers. All the others had to do was take care of the plants and share in the rewards. They couldn't do anything right. How can you say Vogelsang is an unlikable character," he asked, exasperated with my lack of sympathy.

"Unlikable? He's downright sinister," I said. "He misleads his friends; he exploits them ruthlessly, then acts as if he's doing them a favor."

"He *was* doing them a favor," Jul said, suggesting that I'd completely missed the point of the book, that I was a bad reader. Too late, I realized I'd hurt his feelings.

Was I the one who had described San Francisco as the place of enchantment, the point of possibility, the home of reinvention? It was hard to maintain that vision after watching Stretch unfold his frame from the sidewalk or witness the clean needle exchange run by the city in the alley behind the Safeway grocery store. On Wednesday nights, the users lined up for their packets of hypodermic needles, no questions asked. Of course, clean syringes mean a healthier population of users but watching the other exchanges that went on in the Duboce Alley where the needle exchange was located was not very pleasant. This was a San Francisco you didn't see in the promotional material that Curly had so admired. Enchantment? Perhaps up there in Sea Cliff where Robin Williams, Sharon Stone and Cheech Marin lived or on Nob Hill where money has long translated into privilege, dating back to Leland Stanford days, but not on Market Street on the day I counted five reclined bodies between the LGBT and the Safeway and two men shooting up with their new needles while the city walked by, unfazed.

I didn't want to view the city solely through that lens and so I ventured out in search of a place I'd read about, a kind of Vermont meets San Francisco located on Nob Hill. (S)nob Hill still feels off limits to all but the very rich as it did in the days of the Big Four – C.P. Huntington, Leland Stanford, Mark Hopkins and Charles Crocker, the bonanza kings of the 1800s – although the Tenderloin, one of the city's most pitiful neighborhoods, is encroaching up the hill, creating a sub-neighborhood ironically called the Tendernob. Despite my tight budget, I made my way to Powell and Market, paid my $5 and stepped aboard a cable car packed with blondes from Wisconsin to marvel and hold our collective breath as the brakeman and the driver hurled us up and over the hills. At the top of the hill, heart-thumping as I sang the Rice-a-Roni song to myself, I stepped off the cable car and nearly fell into the arms of Marian and Vivian Brown, the famous San Francisco twins, wearing one of their signature outfits – leopard skin coats over red dresses, red heels upon their feet and red hats perched upon astonishing installations of hair. The twins were then in their eighties, about Mae West's age; I wondered if they'd ever met. She would have liked their outfits.

No sign of either the counterculture or the homeless as I wandered through Grace Cathedral Episcopal Church in all its Gothic splendor: bronze doors from Florence, stained glass windows and, best of all, its pair of labyrinths, circular paths of inlaid patterned coils, one inside, one out, then ambled over to the Intercontinental Mark Hopkins Hotel at Number One Nob Hill, a blend of French chateau and Renaissance mansion. I tried not to ogle at its overlarge and ornate everything from the gilded foyer to the three-hundred-and-sixty-degree view of the city available from any seat at the Top of the Mark restaurant and bar on the 19th floor. Although I was dressed in jeans, sneakers and leather jacket, no one chased me away as I strolled from window to window to look down upon the city. It costs about $280 a night to stay there, reasonable by San Francisco standards – that is, unless you want one of those $1600-a-night suites.

I was after something else, however, and eventually found the place I'd read about, the Bigfoot Lodge. There it was, taxidermy trophies and antlers on the walls of a bar decked out to look like a log cabin, complete with a nine-foot-tall resin Sasquatch presiding over the happy hour regulars sitting around a fake fireplace and enjoying the drink specials. Girl Scout Cookie, Toasted Marshmallow, or Forest Fire cocktail anyone?

As Curly had said: San Francisco, what a country.

Glenn, the handsome single man who lived directly above Mae, worked at an upscale jewelry and dinnerware store downtown. In the morning when you saw him out walking Zipper, his big russet dog named for the dark stripe along his backbone, or on his way back from the health club, Glenn wore gym shorts and sweatshirt, a towel around his neck. But in a half hour he transformed himself into a gay blade in blue blazer, a stylish shirt complete with gold cuff links, fashionable tie, sharply creased pants and Italian shoes. I had him in for apple pie the first day we met. After my years mothering a big family and entertaining the flood of friends who traipsed through my Vermont house, I was unable to buy just a few items at the grocery store, never mind resist the cornucopia of the farmers market. Baking pie was a form of therapy. It was great to have neighbors to share pie with so I wouldn't eat it all.

"I exercise to eat," Glenn said as he took a second slice. "I like that you put raisins in your apple pie. I like your politics too," he said, pointing to my "Worse President EVER" poster on the wall.

A few days later, Glenn slipped a note under my door while I was at work: "Many good Protestants are rolling in their graves with the news from the Episcopal Church of New Hampshire, and its decision to consecrate a gay bishop. Thank heavens that Henry VIII isn't around to see this attack on the sanctity of marriage, not to mention his wife Catherine of Aragon, his wife Anne Boleyn, his wife Jane Seymour, his wife Anne of Cleves, his wife Katherine Howard and his wife Catherine Parr."

A subsequent note read, "You're invited to the best fried chicken feast this side of the Mississippi Friday night at 7. We're celebrating the consecration of Rev. V. Gene Robinson, the first openly gay Episcopal bishop. Wear your sacramental vestments."

The front apartments on each floor in my building were laid out railroad style, unlike Ann's and mine and Gordon's, which had a central hall leading to the living room with the kitchen and bedrooms off to the sides. Instead of a roomy entryway as in our apartments, you entered a long hall off of which the other rooms ran in a row with the biggest room, the one most people would use as a living room, at the front of the building overlooking the street, and the kitchen at the opposite end of the hall at the back of the building. Glenn used the big front room for his bedroom, placing the bed against the windows so light bloomed all around him in the morning; he'd stuffed the room with bookshelves and piles of magazines and a swank chaise lounge. Throughout, the apartment was furnished in lavish rococo, red velvet couches and gold candle sconces, elaborately framed photographs of his family, a real dining room set with polished mahogany sideboard, table and chairs, each with its handsome striped velvet cushion.

The table was set with gold chargers, gold-rimmed dishes and wine glasses but the meal Glenn made for me was strictly down home. After a while, or after the third glass of wine, toasting each time, first to us, then to Bishop Robinson, then to Durham, New Hampshire where the minister would serve, we ate the wonderfully juicy chicken with our fingers. At one point I protested the use of damask napkins and retrieved paper towels from the kitchen. Zipper, ever so polite, watched from a distance, never begging, patiently awaiting the moment when he could vacuum the floor beneath our chairs.

All the while, we talked of travel, of France, of dogs and my longing for one, of the upcoming construction of Octavia Boulevard and what it might mean for us. I wondered if Glenn would keep his bedroom beneath those street-facing windows after the demolition began. He confessed it might not matter. He was looking for work on the west coast of Florida, where he had friends and the weather was better than that of San Francisco. After the fourth glass of wine, he confessed his real reason for leaving. He had thought when he moved to San Francisco that he'd find a circle of friends, perhaps a lover. But he had found the social scene hard to penetrate. He'd been living there two years and not made many friends. He was shy and didn't care for orgies or sex for the sake of sex. His family was far away in the Deep South, hence his proficiency in the fried chicken category. He had come to San Francisco, glad to be out of the South, only to find the city a lonely place for a single gay man.

His confession stunned me as I had the impression that San Francisco's gay community was welcoming and open. I, too, had thought I would make friends easily at the university but, although I was in a writing group and a member of both the executive board of the union and the faculty senate, none of the relationships I made in those settings grew into deep friendship. Until I moved to Octavia, I sometimes felt as if I'd come to the Bay Area too late. Everyone already had enough friends. Now I was again feeling part of a circle of people, a circle Jul had been creating for his entertainment, and mine.

"This Gnosticism you two were talking about last week, I could see why you'd be attracted to it, Yvonne." Jay was empty-handed for once, as if he wanted no art by distraction. "Not to say you're not deluded by *The DaVinci Code*, which is kind of Gnostic mysticism meets Hollywood, a ridiculous merger, but I wouldn't mind learning more about the truth beyond the veil myself."

"The truth beyond the veil?" I asked.

He turned his beady browns my way. He was high as a kite, I could see that. Jay was also smart enough to keep up with Wisdom Man's tangents, smart enough to goad him, which made our morning sessions all the more amusing. Was he serious about the Gnostics or just setting us up for one of his routines? Long before I'd arrived on the scene, Jay and Wisdom Man had been competing to prove who was the cleverest guy on the block.

"I do believe in an objective reality, what I think you Gnostics call 'essence.'" He turned toward Wisdom Man. "Do I have that right?"

Wisdom Man just nodded.

"Okay, so this objective reality provides an escape from the subjective mind, which causes each and every one of us so much suffering. I am suffering, you know. The world, the war, the damn cost of living in this city. I could use an escape from all my suffering, an escape more lasting than medical marijuana."

"Well," Wisdom Man said tentatively, assessing Jay's seriousness, "we understand that Gnosis is free of dogma, fanaticism, politics and sectarianism. That's what gives relief. It's as close to purity as the human is capable of achieving."

"Purity, really?" Jay's grin confirmed my suspicion that this was all a set-up. "I don't know about purity and I'd guess none of you do either. I'm interested in something more essential to survival than purity. I'm interested in humor and, of any religious group, I hear the Gnostics have the best jokes. For example, did you hear the one about God giving Adam the ability to stand up and pee?"

Where had that come from?

One thing you had to say about Wisdom Man, he could roll with the changes. He apparently knew the joke. So, rather than take offense, like Jerry Lewis and Dean Martin, he and Jay sat at the Laguna Sidewalk Café and on their second cup of coffee straight-manned one another through the entire routine for my entertainment. It went like this, with them taking turns with the lines:

Jay: God was walking through the Garden of Eden when he came upon Adam and Eve. So he asked if he could join them.

Wisdom Man: No sooner had he sat down than God started digging around in his old bag of tricks. "I'm giving away a few gifts today," God said. "Let's see what I have in here. Oh, here's a handy thing, being able to just stand up and pee."

Jay: And Adam said, "Give it to me, God. Please. I want it. It would be so cool to just stand up and let it rip. Give that gift to me, God. Please, please."

Wisdom Man: Eve just flipped her wrist dismissively and said, "Let him have it if he wants it so bad."

Jay: So God gave Adam the gift to piss standing up.

Wisdom Man: And it was good.

Jay: Eve just watched and smiled and bided her time.

Wisdom Man: Then God looked inside his bag to see what gifts he had left.

Jay: And God said, "Oh, let's see, just one more thing here. What is it? Oh, yes, multiple orgasms."

Wisdom Man: And Eve said, "Okay, give that to me."

They delivered the punch line together: And it was good.

All the time that Jay and Wisdom Man did their routines, while Ted and Tom and I laughed and Elise poured our refills, while we pondered the meaning of the Gnostic joke and the Zen monks came and went from the Zen center, and the neighbors walked their dogs, while all these ridiculous performances were unfolding, all the while, the one I called Silent Guy sat next to us, showing as little affect on his face as a person on Quaaludes. All the while, he rolled and smoked his cigarettes and watched the traffic. His fingers were stained yellow from tobacco. He wore his black beret and his jean jacket like a uniform. Occasionally, he'd take a sandwich, bologna on white bread or peanut butter and jelly, from an inside pocket and eat it silently, abstractly.

What gift, I wondered, would he ask for?

♪

"By the way, that wasn't my girlfriend the other night," Noel said when I ran into him again. He turned those cataracts on me, smiling a daredevil smile. "No siree. We're just friends. Noel, he's a single man. Any time you want to go to a little jazz club, you let me know. I'll be your date. I knew them all, Satchmo, that bad boy Chet Baker, not a nice cell in his body but he played like an angel. And 'Trane, oh what a sweetheart. Yep, I knew them all. And Latin music too. I am your man, the best dancer in this dancing town. Samba. Rumba. You come see me, number 7. We'll paint the town."

He spoke with a slight Latin accent. I wanted to engage him in conversation, to learn his story, but he was gone, strutting with purpose, off I hoped to see that beautiful woman who wasn't his girlfriend.

$

In Boyle's *Budding Prospects*, Vogelsang's girlfriend Aorta was a member of a punk band named The Nostrils. She was thin and solemn, detached and sexy. The other men were drawn to her.

"Who is this Aorta person?" I asked Jul when he came over to gauge my progress on the book and argue politics if I were up for it.

"Oh, that's supposed to be my starter wife," Jul said. "Boyle totally invented her. It's a fiction, remember."

I had asked the question while Mary was in the bathroom. We were visiting over tea and cookies. I didn't want to bring up something that might prove delicate in front of her. She must have heard us, though, because her voice came disembodied from down the hall, saying, "We have a lot in common, me and Jul's first wife. We share a birthday."

When she joined us, I asked them both about that horrible phrase of Jul's, his "starter wife." So dismissive. So rude.

"Everyone starts with someone," Jul protested. "It's not sexist at all, if that's what you're thinking. She can refer to me as her starter husband if she wants."

"Well you might be right," I said. "Most people I know refer to their former spouses in even more deleterious terms. It just sounds so …" I couldn't think of the right word for my discomfort about his comparing his first wife to training wheels on a bicycle or a training bra, but that was exactly what he did mean.

The conversation segued to his and Mary's marriage, which had made its way onto the pages of the *San Francisco Chronicle,* another claim to fame that gave Jul great pleasure. Mary and Jul were in their fifties when Jul got it into his head that Mayor Willie Brown should marry them in City Hall. "His mayor," as Brown was then referred to in acknowledgement of his celebrity status, occasionally married people but the privilege was usually bestowed upon the privileged. Jul was not deterred. He went to Brown's office and began telling the mayor's assistant what he had in mind, turning on the full Jul persistence. Eventually, a muscular black man whom Jul assumed was Willie Brown's bodyguard walked over to ask what Jul needed.

"I immediately recognized that this man had the power to make things happen, that he had the mayor's ear. When I first started telling our story, he had said, 'Take all the time you need.' So I did. I told him, 'I love the mayor. I love this city. I love talking to you. I have all the time in the world.' The mayor's man realized I wasn't going anywhere or that if I did leave, I'd be back – and back, if need be. He picks up the phone and calls the mayor's scheduler. 'Naomi,' he says, 'when is the mayor's next open house?'

"Back then, Willie Brown held an open house once a month with about ten minutes allotted to each of twenty-five people or parties invited in for a private audience. My guy's talking to Naomi on the phone, then listening, then he says, 'Okay, I got a couple here who want the mayor to marry them. You got space available at the next open house? Okay, good. Make them last, number twenty-five.' The fella's right here and I've an inkling he'll want to chat it up with the mayor after the ceremony.'"

According to the article published in the *Chronicle,* the mayor complimented Jul and Mary on the choice of venue for their wedding, San Francisco City Hall, whereupon Jul interrupted His Honor to say, "I heard you come down in disguise on Sundays to work on it," whereupon Willie Brown said, "Actually, I come down to help clean it, too." Although the mayor had held thirty-one open houses up to then, that was the first time he'd officiated as justice of the peace at one.

Being married to Jul must have been a full-time job. He wasn't exactly a poster boy for the up-by-the-bootstraps movement but everything Jul had he'd made on his own, beginning years before the *Budding Prospects* venture. Jul had grown up in Malibu, a restless teenager, bored in community college and eager to see the world when a relative dressed smartly in his Army uniform came by to visit his family. This was the mid-1960s. That uniform had made an impression on young Jul, as had the lure of adventure that the military recruiters promised. Throughout his childhood, he and his father had shared an interest in airplanes. All that and a looming draft notice led Jul to enlist in the Army's pilot-training program. After telling me the story of his and Mary's marriage, Jul told me about Vietnam, describing his tour of duty as months of easy assignments as a helicopter commander, ferrying people from one outpost to another, followed by torturous months during which the base he was assigned to was routinely attacked each night. In this as in other moments of Jul's life, luck and timing were with him. The Tet Offensive occurred just as he returned to the states.

Unlike the stereotypical Vietnam veteran, Jul didn't struggle with guilt after the war. He had seen his share of dead bodies and received several medals of valor, primarily for flying the wounded out of rather dicey battle zones. But he had avoided the worst of that disaster -- exposure to Agent Orange or prolonged hand-to-hand combat in the dense and terrifying jungle. Once home in Southern California, he capitalized on friendships and connections he'd made in the military and at home, sought and took advice from successful people in both worlds, and began investing in property. While some of us were turning on and tuning out, Jul might have been turning on, too, but he also tuned in to his distinctly intuitive version of the American dream. He was instinctively suspicious of corporate America from an early age and remained so. With the exception of his time in the Army, he had never worked for anyone but himself or bought into what he called "the imperial corporate world." His money was in the bank and in property, not in the stock market. Over the decades, he had owned properties throughout the Haight-Ashbury, in Malibu, San Luis Obispo, and in Mendocino.

In comparison with most landlords I'd encountered, Jul was surprisingly generous. He often picked up the tab for dinner or a movie, but he drew the line, of course, on the rent. When it was due, it was due. Money, after all, was the purpose of landlording. (Jul objected to the term landlord, by the way, considering it a feudal title.) He and Mary were also generous with their time, purposefully showing me the city by inviting me to accompany them to art movies and esoteric concerts where, invariably, Jul would find someone with whom to cogitate, deliberate, ponder and debate. All the while, he collected names, people, calling cards, actually phoning people he met by chance and befriending anyone he found interesting, picking their brains on whatever subject or area of expertise had attracted him to them in the first place, a most intriguing fellow.

Mary, on the other hand, was quiet, understandable given the oversize of Jul's personality. We often ventured to the Peninsula together to bird-watch or hike, activities best enjoyed without Jul's long-winded recitations.

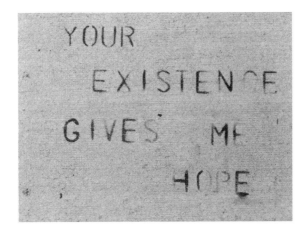

Stencil Outside the Lesbian Gay Bisexual Transgender Community Center

It's always unfortunate when you hear strange things or, worse, uncomplimentary gossip about a person before you meet him or her. Thus it was that when Robin stuck his head out his apartment door, the one next to mine, and yelled in a voice and manner reminiscent of my brother Michael, eerily using Michael's favorite greeting, "Hey, stuck up," that, although I should have known better, I ignored the warnings I'd heard from others in the building to stay away from him. Robin had seemed harmless in our passing conversations, so I accepted his invitation for a drink at the Orbit Room, just a block away.

Robin talked a constant stream of nonsense, or nonsense to me, all the way to the coffee/alcohol bar located in a handsome art deco building with tall windows that opened onto the intersection of Market, Laguna and Hermann streets. I'd been walking by the place for weeks, intrigued by the mix of business suits and punks with turquoise hair who sat around Orbit's curved bar and, somewhat uncomfortably, its oversized drum-shaped tables. Talk about yum: I don't remember what the drink the bartender assembled was called, but it was concocted from about six kinds of fresh fruit, a sprinkle of sugar, a couple of shots of Absolut citron and ice. While I watched her make it, a process that seemed to take forever, Robin segued from one to another comeback scheme or film project or novel plot that he was pursuing. It was hard to follow his stream of conscious ramble because his teeth seemed to slide sideways and I couldn't catch all the words that spilled from him in speeded-up and hopelessly optimistic garbles. And we still hadn't had our first drink. When it arrived, it was so good I almost downed it but just sipped. Robin, on the other hand, emptied his glass in three quick gulps, then renewed his soliloquy mid-sentence. I understood him well enough. I have known and loved men like him most of my life, men with big dreams and talent who took too many drugs or wouldn't play the game, men who got off track and couldn't find the way back, men born as the gender rules were changing and those who bent the rules too often. Most of all, Robin reminded me of my brother. And that, of course, was why I had gone to the bar with him and why I continued to sit while he ordered us another drink. Like Michael, Robin had really been something. My brother was dead, dead from drink, and I missed him at times with a ferocity that would just nail me. And so I listened. I tried to get Robin to slow his ratcheting brain down for a minute, to tell just one part of his story, to finish one story before starting another. His face was bloated, his eyes robin egg blue of course, but hooded, his hair tousled, going gray. He was handsome as an old movie star, the miles embedded in his face.

Robin's legacy was not bravado or hyperbole. His music clubs were intertwined with the city's recent history, which was why Jul had rented to him in the first place, that and because Robin had rarely charged him for drinks and never the cover charge. Of course that had been Robin's problem; he had a hard time charging anyone. Robin's nightclubs were now closed but in the 1980s and 90s, everyone who was anyone had performed there on their way up or down. Robin had partied with them all. I'd been the voyeur; I'd Googled his name after hearing some of the tales about him during my first weeks in the building. He might now be "spinning around like a dreidel in a hurricane," as *SF Weekly* had described Robin a few years previously when his plan to sell one of his clubs to some Burning Man organizers had fallen through. I suspected his problem was not just a taste for alcohol and drugs and anything else available in a city that stretched the boundaries; his brain was worn as much from use as abuse, as much from the rollicking electricity of genius always turned on to discovering the next great thing in rock 'n' roll as it was from whatever substances were routinely abundant in the course of any of his days.

Once we get into our fifties, many of us have histories too complicated and non-linear to tell in one sitting anyhow. That's why couples stay together or break apart; it's too hard to explain yourself. That was certainly true of Robin who seemed to have lived several lives simultaneously and seemed obsessed with telling me his entire saga, all at once, as if he'd never have another chance. He spun out two strands of conversation, each chopped up and laced through with schemes for a renewal. He'd start to explain one scheme, which was to create a live video club with multimedia interactivity between the crowd and the performers, a fabulous idea. But before I could learn more or comment, he'd shift into a lamentation about his grown daughters and his hope of undoing the years he'd neglected them by offering them shelter in our Octavia building or otherwise shepherding them into adulthood. Indeed, if I understood him correctly, his progeny would be moving in soon, one with two children, the other alone. I didn't need the details but there they were, fueled now by the third drink, a sad story, a death, one daughter needing a moment of stability for herself and her children; the other just needing stability.

Eventually, I had my limit of alcohol and defeat. It had occurred to me why he reminded me so much of Michael. Robin disgorged the broken tale of what he planned to do and why he couldn't do it, the list of obstacles, the mea culpas, just as Michael had done until the end. He was a sweet man, a well-intentioned man. With men like him, there would always be a plan but there would seldom be an implementation. And so I bid goodbye.

As I walked by Orbit's big windows on my way home, I could see that Robin was already engaged in conversation with the bartender, rehearsing his reincarnation.

"How do you like your Red Sox now?" Wisdom Man asked, grinning meanly.

"I didn't think you were paying attention," I said. Wisdom Man had been unable to hide his dismissive response to hearing that my husband was a sportswriter even though I told him Chuck could go one-on-one with him on a few other subjects, especially history. "I don't fill my mind with trivia I don't find useful for understanding the deeper meanings of life," Wisdom Man had said rather smarmily. Now, what was he up to, bringing up the dismal ending to the 2003 World Series?

"The come-back kids blew it," I said, playing his game. "Visions of things to come."

"You mean the election," Wisdom Man asked. He was one smart fellow. That was exactly what I had meant.

"Everything has portent about the election," I said. "The good guys never win; that's why the good guys root for the Red Sox. Besides, that's what's so great about baseball. You know who the good guys are. When it comes to politics, it's a bit more tricky."

"What's up with you?" Elise asked. Over the weekend, she had shaved her hair into uneven splotches that resembled a sloppy checkerboard. "Those nuts out there got you down?"

"No, not them."

Elise looked at me purposefully. She stopped steaming my milk.

"Why don't you ask your friend out there how that school of his actually works? That's what I'd like to know. As far as I can tell, all he does is sit there and run his mouth. He's an ass."

"Why do you say that?"

"And that other one with the cigarettes. Those two never tip. They're losers. You work for a living. Don't people who sit around all day talking bullshit or smoking one cigarette after another just frost your ass?"

"Do you think he's a Trustaferian?"

"Ha! I haven't heard that one in a while," she said, finally getting back to my latte. "I think he's a nut, that's what I think. I don't care what he lives on – welfare, disability or family money. I care that he has all day to sit around and blab away to whoever will listen, wants refill after refill, and never puts a cent in my tip jar. But what are you so bummed out about?"

"Red Sox."

"Can't help you there, being from New York. But the coffee's on me," she said. I tipped her what I would have spent on my coffee and went back outside to sit with the nutcases on the sidewalk.

"Just shut up about the Red Sox," I growled at Wisdom Man. Miracle of miracles, he did.

Unfortunately, Wisdom Man's unusual hush provided an opportunity for Tom, the self-proclaimed refugee from Vermont and Paris, to pester me for writing lessons, to read his memoir. Over the past few weeks, Tom had confessed his desire to write about his exploits with women, his inability to make up his mind which one he should live with as if he might find a sympathetic ear from me, taking my distance from home and my husband as a sign that we shared an inability to commit. I had found his descriptions of his two women to be more about him than them. It hadn't taken long to figure out that the one in Vermont, the mother of his children, offered security, while the one in Paris, young of course, offered something else entirely. Poor man.

"Perhaps the professor would give us a writing prompt," he asked.

"I've got one," I said. "Silence."

Out of the corner of my eye, I saw the little grin on Silent Guy's face.

I couldn't get Robin's tales out of my head. In the moments that we spent on the marble steps trading stories or at Orbit bar when I joined him for a second round of fruit juice and vodka, I came to see that his story was the city's story. He had moved to San Francisco in the 1980s from the North Bay and instantly lunged into the whole scene, the music, the drugs, the sex. He was considered one of the founders of music and comedy dance clubs in the South of Market section of the city. His idea for a multimedia nightclub was not his first innovation. He had owned the first multi-show nightclub of the era. One band might be performing hard rock in one room of his rambling nightclub, while an acoustic set was finishing up in another room and a comic starting his routine in a third. Often enough, perhaps too often for Robin's financial success, the performances benefited some non-profit organization or other cause to which Robin had donated the space, half the proceeds and his own organizational talents.

As he explained, he was never good with the math, the keeping of records and the filing of forms. It all eventually unraveled. Just as what was so essential about San Francisco, how mind-altering drugs and the influence of the East had transformed the way people conducted commerce and politics there, resulting in the quirky freedoms of the place and its excesses, both dazzling and unfortunate, so too did Robin's undisciplined joyride though the seventies, the eighties, and so on taken a personal toll. No one could say he hadn't earned it.

He was certainly not alone. If the rest of the world had experienced a kind of wonderful debauchery in those eras, San Francisco and its residents had immersed themselves in the surfeit. Tens of thousands drank too much, slept with the wrong people, and got into situations from which they couldn't extricate themselves, burned out, went broke and died of the new disease called AIDS. Robin had seen it all. Yet he sought to reinvent himself and his club, to save his children. I admired that.

Late at night, when he knocked on my door, if I were up and inclined to listen, I'd let him in to ramble over a glass of scotch or vodka. Eventually, he'd get frisky and I'd have to send him home. Other nights, one of his ex-wives or ex-girlfriends would show up and need a place to stay and he'd paddle off to his apartment to give them comfort. Robin's women took to ringing my bell if he didn't answer his own. I was glad I'd not heeded the words of warning. If this was indeed the city of renewal, Robin might have enough for another performance.

Gail lived in a handsome green Victorian on the corner of Page and Octavia with two Shih Tzu dogs named Molly and Dolly. When I first met her, Gail had only Molly, whom I showered with the kind of affection a wannabe dog owner brings to these sidewalk encounters. Gail inherited Dolly after her ex-husband, for whom she'd bought Dolly, sent her back. I'd been listening to the saga for weeks as we passed on our way to the coffee shop: the purchase of the puppy, the delivery of the puppy, the refusal of the puppy. Now Gail was struggling down the street with these two adorable dogs, one old and settled and well behaved, the other, young and sprightly and full of mischief. I wanted a dog of my own, of course, but I was willing to help Gail around the block. She was scheduled to have an operation on her leg in a few weeks. The young Dolly would be a problem.

"I'll take her," I said, more than once, shamelessly. Dolly was certainly my kind of dog with her willful manner and pretty face.

"We'll see," Gail said, but I held out little hope, she was already smitten.

I loved San Francisco in the fog, especially at night when the clouds were layered low, making the air otherworldly, psychedelic. Light pulsed. The din of cars and people throbbed, skin breathed. Pink and turquoise blotches of light vibrated faintly against the damp pavement in front of the Baptist Church but its neon sign that spelled BAPTIST was shrouded in mist. Jack said the white cross atop the church roof used to rotate.

As I rounded the corner from Octavia on to Market in the haze, the colors and sounds of the city were suddenly magnified: traffic lights bled yellow, red, green. Car horns were a rude intrusion over the thump of engines, the thrum of tires. When I walked my Vermont neighborhood at night, even though Rutland was one of Vermont's larger cities, only a few cars would pass by and rarely a pedestrian.

San Francisco walked. And because I am a gawker, I was phylum *Porifera*, a human sponge, absorbing all I passed. That may have been why I loved the fog when the traffic of people and cars were cloaked in haze. The fog insulated me from the harshness of the city so that I felt less alone, less isolated, less visible. Walking through vapor suspended in air, I'd revert to an old habit of singing to myself, old favorites like Dylan's Chimes of Freedom:

> Through the wild cathedral evening the rain unraveled tales
> For the disrobed faceless forms of no position
> Tolling for the tongues with no place to bring their thoughts
> All down in taken-for-granted situations

And singing that song in the moody fog brought to mind, in the way that one thought can lead unpredictably to another, my parents, who had abhorred Dylan as much as I had been enamored of him. I didn't know before my parents died that I would miss them so much, how I would wish I'd asked them more, told them more when I had the chance.

They'd hate to hear me say that I owe everything I am to their repressive upbringing, a line I've used many times because it sums me up. Growing up in my parents' home, I heard a litany of negativity: "Why do you ask so many questions," "Get your nose out of that book," "Stop gawking," "Girls can't do that," and "Mind your own business." My parents' childhoods had left them battered and untrusting. My father had been abandoned on the altar of a Catholic church at age four; he'd essentially raised himself. My mother's father came home to Nova Scotia periodically, impregnated my grandmother, then left again, a perpetual roamer. Years after their appalling childhoods, my parents reinvented themselves and raised us kids in relative comfort. But their pasts, over which they had no control but felt great shame, had made them deeply secretive. No matter how I pried, they held their cards close to the vest, as my father used to say, never revealing their motivations, hopes and fears. They cautioned us to do the same. I could not tell you how many times I got in trouble for smiling in public, for talking to strangers. In their household, striving to be unlike them, resisting their paranoia and fear and longing to unravel their secrets, to know my past through theirs, I became a sleuth, a solver of mysteries, a questioner. In their house, where books were nearly absent and smart people were called eggheads, I became a reader.

My parents characterized people by the color of their skin, their last name or the shape of their nose, by the aroma of their food or the place where they worshipped. They made me a defender and a debater. I couldn't understand their need to compartmentalize, to label. My brothers and sisters got in trouble for sneaking out bedroom windows or stealing my father's cigarettes. As the youngest, I learned from their mistakes and didn't repeat them. My transgressions usually involved opening my mouth to ask what seemed like an obvious question or to come to the defense of someone or some idea, only to learn that I'd uttered the blasphemy of independent thought or committed yet again the unpardonable sin of being curious.

In this perverse way, my parents trained me well for the career I stumbled upon and have pursued for more than twenty years, that of the journalist, the paid gawker, the minder of other peoples' business. I was thinking all this as I rounded Church Street, the fog a mantle of disembodiment that gave everything an otherworldly softness, because earlier that day I had seen my father. He was standing with his back to me, the perfectly shaped "u" of his hairline where it met his collar, the slight wave in his brown-going-to-silver hair, the assurance even from a distance in the way he held his head. My heart literally knocked. I was rushing toward him when logic knocked back so that by the time I'd caught up to the man, I knew not to be disappointed.

My parents never knew what to make of me and I'm sorry for that, or sorry they had other dreams for me than the ones I followed. In their last years, they were pleased to find my name in national magazines, to point out my byline to friends. But they would not have been pleased with the means a journalist used to get her stories, the very actions they cautioned against. And they would be even more displeased now, to see me stopping to chat with Stretch as he sat in the church alcove eating the Twinkies I had purchased at the Safeway to bring to him. So sweet was the moment, there in the shadow of the church overhang, there in the damp fog, that I ate one myself.

Moments later, back home and walking past Dad smiling at me, one of the cigarettes that killed him still burning in the framed black and white photograph atop a bookshelf, I told him not to worry. With friends like Stretch in the neighborhood, I would be all right.

Robin's daughters, long, lanky, tattooed beauties, moved in. Along with Star's babies, the boy a nimbus of blond curls as he shrieked down the hall, the girl a streak of energy trailed by a red ponytail, they also brought an entourage of misfits, orphans and abandoned pets. Robin loved it all. I think he fashioned himself as the guru of strays, both the ones he had fathered and the others who showed up at his door, sniffing out the luscious daughters. Smoke of all kinds oozed from under his door as the homeless butch women who lusted after Robin's beautiful progeny dragged their pit bulls down the hall and boy punks in fuchsia hair and leather crowded the marble steps outside, making deals and selling bootleg CDs, longing for the babes (the older ones) inside. It was simultaneously entertaining and annoying as I stepped over the bodies or wondered how many keys to the building were out there in illegal land. The pit bulls were banned from Robin's apartment when Acacia, the younger daughter, brought home six newborn kittens, abandoned on the street. The kittens, barely alive, mewed from behind Robin's door and, over the next few weeks, died, one by one, until only two little toughies survived. The older daughter moved out, children and all, within a few weeks, heading north to Mendocino or Ukiah, I never got the details right, to open a dude ranch. But Acacia was there to stay.

Robin had a new version of the drama each time I saw him. He'd start mid-sentence, mid-story, using names of people I didn't know, picking up plots I hadn't heard the opening chapters to, sometimes frantic, running fingers through his rumpled hair, sometimes hopeful, winking in open lasciviousness, asking to be asked inside.

The butch women tied their pit bulls outside so they wouldn't eat the kittens, hardly a better solution as the dogs growled and snarled at anyone who walked by. And the butches themselves, two brassy blondes with leather and spikes at all the appropriate places, wrists, necks, ankles, who slept in a blue van parked on the street and did their laundry downstairs, right under my apartment, at all hours of the night, they snarled too.

"Oh, them," Robin said when I complained about the slamming of dryer doors at 2 a.m. "It's just an act. Acacia sleeps with one, then the other, so they do get a little worked up. Keeps life interesting. She's exploring her lesbian side but she doesn't see herself as a lesbian. Or even bi. She's just not into men right now. But those girls are harmless, better than some of the guys she brings around. You can't trust junkies, you know."

"Girls?" I asked.

Robin was deaf to the complaints from his fellow apartment dwellers, which included me, that the smoke from his apartment permeated the building. Talk about ashtray. His apartment had locomotive breath.

"Hey, this is San Francisco," he'd say. "Get with the program. Free will. Free love. Free me."

Which would be when I'd wander back to my apartment.

The most frequent of Robin's visitors was a woman who looked like an expensive call girl with a mighty active cocaine habit. She always gave me the hooded glare as she slithered down the hall, all perky tits and tight jeans. She never walked but rather seemed to balance on the tippy-toes of her high heels, half scurrying, half slinking into Robin's apartment after waking me to let her in the building for the umpteenth time.

"Are you running a harem or a brothel in there?" I asked the day after I'd encountered four or five different women coming from or going into his apartment in a matter of hours. I would have thought it orchestrated if I believed that either Robin or the women were capable of such coordination.

"A brothel?" Robin asked as if he wished he'd thought of the idea. "No, it's just the ex-wives, looking for a little. Don't worry. I'm saving it for you. Only kidding. Or, I wish I wasn't only kidding. Rita? The skinny one? She's not a prostitute. I know you think she is; everyone does when they meet her. She's a sex therapist. She gets paid to talk to men about sex, that's all. She's been through a bit of a bad time and we're helping her out. She's one of our projects, Acacia and me."

Remembering my first conversation with Gordon, I wondered how many projects were going on in this building, anyhow.

"Here you are, fellow Terran," Wisdom Man said before I had even ordered my latte. "We're starting a branch of the Uniterran Church. We need you to fill out our membership."

"Membership? In the Unitarian Church?" I asked.

"No, not Unitarian. I thought so at first, too. It's unite and terra, Unite the Earth," he said as Tom gave me his chair. Brown noser.

I was quite entertained by the idea that Wisdom Man needed me for anything intellectual or spiritual. As a recovering Catholic who majored in philosophy, I could fake it through our morning conversations. But honestly I was often lost as, for example, when he spoke quite seriously one day of "the gender of the seed," which had been the subject of his master's dissertation. I hadn't a clue as to his exact meaning, something about the Greeks and Hippocrates and early man's understanding of power and reproduction and sexual roles. He had tried to explain it to Silent Guy and me for an entire hour; by the time I gave up trying to understand, I had needed a nap.

I did like the Gnostic mandate, Know Thyself. Wisdom Man used it liberally. And if I did believe in God, which I was not quite sure of, I might be able to accept that, as Wisdom Man taught us, within each person was an "inner" person, a fallen spark of divinity. I used to believe something like that but two decades as a journalist, even in Vermont, had cured me. There are two words a journalist might use to sum up the themes of her career and they were senseless and humbling. Too many people and deeds fell under the first category – senseless murders, senseless greed, senseless bureaucracy, and so on. For a long time, I had kept at the profession because of the humbling experiences in which I got to celebrate remarkable people who had made a difference. More and more though, I found it hard to feel good about my own species, the human, the Earth Dwellers or Terrans, as Wisdom Man was now calling us. We seemed so entirely damaged, so far from partaking in divinity, so stuck in clannish behavior that I came to the café filled with dismay, hopelessly depressed after listening to the morning news.

Wars dominated the news day after day, all this killing and shaming in the name of Judaism, Islam and Christianity. Nations called what they did self-defense but when it was done to them by their enemies, they called it terrorism. And with the run-up to the presidential primaries in full gear, I had little hope that the killing would end any time soon. Even the supposed forerunner for the Democrats, John Kerry, had taken to war mongering.

But it was too depressing to start the day that way. I gave myself a mental slap, put *Morning Edition* behind me and listened up. The men were sitting around the table, each with his preferred form of caffeine, waiting for my response to Wisdom Man's question.

"Okay," I said. "What's up? What is this church you're so interested in now? And by the way, don't you have enough going on with your interest in Gnosticism and your meditations at the Zen center and your Wisdom School? Don't you have enough to keep yourself busy rather than join another church?"

"Do I look busy?" His cheeks were a particularly vivid shade of red and his fine blond hair shone with cleanliness. The part was perfect.

Wisdom Man had learned of the Uniterran Church, a "neo-pagan" group founded in Florida of all places, from one of his students and had spent the last couple of days "doing research" and making contacts with other members of the "church."

"Don't confuse it with the Unitarian church," he warned, "although they're both rather unspecific in their doctrine. Central to the Uniterran Church is a belief that the Earth is sacred and alive. It's totally sympathetic with my existing practices and interests. Listen to this: Uniterrans believe it is the *duty* of all Earth dwellers to care for the Earth and preserve it, a duty to teach tolerance and provide service to humanity. It's Christianity with responsibility but without the condemnation. You gotta' love it."

Wisdom Man said the word "love" with gusto. He was the most earnest person I'd known in a long while. Nonetheless, as a recovering Catholic, I was interested in rituals. If I were going to join any church, I wanted it to have rituals. Wisdom Man told us we were already performing the kind of rituals Uniterrans considered most significant. We met and shared sustenance together on a regular basis, our morning coffee. We cared about the planet and meditated on ways to make it healthier. Several of us were teachers. And, to top it off, he noted that we each in our own way practiced the basic principles of the Uniterrans, which he referred to with the group's acronym, DART, for Diversity, Acceptance, Respect and Tolerance.

"We're already Uniterrans," he said again fervently, opening up his thin arms to signal the inclusion of Jay, Tom, Ted, Silent Guy and me. "We just didn't know it."

The first order of business was to give each of us a job and title. I got my coffee and let it roll. Since he was our organizer and resident specialist, we let Wisdom Man be our Abecedarian or Education Coordinator. I accepted the role of Master Bard, even though poetry was not my genre, while Silent Guy granted that his title, Master Fire Tender, was most appropriate since he was the one with the stick matches. He didn't articulate any of this, of course; he just held up the match that he would later strike against the side of his jeans. Jay was thrilled to be Master Healer and said he'd provide earth-based art therapy and give us all medical marijuana prescriptions immediately. Old Ted the politico wanted to be our Master Guardian, protecting us from false claims and insecurity. Tom, whom I'd begun to view as an annoyance, announced yet again that he was heading to Paris or Vermont in a day or two. Either way, if we would allow, he would like to be our Foreign Ambassador.

We toasted the creation of the latest branch of the Uniterran Church over our coffees while Silent Guy and Jay and Ted lit up, all from Silent Guy's single matchstick.

You can learn a lot from a person by the way he or she treats his or her spouse and friends. Gordon was so liberal with his generosity to us, his neighbors, that I quickly regretted my rudeness when I had first met him. He ran errands for Mae and Noel, the senior members of our family. He called Noel *Tio*, uncle in Spanish, and now that Noel was old, Gordon went out of his way to wait on him. Gordon was a cab driver and occasionally used the cab to haul in various items he knew the older members of our family there on Octavia might need, no questions asked. Noel might have twenty cans of Ajax and a hundred rolls of paper towels stashed in his overcrowded apartment but if he asked for another of something he already had too many of, Gordon obliged. He moved Noel's stacks of magazines from one place to another and gave up on suggesting that it might be time to throw some of them away. Gordon sat with Noel to watch the Giant's games, their mutual favorite team. He brought Mae books on tape and boxes of chocolates. He helped Ann with her groceries, with the many things a mother had to carry from the car and up and down the stairs. He fixed things when they broke – garbage disposals, locks, toilets – without asking or accepting recompense. He spoke of his wife, Liya, in the most tender words, describing how he'd met her when she worked at Fisherman's Wharf and how she'd rejected every other male who came to court her. "She was an Ethiopian queen, so regal, so beautiful, so centered," he said. "Everybody wanted her." Now, twenty-five years later and still married, they had seen their only daughter graduate from the now-defunct Baptist school next door and go off to college.

When the ants invaded my apartment one weekend while I was away, Gordon helped me sweep them up and we traded remedies for eradicating the pests. I showed him the pyramid of tiny ants that were freeze-dried just inside my refrigerator's freezer and we stood there speculating as to whether they had piled themselves up like that to keep warm or whether it was a form of mass suicide. He had never seen the Chinese chalk that you could use to keep ants out, drawing a line across which ants would never crawl. We don't have ants like that in Vermont, Argentine ants that invade by the thousands and were not deterred by boric acid, ant traps or poisons. You bought the Chinese chalk at one of those jam-crammed stores in Chinatown, three pieces for $3.99.

"What do you think is in it?" I asked.

"Don't know and don't want to know, but let's draw a line around the outside of the building," Gordon said. "The ants come inside for water when it's dry and come in to get out of the water in the rainy season. Twice a year, they invade buildings all through the Bay Area. We'll declare ourselves an ant-free zone."

Gordon had never heard the story of how I had gotten my apartment and I told it to him as we drew our chalk line. I told him I thought Jul had picked me because he thought I'd provide ample opportunity for provocative conversations.

"Don't be deceived. No one buys a rental building because they like people," Gordon said, suggesting I might try being a little self-protective when it came to Jul, a little less naive. He had worked six years for Jul, during which he'd been fired and rehired at least twenty times. "Don't try to understand the logic behind it," he said when I asked why he kept going back to work, why he cleaned the building even when he'd been fired.

"I accept money to do what I would do anyhow, simply because I live here," he said. A fellow with that attitude had all the right in the world to be proprietary, I thought. I couldn't help but wish that Jul would make Gordon the official building manager and give him a little extra income. With their daughter in college and elderly parents, Gordon and Liya's money was tight. Not that either one ever told me this or complained. They had a wonderful attitude about money; when they got a little extra, they sent it to Lydia or to their parents and continued to live on as little as possible. Liya had grown up in Ethiopia where her father had been a preacher in the Seventh Day Adventist church and her mother a schoolteacher. By the time I moved into the building, Liya's father was more than one hundred years old and, although still preaching, he and her mother needed money for medical care. Gordon's parents lived on the East Coast and he worried about them and helped them out when he could.

But each time I suggested that Jul make Gordon the official building manager, Jul would say, "I've told Gordon a dozen times, 'You have been a tenant too long; it's time for you to buy your own apartment building so that you can run it the way you want.'" By that, he meant that if he asked for something to be done, he didn't want suggestions as to how it should be accomplished. Which, again, Gordon would say was Jul's right. The last thing he wanted to be was a landlord. After living in a twelve-unit building that he cared about for thirty-four years, Gordon could recite a catalogue of miseries that came with property ownership.

"The one thing Jul doesn't understand is that I'll be here in this building long after he's gone. Soon enough, when the right situation presents itself, he'll sell the building but, unless I die first, which I doubt, I'll still be here. I plan to spend my last thirty-four here."

"You really think he'd sell?" I asked. "It seems like he's invested a lot into choosing who lives here for reasons that go far beyond money. I had the impression he was in for the long haul." Indeed, the best way for Jul to make money on his investment would be to outlast some of the long-term tenants like Gordon, Noel and Mae. Our building was rent-controlled, which meant that I paid a substantially higher rent than the tenants he'd inherited when he bought the building. It made sense that Gordon planned to remain here as long as possible. He'd never get a comparable rent.

The point I was trying to make was that being a landlord was more than just an enterprise to Jul, that of course he wanted to make a good profit but he was also interested in surrounding himself with people he could learn from and impress with his own acumen.

"Don't let Jul fool you," Gordon said without rancor or malice, more as a point of reference. "When the price is right, Jul will sell. That's what he does. You think he's interested in us as individuals but you forget he's a businessman. You're a big Dylan fan, right? You'd better go listen to his "Dear Landlord" one more time. Don't underestimate the power of money."

And just as Noel had sung "Star Dust" as he ambled upstairs a few months previously, I watched Gordon take the stairs two at a time, singing, "Dear

Landlord, please don't put a price on my soul. My burden is heavy; my dreams are beyond control."

As I rounded the corner, I saw that Tom and Jay, Wisdom Man and Silent Guy were already gathered around our table deep in conversation. It was early but the sun felt luscious. October is the best time of year in San Francisco, sun-drenched days with cerulean skies. Unfortunately, my café comrades and I were not in sunny dispositions. For the past week or two, we had spent our mornings in dark conversation, analyzing the voters' moods, amazed, appalled, enthralled. Would the people of California actually elect Arnold Schwarzenegger governor?

"Know why he's a Republican?" Wisdom Man asked after his usual salutation.

A tired, unanimous yes from the rest of us.

"So he can screw a Democrat."

A universal groan.

Tom could do a dynamite Schwarzenegger, puffing up his neck muscles and talking with a thick Austrian accent, while Wisdom Man was fairly convincing as the unfortunately named Gray Davis, the Democratic governor now being blamed for every problem the state of fruits and nuts faced, so much so that I had recently seen a cartoon that showed two women sticking their toes in the Pacific Ocean. "The water's unusually cold," the first one said. "I blame Gray Davis," her companion responded.

My companions liked to open the pages of the *San Francisco Chronicle* and devise an impromptu debate or create a made-for-TV plot or invent a bizarre advertisement from the headlines. Our latest form of entertainment involved Tom and Wisdom Man doing their Schwarzenegger and Davis imitations, far less entertaining than the Adam and Eve joke of a few months previously. One installment went like this:

Tom as Schwarzenegger: Ven I kick you out of Sacramento, Gray, I vill bring color back to Kali-forn-ia politics. Ve have been gray too long.

Wisdom Man as Governor Davis: Arnold, may I call you Arnold? No, no, this is better. May I call you the Austrian Oak? I'm wearing my special Austrian hunting jacket for this special opportunity to kick your butt, I mean debate you.

It went on like that for a while. I'd stopped listening. I was tired of it all -- the celebrity politicians, the celebrity drug addicts. I guessed Jay was tired of it, too. He looked particularly ill in his shabby clothes, his scruffy beard, his thin face oddly pale.

"You okay?" I asked.

"I am. I am," Jay said absentmindedly. "I was just thinking of the movie they could make from this. They could call it *Arnold: The Term-Eliminator*. He names himself King of California, dares anyone to oppose him and for good measure orders the annihilation of the Bay Area."

From somewhere deep within his throat, in a voice and accent much more convincing than Tom's, Silent Guy croaked, "Vong movie. Vong plot. Don't you remember *Demolition Man*? That Sandra Bullock, she knew vat she was talking of."

As if we were one body, we all turned, equally astonished, to gawk at Silent Guy. To imagine that he was some sort of movie hound, to imagine him pulling this chestnut out of his video file, complete with perfect Ah-nold accent, caused all of us to stare like morons, even Wisdom Man, our mouths open in amazement.

Silent Guy dropped the accent. "I saw it on late night TV years ago, *Demolition Man*. It takes place way in the future. Sandra Bullock is a cop trying to bring Sylvester Stallone up to speed on what has happened in the world in the last thirty years while he's been in a state of suspended animation. Somehow, the Schwarzenegger Presidential Library comes up.

"It seemed so absurd," Silent Guy continued. "Stallone's saying, 'Wait. What? Schwarzenegger gets to be president? He wasn't even born in this country. He couldn't be president.' And Bullock tells him about some amendment Congress passed so he could run."

Silent Guy had just uttered more words than I'd heard from him in the months since I first drew up a chair outside the café. From the little bits of biographical information I'd harvested, I'd constructed a back history for Silent Guy in which he had lived hand to mouth on the streets and in shelters all these decades since his youth, before he got sober a year or so ago and moved into a group house located nearby. And now, the fellow who hadn't said twenty words in all our mornings together had just strung together several articulate paragraphs about Schwarzenegger and Sandra Bullock and Sylvester Stallone. When I asked where he had watched this movie, was it when he was living in a shelter, how he had remembered all these details, Silent Guy turned my way and, looking over his rimless glasses, said, "You got me wrong. I never lived in a shelter. I was never homeless. Me and my mom, we watched movies all the time. Mom loved a good movie."

So much for assumptions. And what was his story anyhow?

I was the middle-aged woman gawking in disbelief as a naked man was actually beating off in public while a leather-clad woman squirted oil from a rather elaborate brass mister onto the man's engorged penis. Gawking not just that a penis could be that big but that someone could masturbate in public while dozens of other people took it all in stride as they moved on to the next exhibition at the Folsom Street Fair. There were men dressed in leather chaps with naked butts bursting forth; others wore harnesses or muzzles or both. One essentially naked man – he wore a leather mask and bracelets with big brass spikes and a kind of thong tied tightly around his penis -- was kneeling down to be paddled while nearby a bare-chested woman with black Xs taped to her nipples writhed against the splintering wooden pole she was tied to, her wrists pulled tightly behind her back. Her "keeper" stood by grasping a metal and leather chain that was wrapped around her neck. I was about to make my exit when I saw a couple pushing a stroller down Folsom Street with two golden-haired toddlers inside.

"We have no secrets from our kids," the couple said in stereo when I asked if they knew what the Folsom Street Fair was about when they decided to bring the kids. Stupid question given that the man was enveloped in Saran wrap over what looked to be thorny rose bushes while the woman wore high heels, a bustier, garter belt, thong undies, and nothing else. The twins wore diapers and Gap shirts.

Bodies. Leather. Bondage. Piercings. Beat and Suck and Kink and Cock. Anything goes. That was the Folsom Street Fair. And if you're reading this and thinking it's just a few enthusiasts showing off at the annual let it rip festival, think again. For twenty-three years, according to its official website, the Folsom Street Fair has been "the largest leather, alternative and fetish street fair in the world (and) has attracted more than 400,000 attendees annually and raised thousands and thousands for a host of charities."

I've seen it once.

You could always tell whose car had been broken into during the night by the blue glass that sparkled across the sidewalk. With the knock of a knuckler, some punk could smash a car window into shards of blue-tinged marbles. They glittered in the morning light as I made my way to the coffee shop, petty crime committed by crack heads and hoodlums, people looking for a place to sleep or anything to rifle and sell on the streets. Another reason not to have a car.

It was my first time at the Fillmore in forty years. The last time was during the Summer of Love when I traveled to California with my first husband and our old friends Harry and Joanne during our lengthy expedition across the United States in the late 1960s. We were at the Fillmore for the Electric Flag and Blue Cheer concert. We'd lined up to buy tickets, not knowing it was a historic night, that it would be the last performance in the original West Coast location of the Fillmore for twenty years. We weren't part of the San Francisco scene, just young hippies making our pilgrimage to the City of Love, in retrospect so pitifully guileless that I wonder how the four of us survived that year's wanderings. My most vivid memory of that night was not the music but seeing Harry atop a twelve-foot-high speaker set up in front of the stage. He'd taken about a hundred hits of acid and from his position on top of the speaker, he sat lotus-style, a skinny god meditating, his middle fingers touching his thumbs while the music blared from the speaker beneath him. How he'd gotten there, I never knew.

At that time in my life, I'd been to concerts and performances in coffee houses and music halls, at Newport Folk Festivals and Madison Square Garden, but this was my first concert in a place like the Fillmore, a place that embodied the counterculture. After that night, Bill Graham moved the Fillmore to a bigger venue on Market at Van Ness, now a car dealership. After his death in a helicopter crash in 1991, Graham's friends reopened the original Fillmore.

I hadn't thought about that Electric Flag concert in years, but it came back to me whole as I stepped inside the Fillmore with my friend Denise for a Zap Mama concert. Imagine me there back then, a girl just over twenty, mini-skirt up to my butt and hair half way down my back, believing I was immune to anything bad until I found my husband at the end of the concert, crouched in a corner, frightened by something he couldn't articulate. There we were, three thousand miles away from home. We had been on the road for months; it would take longer to make it back, and the fact of the matter was that not all of us made it back whole.

Denise and I took the 22 bus there, arriving early so we could take in the posters from Bill Graham's productions, the artistic and musical history of San Francisco that lined every wall. I was admiring the posters that recorded my twenties and thirties, disoriented from the sudden recollection of that night with Blue Cheer, which we may have been on all those years ago, when Zap Mama came on stage. One minute I was trying to bring back the details: Joanne's russet hair reflecting the light show: Harry, magically there and not there for all to see; the blue cheer acid not particularly harmonious with the Blue Cheer band, which had earned its reputation as the loudest band in rock and roll, precursors to heavy metal, while Owsley's Blue Cheer, named for the detergent, was a fairly mellow product. The next, there was Marie Daulne, golden curls above bronze skin, stunning with her band of equally gorgeous women (and one man), creating their unique form of polyphonic music. Zap Mama's founding singer could have been Jul's model of someone who overcame a gazillion obstacles. She was the daughter of a Belgian father and Zairian Bantu mother. When her father was killed in the Congo, Daulne's mother took refuge with the pygmies. Daulne was born in Africa but grew up in Brussels. Her songs are filled with pygmy chants and Zairian melodies; they resonate with Arabian and antique Spanish influences, complemented by Belgian and French and by the human beatbox of vocal and body percussion. And then there was the dancing! There are very few places to sit in the Fillmore, maybe ten tables set up along the balcony with a couple of chairs available at each. Everyone stands in front of the stage, one congealed mass, shaking bootie like the African descendants we are. It was tribal.

But there was something else in my head, that memory from my past, and with it so many discomforting questions: what might have happened to that hippie philosophy of peace and love, the belief that the world was a place of perpetually unfolding enchantment, had it not been demolished during that springtime and summer of assassinations that took the Reverend Martin Luther King Jr. and Bobby Kennedy? In place of that tender dream, what did we have today? Was it there all along? Were we deluded? Sometimes I hated my head, the way that I couldn't escape my thoughts. There I was at the Fillmore with one of my favorite musical discoveries performing, and I was still pained by memories long past and the possibilities that went with them.

Hours later, Denise and I stepped from the bright light and loud music of the Fillmore onto the street, joining the other lovely, engaged people stumbling from the concert hall, the workers who had bussed tables and washed dishes in the high-priced restaurants along Fillmore Street just now getting out of work, the shoppers and late-night revelers who had been at other clubs in the neighborhood, when there, on the sidewalk, I saw another ruined one, dazed and confused, long hair matted and dirty, crying out his misery in crazy fragments of words, another burn-out, another refugee.

I did not know his history. I did not know if he took too many drugs or had a chemical imbalance or drank himself into delirium. From his age and attire I couldn't help but think he might have been one of those who came to San Francisco seeking something outside himself and got lost somewhere after those hopeful, guiltless days in which we fought against the senseless war of our generation, the one in Vietnam, but didn't have the courage or stamina or whatever it would have taken to actually address the causes of conflict and human self-destruction. In the end, we were a lazy, spoiled generation, one with great promise but little endurance for the hard work, the long haul, for living outside our own small circle of need and comfort. I was glad Denise was with me. Denise was always good for getting my mind on better things, like chocolate cake at Citizen Cake. And that's where we headed after I dumped a handful of change in the beggar's cap, singing Zap Mama all the way to Citizen Cake where I confirmed my disgust with myself in a most delicious manner.

My students taught me. They brought me their lives, their families, their music and stories. They schooled me about a San Francisco I might never have discovered on my own. They labored in the city's restaurants and bars, and snorted cocaine between tables. They were vegetarians who got fired for refusing to serve foie gras. They volunteered with the homeless, the handicapped, and the poor. They prayed before class or danced all night and arrived hung over, reeking of cigarettes and sex. One had driven a cab for thirteen years; she had been mugged, proposed to, cheated and died on. She wrote about the city with an authority I would never achieve. My students were a United Nations of color and religion and place of origin, of class and ability and gender in a minority-majority city, defined as one in which non-Latino whites comprised less than half of the population. They were the perfect antidote to living twenty-five years in a white state.

My students eloped and broke up with lovers. They got pregnant, had their babies or didn't. They sobbed out their dramas in my office. One student announced his virginity in class, and then wrote about his decision to abstain from sex until marriage; his chastity briefly made him a celebrity. On the other hand, my students taught me about fetishes I'd rather not have known about and took me, through their words, to clubs I'd never visit, clubs where couples traded trysts or gambled their futures away. I studied the history of the city, walked its streets, tasted its food, talked to strangers, went to concerts, tromped through museums, hung out at gay bars, adopted homeless people and tried to educate myself about Baghdad by the Bay, as the late journalist Herb Caen called San Francisco to reflect its multiculturalism and exotic nature.

There were aspects of this city I would not experience myself. At least once a semester, someone would write about the Tranny Shack where the drag show started after midnight, which dampened my enthusiasm for attending, or The Twist, a two-story warehouse in North Beach where couples traded sex, or the Fairfax Gym, where men and women beat each other up in something called mixed martial arts; or the Power Exchange Sex Club, where people went to get flogged or fucked or watch people get flogged or fucked. I didn't even like reading these stories and I wished my students wouldn't write them. I discovered in San Francisco that, while I believed everyone had the right to his or her own pleasures, obsessions and entertainments, as long as the other participants were adult and consenting, I was personally, at least by San Francisco standards, a prude. I had embraced all the freedoms of the Sixties but there in San Francisco, I wondered how far was too far. On one hand, I wished I had witnessed some of the outrageously campy antics of the Cockettes and the Angels of Light whose drag shows and costumes mixed all the elements of the Seventies from David Bowie androgyny to sex on demand. The Folsom Street Fair was a peepshow into that era. But there was another hand, the consequences of excess there to be seen in the ravaged bodies all around us.

My students taught me other things too: about the raven's manzanita, the last plant of its kind being kept alive by botanists and volunteers working in the Golden Gate Recreation Area; about groups that recycled computers for low-income children; about cars fueled by hamburger grease; about the new ways to wage activism, on the Internet, in chat rooms, in the blogosphere. I was grateful to them in so many ways, not just that they so often trusted me with their disasters and dreams but also that they were there, young, hopeful, smart, reinventing journalism before it was too late.

One of the courses I routinely taught, Reporting, was the boot camp of the journalism curriculum. In this class, San Francisco was our laboratory with each student learning and writing about one of the city neighborhoods throughout the semester. That was where I could be of most use, teaching them how to gather information, to talk to strangers, to ask the questions they were afraid to ask. And it was there also that I taught students how to build stories around the facts of a place, to step out of their comfort zones to look at how elderly tenants in rent-controlled apartments were being forced out of homes they'd lived in their entire lives, for example, or how children living near the former military shipyards in Hunters Point had been diagnosed with asthma at rates higher than most anywhere in the world. But I also challenged their (and my) natural inclination to side with the underdog, to fail to investigate both sides of an issue.

Jul was most helpful in this regard. He often asked me what my students were writing about then challenged their and my proclivity to side, for example, with the renter over the property owner. He challenged me to consider the impact of rent control on high rents, to see how one had led to the other, how the system of ownership had been subverted by laws that, he believed, favored the tenant.

My understanding of all these things was superficial at best, undoubtedly flawed, but any student of San Francisco could see the difference that money made. We took to the streets and explored what was happening to San Francisco's famous diversity at that very moment in time, how the high cost of living was forcing middle and lower-income residents into the poorer neighborhoods or out of the city altogether. We catalogued the exodus of artists and musicians, of African Americans, and the ways in which those who couldn't get out were trying to get by.

Students learned soon enough that marginalization was nothing new as they studied U.S. and San Francisco history. During WWII, President Roosevelt had ordered people of Japanese origin moved to internment camps. In San Francisco, many Japanese had lived on and around Fillmore Street in an area called Japantown. About the time that the Japanese were sent to the camps, African Americans arrived in San Francisco to work in the shipyards and the burgeoning war industries. Many moved into the homes that had been vacated by the Japanese. By the early-1940s the Fillmore was the heart of African American culture in the West with black churches on almost every block and nearly as many jazz clubs, places like Shelton's Blue Mirror, Wesley Johnson's Texas Playhouse, Jimbo's Bop City and Leola King's Bird Cage. Billie Holiday, Louis Armstrong and Duke Ellington performed there regularly. When the war ended, African American GIs came by the hundreds, attracted by the city's reputation as welcoming, the lure of jazz and a thriving black culture. Once the internment camps were closed, some Japanese families moved back as well, but the new Japantown was much smaller, encompassing only six square blocks where it had once been twenty or more.

Over the next decade, the area's commercial district continued to attract jazz musicians followed by the Beat poets, who heavily influenced the jazz scene and vice versa. Together, the Beat poets and the jazz musicians created the San Francisco Renaissance, a phenomenon that encompassed avant-garde poetry, music, philosophy, Asian art and spiritualism, and alternative sexual practices. At 3119 Fillmore Street in a place called 6 Gallery, Allen Ginsberg read his poem *Howl* for the first time on October 13, 1955.

My students and I studied these movements, learning how history had led to today's challenges. We learned, for example, that despite that renaissance, the city's Redevelopment Agency declared the area a slum and began demolishing hundreds of older Victorian buildings in the greater Fillmore district and replacing them with large housing developments that were planned to include subsidized and low-income housing. Many of the families forced out during the redevelopment were poor; many were black. Many sold their homes to the Redevelopment Agency at a deflated rate or moved out of longtime rentals in exchange for certificates they thought would ensure priority status for housing once the redevelopment was completed. But the redevelopment project took much longer than expected and when it was completed, those certificates were next to worthless. In all, the project wiped out more than 4,700 households and demolished about 2,500 buildings. In 2000, forty years after it had begun the project, the Redevelopment Agency moved out of the Fillmore and city officials conceded that the venture had been a disaster.

Whether intentional or not, the end result of the renewal, or removal, project was that many blacks left San Francisco or moved to the city's poorer neighborhoods, the Tenderloin and Bayview-Hunters Point. The Tenderloin, perhaps like a similar neighborhood in New York, was named by police officers who earned extra money patrolling the neighborhood, enough to buy a tenderloin steak. Like the 'Loin, Bayview-Hunters Point had been marginalized for decades, its shoreline polluted with toxic wastes from military and industrial shipyards. Nonetheless, that neighborhood had the highest percentage of home ownership in the city and many of those homeowners were African Americans who had been forced out of the Fillmore and Western Addition.

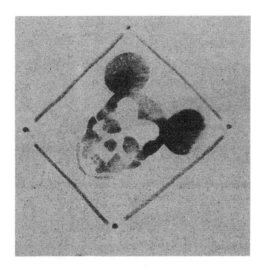

Stencil on Market Street, just a few blocks from Octavia

Now, the developers had their sights set on those long-neglected neighborhoods, especially Bayview-Hunters Point where the city was promoting a $7 billion project that could create more than 10,000 much-needed homes, nearly 4 million feet of commercial and retail development, more than 300 acres of parks, an artists' colony and performance center. First, however, developers needed to remove hazardous waste left behind at the long-abandoned Hunters Point Naval Shipyard. While many saw the project as a way of reconnecting this long-neglected neighborhood with the rest of the city, others saw it as another in a long line of land grabs in which the poor and disenfranchised would be left out of the renewal.

This was especially true among the city's few remaining black residents, at that time only 6 percent from a high of 19 percent of the population fifty years previously. Activists worried that the few remaining blacks would be exposed to further contamination during the clean-up process, then forced out of the neighborhood once the project was completed.

All this provided great material for class projects. We could explore the conflict between San Francisco's reputation for liberal social action, tolerance and protection of the disenfranchised, and the realities of gentrification and capitalism. Students who covered the wealthy neighborhoods of the city, St. Francis Woods, Seacliff, Nob Hill and the like, and the more suburban neighborhoods such as the Richmond and Sunset complained that their "beats" were boring, that there were no characters to write about, and few issues of import. That was the kind of place it was, San Francisco State University. My journalism students wanted to chronicle the struggle, they wanted to change the world. Or, at least, some of them did. Maybe they would someday. If indeed anyone could make a difference.

For four days, when I'd rounded the corner, only Silent Guy sat at our table, alone as he rolled his cigarettes, smoked and hacked, drank his coffee and watched the traffic. I'd used one of those mornings to apologize for assuming he had lived in a homeless shelter, for being surprised that he knew the plot to an old movie.

"One step up," he responded and then, haltingly, explained that he now lived in a halfway house for recovering addicts and alcoholics, that he had a roommate he tolerated, and that the rules of the house required him to leave the building from 8:30 in the morning until 4:30 in the afternoon. Hence, the pocketed sandwich and time on his hands.

I could only speculate about the whereabouts of my other morning chums. I knew Wisdom Man lived across the street in a mauve building. (He'd corrected me quite strenuously the day I'd called his house pink. "It's mauve, darling," he'd said, "mauve as in the Mauve Decade, pink trying to be purple, the celebration of decadence over New England Puritanism.") The house itself was very grand, multi-floored with a kind of turret on the top and lots of architectural details, handsome plantings all around. I would no more go knocking on Wisdom Man's door than I would have tried to track down the halfway house where Silent Guy lived or Tom's son's apartment. Just as the men had a general idea where I lived, I, too, had observed the direction from which each of them approached the café on the rare occasions when I arrived before any of them. Ted lived in an upstairs flat somewhere down Page Street. I knew it was on the third floor because he complained so regularly about the stairs. We didn't take seriously Ted's pitiful and often prolonged goodbyes. It would take a Herculean effort for him to move, unless the only things he had to move were the clothes on his back, which was also possible. And even though we didn't discuss it openly, we neither expected Tom to depart any time soon nor did we expect him to show up with any regularity.

I had an even vaguer sense of where Jay lived but I'd built an image of him living in an ark of a building on Market Street that housed a tattoo parlor, a drug-shooting gallery, a hash bar and dozens of illegal apartments. I had built this image from his description of an apartment in that building that he'd been paid to clean after the occupant had been taken to the mental hospital. Amongst the refuse of someone who had holed up against the world for a decade, he had salvaged enough material for an installation that he tentatively called "A Life Unobserved."

While we six often talked about the dilemmas of the universe, our friendships did not extend past that sidewalk where we traded only the smallest bits of personal information from which we each constructed our flawed understanding of one another. And even though Silent Guy and I sat together on the corner and conjectured about Wisdom Man's whereabouts, me doing most of the talking, awkwardly, Silent Guy acquiescing to my speculation with a nod of a head or a phrase or two about the miniscule details of his own life, you could not call what we did conversing. Then, on the third morning came a breakthrough of sorts as he shyly asked if I had an extra dollar for tobacco.

Me: You broke?

Silent Guy: It's the end of the month.

Me: Let me get your coffee.

Silent Guy: Nah, I'm fine but I will need tobacco.

Me: You could quit.

Silent Guy: Can only give up so much.

$

Jul was a health nut. I kept fit enough but I was not into colon cleansers or pummeling my joints jogging up and down the hills of San Francisco. Jul regularly ran up Twin Peaks, the second highest hills in the city at more than 900 feet. It was always worth the trek up those peaks, which have a 360-degree view of the city, but I had enough trouble climbing its steep, rugged incline. Frankly, I've never thought runners looked all that healthy. Jul dismissed my concerns about his middle-aged knees. He also liked to bike the most demanding routes he could find, adding weights to his ankles to increase the workout. I'd come to think of him as the indestructible man. He climbed around on ladders and pounded nails all day and when evening came he called to invite me to a political debate or esoteric art show. He sought out natto, a stringy, strong-smelling fermented soy product said to cleanse the blood. His claims were backed by Asian nutritionists and medical researchers who had found that natto reduced the likelihood of blood clots and might help prevent strokes and heart attacks. When he went to the VA doctors, he'd engage them in complicated conversations about natto and other health foods. He brought them questions he'd culled from reading Doctor Roizen's *Real Age* books and printouts from the U.S. Department of Health. Jul challenged anyone and everyone to find the flaws in his approaches to keeping fit, as well as making money and navigating the world. He could be relentless, as in his oft-repeated entreaty regarding Burning Man.

"I can't believe you're so close-minded about the Burn?" he said when I declined for the umpteenth time. "You strike me as an open-minded person."

"Well, I guess that's where you're wrong, Jul."

"No, really, Burning Person is an event you shouldn't miss, if only for the experience. Just imagine the stories you'll get out of it."

"Burning Person, that's pretty PC of you, Jul," I said, changing the subject from me to him. "Where did you come up with that?"

"Oh, you like that? It's an original. I never told you about the time I told Larry Harvey he had to call it Burning Person?"

Larry Harvey had founded Burning Man at San Francisco's Baker Beach in 1986 as one of the pranks organized by a group called the San Francisco Cacophony Society. The event had grown so popular it was moved to the desert –

a safer place for those pyromaniacs and exhibitionists and utopians to gather – to federal land administered by the Bureau of Land Management. I could just imagine Jul sidling up to Harvey at the height of Burning Man, with all its zaniness and potential for meltdown, and telling Harvey that the feds were displeased with the event's politically incorrect name.

Jul told the story this way: "I said, 'Larry, you know I've got connections with the BLM, right?' I'm just bullshitting, of course, so I didn't give him time to answer. I said, 'Last time I was in D.C., my buddies there started asking me about Burning Man. What's with the name, they wanted to know. They're quite fascinated about us out here in the Far West. Seems they were worried about some radical feminists threatening to bring a suit against the government for allowing such a sexist event to be held on federal land. I hate to tell you this, but you're just gonna have to change the name. I suggest Burning Person."

Jul was so excited with the story that he rose from his seat. His Adam's apple worked overtime. "Larry got immediately all worked up. 'They can't do that,' he said. 'Burning Man is a copyrighted name.'

"I told Larry, 'You don't want to endanger the Burn over a little thing like semantics. You know how sensitive everyone's become. You know these liberated women…and there are plenty of them at the Burn. I'm surprised they haven't picketed you already.'

"I saw Larry a few times over the course of the week and every time I brought it up. 'You thinking about changing the name yet?' Finally, I told him I was only joking. I think he half took me seriously."

"Doesn't everyone?" Mary asked.

"Schizophrenia is an airborne disease in San Francisco," Wisdom Man said. "I should know. They gave it to me when I was in the mental ward. I've been cured, though. Want to know how I got cured?"

Of course we did.

"By going to jail. You don't want schizophrenia in jail."

Wisdom Man might have been giving out a piece of the story about where he'd been. Then, again, he might have been talking theoretically as if we were his students.

"You were in jail?" I asked, taking the direct approach.

"I have been," he said, feigning nonchalance.

"That's where you were last week?"

"No, I was in the library. Big research project."

I was trying to imagine his scrawny frame in a city jail. "Why were you in jail?" I asked. The last thing I wanted to hear about was his big research project.

"For crying in public," he answered. "Just like there's no crying in baseball, there's no crying in public."

Of course I asked for details, an explanation. But Wisdom Man liked to bait you into a particular avenue of discussion and then take an excursion through some esoteric argument about the Feminine Attribute or Jesus' offspring with Mary Magdalene, holding out the promise that he'd return to the original question if you were patient enough. Then, maybe, he'd give you another nugget of information about himself, his Wisdom School and how it functioned. If I became too persistent, he would retreat to the mauve building.

So far, what had I garnered of his story? That he came from the East Coast, that his family was well-to-do, that he went to Oberlin, that he was married briefly and now had total disdain for the former wife, that he was waiting for family money or for his school to start making a profit. In the meantime, he was on an austerity campaign. These personal details were nestled among the Gnostic and political minutiae he handed out for free. And, for all I knew, as with the story I'd constructed about Silent Guy having been homeless, it might have been a fiction.

"There's no law against crying in public," I said.

Silent Guy had turned our way. This was clearly a story he had not heard before and he had spent many more mornings on the sidewalk with Wisdom Man than I.

"That's what I thought too," Wisdom Man said. "You'd cry too if you couldn't see your kids."

"Your kids? I didn't know you had kids," I said.

"Twins. You couldn't imagine what we went through to get them. I think the shots made my wife crazy. She got those kids and all of a sudden, she turned on me. She said *I* was crazy. First she divorced me. Then she got a restraining order against me. And then, she got a court order that prohibited me from seeing my kids. I pleaded with the judge. I said they were made with my sperm, the fruit of my loins. I said they were everything to me. But the judge agreed with her that I was crazy. It was not seeing my kids, not being part of their lives that was making me crazy. *That's* not crazy.

"So I went public with my case. I went down to KQED. It's public radio, right? But they wouldn't let me tell my story on the air. And when I started crying and wouldn't leave, they called the cops. And when the cops and the judge heard my story, they sent me to the mental ward for crying in public."

With his references to Plutarch or Heraclites, Wisdom Man's lectures were often too convoluted to follow. Not that day. I was entirely astonished with this speech, all this personal information spilling forth in uncensored candor.

And Silent Guy? Silent Guy hung on every word. Then he reached out and touched Wisdom Man, placing just a few fingers on his arm.

"I loved my mother," Silent Guy said sweetly. "I'm sure your children love you too."

An apartment building is a microcosm, a small village. Our noises, smells or bad habits had ramifications that identified us as considerate or not, reliable or not. There on Octavia, this is how we functioned: We had Gordon, whether official or not, as our building manager. Several afternoons a week, he unwound the long orange power cord and sucked up the city debris we'd all hauled in, wiped down the washing machines and dryers, emptied the mail trash by the door. Gordon knew our dirt. Better yet, if my gas heater wouldn't turn on and Jul wasn't around to fix it, Gordon would figure out the problem and have it working in no time. As he was leaving, he might notice the music I was listening to or the book I was reading and the next day I might find outside my door a different CD by the musician I had on the CD player or another book by the author I'd been reading.

There were the predictable sounds of the comings and goings of Ann and Alexandra. In the morning, there was the struggle to get to work and daycare. And in the evening, when the two arrived home, they stopped at the mailboxes in the hall not far from my door. Alexandra loved junk mail. She loved envelopes. Her voice and Ann's filled the hall, the mother patient or not, the child happy or not as the ritual unfolded. Ann would attempt to limit the amount of junk mail that would make it upstairs to their apartment while Alexandra didn't want a bit of it thrown away. She loved the flyers from Bed Bath & Beyond or Safeway. She loved the Walgreen's advertisements. Each provided opportunities for cutting and pasting, for pretend shopping, for working at her "office." Ann was the kind of mother who liked to reason with a child, even when the child was tired and hungry and beyond reason. It was often at that moment, the moment of meltdown I remembered so well from raising my own brood, that I'd lend a hand with the hauling. Later, Alexandra would sit for hours with crayons and glitter sticks, "writing letters" that would appear under one of our doors, a gift from our building's only child.

Mother Mae, as the Jewesses called her, ruled the house. We took our turns bringing her raspberry turnovers and chocolates, running errands, taking her trash down to the basement. She was our fashion statement, stepping out on her Sabbath in winter white, a gold broach perfectly situated upon her fuchsia scarf one week, or in an old-fashioned black suit and pearls another.

Noel was our rock. His steadiness grounded us with the smallest of actions: the tip of his hat in the hallway; the warmth of his smile; the stories he told of life in the city when jazz ruled; the salsa clubs in the Mission where, week after week, he promised to take me dancing.

Robin was our reprobate. His life unfolded in one drama after another. Like nearly everyone else in the building, Robin was generous to a fault, only what he had to give away, his affection, for example, came encumbered with things you might regret in the morning. Everyone loved him but, when we gathered in Ann's apartment for potluck, or in my apartment for pie, we didn't invite him.

We invited Glenn for the lovely acid of his wit and the joy of watching a toddler climb over Zipper. Zipper was our mascot. If one of our doors were open, he'd wander in. He might even clear the table. We didn't take offense. Glenn was our aristocrat. He raised our cachet.

There were others in the building who were peripherally part of our little family. Brendan, our resident queen, sang at The Mint Karaoke Lounge a block away on Market Street; Patrick and his wife lived with an Italian greyhound upstairs, next to Lance. Lance had once been a successful computer programmer. Now, he loomed over the banister. He stumbled in the door. You didn't see him for weeks then heard him on the stairs, traipsing up and down, dragging garbage bags of clanking Jack Daniels bottles and stacks of pizza boxes to the basement.

Mary told us there was a brilliant man in there, a sweet man who had been broken by love. I wished I had known him when he was whole, but when I tried to talk to him, his pale eyes turned watery and he drifted away.

The girl on the Muni had a tiny silver stud pierced into the tip of her tongue. She could roll her tongue along the inside of her teeth so that the silver ball flowed across the outside of her teeth like a metal bubble. I wondered if her professors were as fascinated as I was, watching her from across the aisle. She was so young, clearly a freshman, as were the others in the group that boarded the M-train at the university platform with me, students from across America thrown together by the chance occasion of attending the same university, San Francisco State. It was after midnight. I'd gone out to dinner with colleagues than returned to the university for the papers I needed to correct, catching the last train downtown.

Meanwhile, the kids were just going out for the night. I listened as they shared a soda bottle filled with a cloudy liquid that made Silver-ball's seatmate choke. Still she took another chug. This one looked so put together, so clean and tucked in her plaid skirt and starched white shirt, knee socks and saddle shoes of all things, that I pictured parents back home in Iowa or Ohio, envisioning their perfect daughter just going to bed in her dorm room while she was actually heading downtown with a group of virtual strangers. The boy beside me barely said a word. He was dressed in that mix of military refugee apparel kids adopted to be anonymous, his long blond hair in a loose ponytail, indifference on his face. The other two boys sat sideways on adjacent seats so there was an intimacy between them without them having to actually touch while they traded their stories. One dismissively put himself and his hometown down, lamenting how little he actually knew about LA, how little there was to do where he came from, admitting he didn't know anyone until the third female, the obvious ringleader, began to hold forth as if she were the authority on all things young and exciting in the city of angels. She sat across from him and threw out names of people she knew and high schools and music clubs and record stores, all around LA, becoming more and more astonished at the boy's ignorance about the place he came from. "What are you, the Bubble Boy?" she asked cruelly.

Oddly enough, she spoke in a pert British accent that made me wonder how she knew so much about LA. But then she revealed to the other students and by extension the rest of us on the train that she had moved to LA from London when she was nine. Then, sitting there in her self-admiring self-confidence, she guzzled what was left in the bottle and threw it at the boy, who caught it in one hand and slammed it down on the seat next to him in obvious humiliation. She was dressed like a feminine Nazi in leather and chains and a ridiculously short skirt over a lacy slip and tights that were more holes than material. Her hair was badly buzzed, all uneven with patches of scalp between the tufts of Bozo orange and puke green. Midwest wanted to know where they were going but she asked the question as if she could care less. LA Queen of the Night answered that they would "go to the Castro and look at the queers. We'll get off on Market Street and check out what they're wearing." I was thinking about my own sweet grandchildren, envisioning the dangers that awaited them, when LA announced they'd forego the Castro for the Civic Center to watch the homeless sleeping in the shadow of City Hall. I wanted to tell the five of them to dump their ringleader, to go home, rent a movie.

I was simultaneously wondering if the students' outing was part of a course in mercy they were undertaking or one of ridicule. Was this viewing of the homeless a preparation for where they might end up or what they wanted to avoid, as if it were ever that simple? Silver-Ball saw me staring at them, preparing to say something, and the way she rolled the little sterling ball between her upper and lower teeth essentially said, Mind your own business.

There, on the sidewalk, I saw him again as I stepped onto Market Street from the subway, leaving the college students to their own futures. Hudson Bay Blanket Man sat on the curb outside a restaurant called Home, which served meatloaf with creamy, buttery mashed potatoes. It served country-fried chicken, macaroni and cheese, apple pie with vanilla ice cream. Hudson Bay Blanket Man's shock of yellow hair matched the yellow stripe on the blanket, which he had wrapped around his shoulders. I was so surprised to see him awake, desolately begging money from the late-night diners as they stepped from Home, bellies full of comfort, that I pulled out the four one-dollar bills and the twenty I had in my pocket.

"You're up," I said. He blinked, his blue eyes dazed and huge under the street lamp. What a dumb thing to say. But as he took the money, smiling over perfect teeth, he stammered, "Oh, you, thank you, thank you," as if he'd recognized me.

"I'm glad you're okay," I said, sounding even lamer. I wanted to say more but he was wrapping himself up in his Hudson Bay blanket and moving toward the Safeway grocery store. I was following just a few steps behind him when my cell phone rang. It was my husband calling from Vermont. It was the middle of his night, actually the middle of the morning, something like 3 or 4 a.m. his time, but Chuck had been traveling and we'd not touched base all day.

"I just gave Hudson Bay Blanket Man a couple of dollars, well, maybe a few more than a couple. I'm going to see what he spends it on," I said casually as I started to follow him into the store.

"Don't start following homeless men around," Chuck said. "It's not your money anymore." I could hear the concern in his voice. Miles away, he was aware of the city's dangers while I was blithely spying on a homeless man I'd just given money to. Bright lights, big city: Like those callow students, I had no fear. I realized Chuck was right, wrapped my scarf tightly around my neck, and walked on home.

In the morning, Hudson Bay Blanket Man's usual spot in front of the Redemption Center was vacant and the cart-wheelers entered, unimpeded.

Wisdom Man again, on a roll: "Christ spoke of the Logos and how there are people with minds like rock, solid and infertile, who will never be receptive to the Logos. That's what the problem is today. No reason, no logic, no Logos. You're the professor, Yvonne. How can we turn young people's minds into fertile soil?"

"Hmmm … Logos," I said, recalling the students on the Muni and as swiftly my own college years, which had been far from reasoned. Why had I worried about them; angels had certainly watched over me in my youth.

"I might be as bad on Logos as I am on physics," I said. "My philosophy professor once said to me, 'Yvonne, you might know a lot about mythos and pathos but you know nothing about Logos.'"

Wisdom Man: "But you *have* to dedicate yourself to Logos. You owe it to your students. When we fail to project our consciousness to the other side of the frontier, we fail to see the deceptions on our side."

"What do you mean by the other side of the frontier?" I asked. "I keep hearing about this other side. What did Jay say the other day, 'the other side of the veil?' Haven't there always been people who would rather be deceived than risk the comfort and security of their perceptions, who would rather live in ignorance?"

Wrong questions for so early in the morning. Silent Guy couldn't stand it when we got too esoteric in our conversations. He particularly disliked when one of us raised our voice, even if only with the passion of the moment rather than in argument. Sometimes he would just get up and leave, as he did on that morning.

"You see what you've done with your philosophizing, all that Logos so early in the morning," I said to Wisdom Man. "You've chased him away."

"Guy? You mean Guy just now? I didn't chase Guy away. He's going to the library to read some Plato. He asked me what he should read in order to more fully understand our morning dialogues and I ..."

"Guy?" I interrupted. "What did you just call him? Guy? His name is Guy?"

I was astounded that the person I'd been calling Silent Guy in my head, my journal and emails to Chuck for months was actually named Guy. While the others had told me their names, the man Wisdom Man was now calling Guy never had offered his.

"Yeah, what's the big deal?" asked Wisdom Man.

I had never told my Laguna Sidewalk Café acquaintances that I'd been jotting notes about our morning conversations in my journal, nor that I had made up names for them. But I did then, laughing over the likelihood that, of all the male names in the world, the person I'd named Silent Guy would actually be named Guy.

"And what do you call me?" Wisdom Man asked.

"Wisdom Man, of course."

"I like that," Wisdom Man said. "Guy's actually pretty smart. He just never finished high school. He took up drinking early, you know. Now, he says he might want to join my Wisdom School."

"Okay," I said. "Since you brought it up, explain this Wisdom School of yours to me, will you for God's sake? When and where do the classes meet? Seems like you're always out here on the sidewalk."

I sounded like Elise now.

"It meets when and where I want it to. It could be meeting right now. My school has no classes in the traditional sense of the word. It has no walls or schedule, no rules. It's *wisdom*. You're thinking through the world of senses; we live outside of that world. You should know that; you studied philosophy."

And so another morning began.

"Do you ever talk to Mae about her Judaism?" I asked Ann. Since Ann was Jewish, I thought she might know something about the black Jews.

"Mae's not Jewish," Ann said, laughing. "What are you talking about?"

"I don't mean Jewish, the way you are ethnically Jewish. Or maybe I do. Maybe I mean Hebrew. Mae says she's descended from Abraham, Isaac and Jacob. Each Saturday, her Jewesses bring her to temple."

"What do you mean, her Jewesses? Did they look Jewish?"

"That's funny, Ann, you asking me if someone looks Jewish. What does Jewish look like? Actually, they looked black. I've heard about black Jews before but I don't know anything about them. That's why I asked you. She worships on Saturday. She called it her Sabbath. She says she's been a member of the Hebrew Cultural Community for thirty years. She tried teaching me the names of the months in the Jewish calendar. The only one I remember is something like Tishree. Do you use the Jewish calendar?"

"No, I wasn't raised Orthodox so I don't know any of that. Maybe you misunderstood," Ann said. "Maybe she's a Seventh Day Adventist. They worship on Saturday. Ask Liya. She's a Seventh Day Adventist."

"I don't think so, Ann. Seventh Day Adventists believe in the *next* coming of the Messiah; Mae believes in the *first* coming," I said. "She talks about the Old Testament, and the Exodus from Egypt, and the freeing of her black brothers and sisters. Do you know about any black Hebrew synagogue around here?"

"Never heard of it. Maybe my Dad has. He knows everything."

Ann's father was the one who told me about the Beta Israel community of Ethiopia who followed the Jewish faith and were formally recognized in the mid-1970s. He said many of them were airlifted to Israel twenty years ago.

"Mae," I asked the next time I saw her, "can I ask about your church, this Hebrew Cultural Center? Is it only for black Jews?"

"Right now, everyone there is black but you could come, except why would you? It's for those who followed Brother Abraham into Egypt and were scattered by the evil pharaohs. We are descendants of the tribe of Dan, one of the Ten Lost Tribes. We is ancient, girl. Don't you have your own story?"

"Oh, I do, Mae, but I'm intrigued by yours. Actually what I wanted to know was whether your church is related to the Falasha of Ethiopia. You know. The people who were formally recognized as Jews, I don't know when exactly but in the last thirty years or so. Some of the words you use sound Hebrew, but I heard the Falasha spoke another language rather than Hebrew, something I think Ann's father called Ge'ez."

"No, we older than them. Twenty years," Mae scoffed. "We are the original exiles. And did you say Ge'ez? What kind of language is that? Don't you go talking to no white folks about me, girl. They will never understand. You's special. I knew that the first time I saw you."

"Saw me?"

"You know what I mean," she said, and I think I did.

"You know, last week you told me you went to jail for crying in public but then you never told us the part about being in jail. You told us about being in the mental ward. Or did I get something wrong?"

Wisdom Man was wearing his Austrian hunting jacket again. He often referred to it as his cloak of valor. He had recently developed a tremor in his cheek. He inhaled coffee like hope.

"I only told you half the story," he said. "The other half has to do with what I published about the judge. The judge called it contempt of court, which it was. Contempt of court is willful disobedience of a court order or misconduct in the presence of the court. I was guilty of both. I had contempt for the court, specifically that judge, and it was my moral duty to show that contempt, which some would consider misconduct."

"You published something? What are you talking about?"

"First you should know that I broke the restraining order when I got out of the mental hospital. They let me out of Langley and immediately I went to my kids' school to watch them in the play yard. Of course I knew I wasn't supposed to but I couldn't help it; I *had* to see them. I had this idealistic vision of the court as just and fair. I thought the judge would eventually see my point, acknowledge that I had equal rights to my children. My wife found out I went to their school and she reported me to the court. That probably would have been bad enough, but when I got charged with violating the restraining order, I wrote flyers about the judge, charging him with being the Antichrist. I said he was denying me my basic parental rights, that he was anti-father, that his ruling denied me the simple pleasure of seeing the progeny of my loins, my own children, flesh of my flesh. I got a bit carried away. I quoted liberally from the Old Testament. I passed the flyers out on the sidewalk before I went into court. One of the marshals actually handed one to the judge. He wasn't amused, sent me right to jail. But I learned a lot in there. I learned that some men don't want to be free, that freedom can be a burden."

"So," I began, not responding to his observation about freedom, enticing as it might have been to follow that thread of thought. I had to know. "So, did you give up on seeing your children?"

"I have," he said. "I didn't like jail, but I did like the prisoners. I tutored a lot of them while I was there. I served three and a half months of a two-year sentence, then probation for another year. More than anyone I've ever met, prisoners understand that truth is relative, that it is based on shifting paradigms. I could argue the wrongness of a father denied the right to see his children, but of course I had been placed in that category of men who are considered a danger to their offspring, although no one actually thought I might hurt them physically. What I did learn is that prison demonstrates one of the basic tenets of Gnosticism: There is a role for slavery in a free society; it is an example of what to avoid. I would not survive long in jail, not because I might be harmed. Prisoners have no fear of me, nor I of them. One could argue that the mind is free wherever one is but a man needs something more than his mind. He needs honor. The inhumanity of the prison, the constant noise, the degradation of the spirit, none of these would I survive for long. Sometimes the city is even too much."

That was when Wisdom Man provided another small nugget of personal information, explaining that when he disappeared for days at a time he was not necessarily in the library, as he had claimed previously, but rather was out walking, that he often took public transportation east into the Oakland hills and beyond, then set off on foot, hiking and sleeping wherever the weather or lack of human domesticity allowed. "I would sort of die if I couldn't take my restorative hikes," he said, "something they're not too keen about when you are on probation, either. So, yes, I've had to give up seeing my children. At least until they are older and perhaps then they will choose for themselves to have me in their lives. Their minds and hearts may seek out mine. That thought is what keeps me alive."

In the evenings, Ann, Alexandra, Liya and I often gathered together in Ann's snug apartment. If it weren't for Ann, I would have remained ignorant about the dramas that unfolded each week on *American Idol* and *The Nanny*. But mostly we were entertained by Alexandra whose language skills began slowly, then exploded into complex sentences. We were fascinated by the development of language, of dexterity, of a small person already showing big determination. Alexandra particularly loved Liya, who babysat regularly. But the best thing was to watch Alexandra with Gordon, who became a child in her presence, down on his knees to help her line up her stuffed animals or put on her shoes. He was carrying on the tradition that Noel had begun when he'd acted the role of *tío* for Gordon and Liya's daughter Lydia. Noel was old now and slowing down. Some days he didn't leave his apartment. He'd seemed tentative when I visited him last.

"He'll be okay," Gordon said when I expressed concern. "He's been under the weather but he's a tough old coot."

"What's a coot?" Alexandra asked.

"Ask Yvonne," Gordon said.

"A coot is a black bird with webbed blue feet," I said.

"Noel doesn't have web feet," Alexandra said, laughing with the sheer idea of an old black man with webbed blue feet. That child was brilliant.

You didn't want to go out into the Castro too early on Halloween night or too late. Too early and you caught the amateurs. Too late and the annual street party became a bit scary with roving bands of gay bashers and too many fucked-up people. After donning my usual costume of gypsy funk, I headed out about 10. I was meandering past the Lesbian Gay Bisexual Transgender Community Center, which was, of course, replete with revelry, when Robin grabbed one end of the gypsy scarf I had wrapped around my head and renewed his circuitous conversation as if the week or more since we'd last talked had never happened. We made our way down to the Orbit Room and ordered vodkas, then snuck around the corner to smoke a joint. You did not want to be straight on Halloween night in the Castro.

The crowd was electric, some quite literally with costumes that ran on batteries. One couple came as the female and male ends of an electric circuit plugged into one another. Another person was dressed as a Christmas tree complete with racing lights and a flasher Santa Claus on the treetop. Still another was dressed head to foot as a refrigerator with an open door full of mustard and ketchup and other condiments, all lit by a single little bulb.

The only hassle was the teenagers, already out en masse and roaming through the crowd in rough gangs, self-segregated into black punks and white punks, Asian punks and Latino punks, pushing and shoving and talking jive jingo lingo rap crap.

"Slap my fat," one girl shouted to another. And the other did.

Few places do Halloween better. Among the tens of thousands in costume, there was someone dressed as the Tower of Pisa, or was it the Tower of Babel, a Samson carrying Delilah's head, and a creature with two heads – an elephant on the front end, leading the way, with a donkey on the back end, heading the opposite way; a sign in the middle of the two-person animal read "Politics in America: white elephants and asses, working at cross purposes."

At the corner of Market and Laguna streets near ACT-UP, a group of incredibly skinny white guys in tight black jeans, black jackets and black wigs were setting up instruments on the sidewalk. They had tacked a sheet to the front of the building behind them announcing their band's name, The RayClones, and that they would be performing for free at 11. I loved their name, a play on the punk band The Ramones, whose lead guitarist Johnny Ramone had just died of prostate cancer. Robin was trying to get me to go to another bar when I noticed Jason F, one of my students, helping the RayClones set up, then grab his camera to shoot photos of the RayClones as they did fantastic renditions of the Ramones' songs, one after another, shotgun style, including my favorite, "Bam, bam, bam, bam, I want to be se-da-ted." A crowd had gathered round and they threw themselves onto the sidewalk and hurled themselves into one another, punk style, to the blaring music. I was dancing in the back, out of sight of Jason. The RayClones' music was so full of percussion that you could feel the beat on your shins and chest as the vibrations bounced off your body. And these kids just had crash-pad speakers on the sidewalk, nothing fancy. They were good. Robin hung around dejectedly, annoyed with my lack of attention. He'd certainly heard better and maybe the real thing in his day. Eventually, I either got tired of his sulking or he talked me into heading deeper into the Castro to catch more of the scene. Robin resumed the story of his convoluted life, as if I could hear or follow in the din. Sooner rather than later, I'd had enough, ducked Robin and headed home. The RayClones were winding up, too, and I joined the throng for the finale, dancing in the back of the pack with my student.

Back on Octavia, Robin was waiting. He had more chapters he wanted to share.

Kali-forn-ia had a new governor. Gray Davis had been recalled. I walked up the hill to the café hoping to yuck it up with my colleagues, but just old Ted, the politico, sat at our table. It would take more than a Superhero to straighten out California's financial mess, a mess caused simply by poor economic management over many administrations.

"I didn't even turn on the TV yesterday," Ted said after explaining that his arthritis had kept him away the past few weeks. "I had to get out this morning. I couldn't stand another moment with the TV on and the TV is always on. My roommate listens to every crackpot, right-wing wing nut on the air. Meanwhile, I'm thinking, is it possible that the people of California are that stupid? Maybe that's what Ronald Reagan had in mind when he dismantled the state's educational system. The Gipper brought us Schwarzenegger. If he only knew."

Gray Davis or Arnold Schwarzenegger? Really, it made little difference. I'd just about had it with politicians in general. There was the war, always the war, which consumed my attentions. And the primary race. I had my own addictions with the news. But having Ted to myself presented another possibility, one that I had to handle carefully.

"Ted," I said gingerly, "help me with something that happened here last week, will you? It has to do with Guy. Tell me if I'm being rude but I made a big faux pas when we were talking. I'd assumed he had been homeless and said something to that effect, and he said he'd never been homeless, and then told us a story about his mother and …."

"Ah, Guy's mother," Ted said. "Well, I probably don't know any more than you, Guy not being big on words. I don't know whether I should be speaking of this, since he told his tale drunk to drunk, but he never said to keep it secret. You were wrong. Guy never lived on the streets. He lived with his mother, the two of them holed up in the house, her old and senile, Guy getting drunker and sicker, just sitting around watching TV and drinking and smoking, I guess. Finally, someone, a sister I think he said, called in the health people to check on the mother. They moved them both out – her to a nursing home, him to a dry-out tank. He's been sober ever since. Never took a drink again. Unlike me, the rubber-ball man. He lives in a halfway house for former addicts. He's smart, I can tell you that, but shy as hell."

"And what about you?"

"Oh, shyness was never my condition. No, I drank in the beginning like everyone else because it was the social thing to do and it gave me a good excuse for outrageous behavior. Then I got to like it more than work or the wife or the kids or anything else. My wife was a Holy Roller. You know what they are? She had her whole group of women come to the house one day to pray over me. She paid for it when they left; I was a mean drunk. That was the end of that marriage. There's not a day goes by that I don't recall the many swell opportunities I had and blew, how often someone, usually a woman, gave me a chance at something truly wonderful, at belonging to a family or starting over. But I always blew it."

"How'd you stop?"

"Had to," Ted said, lighting a cigarette. "Had to or die. Probably it's already killed me; I just don't know it yet."

My neighbor Lance on the top floor was a big guy with pasty, puffy rolls of skin and yellow hair that clung to his scalp like old cellophane. He was on so many antidepressants that he just sort of stumbled around our building, still depressed, or holed up on the top floor, inside his apartment with his bottles, large and small. We seemed to be all he had, he was that pitiful, a fellow traveler on the landing, crying softly for the things lost, the lover, a job, his sanity, it was hard to tell what exactly. His breath was that of a smoker, an alcoholic, a person who ate a lot then nothing at all, a person who wallowed, who vomited, and stumbled about, another lost soul in San Francisco.

Jul and Mary worried about him. Jul called Lance's parents to report his deteriorated state, but they seemed either incapable or unwilling to intervene. Gordon cleaned up after him. Ann avoided him. We worried about him separately and together. I vowed to invite him for Thanksgiving dinner. Chuck was traveling to San Francisco for the month of November. We planned to celebrate Thanksgiving with my niece Bonnie and her girlfriend Birdie. As usual, we would have enough food for half of San Francisco. Maybe I'd even invite Stretch or the guys from the café.

Laundry time and I didn't smell Gordon's chlorine. I definitely wanted clean sheets and a tidy house when Chuck arrived to see for the first time my apartment – our apartment – in San Francisco. I had sixteen things going on, of course. Besides laundry, I was baking a pie, correcting papers and preparing lessons so I'd be free to play with my honey on my days off. I had also bought an old dresser from Gordon for Chuck's clothes and was polishing it with wood wax. With all this going on, I wasn't paying attention as I maneuvered the stairs, the clothesbasket balanced in front of my face. Suddenly I heard a shriek so piercing I dropped the basket. Towels and underwear went flying. Patrick's wife – I didn't even know her name; every time I'd tried to introduce myself to her, she had cowered behind him or skulked upstairs – had retreated to the corner of the room. Patrick and his wife lived on the top floor next to Lance. Patrick was a very nice guy with a very nice dog, which was how I got to know him, admiring his Italian greyhound and repeating my lamentation about wanting a dog of my own. He had explained that his wife suffered from a severe form of agoraphobia, coupled with xenophobia. She couldn't talk on the telephone or walk the dog.

I started to say something to assure her, calm her down, but as soon as I opened my mouth, she started throwing her laundry at me. While undergarments and T-shirts don't hurt, it was too bizarre to be pummeled by someone else's panties. An hour later, when I returned, my clothes still littered the floor and hers filled the machines.

I was delighted to find the Laguna Sidewalk Café gang gathered around Wisdom Man's table. Wisdom Man greeted Chuck with his usual, "Hail, there, fellow Earth Dweller," then actually winked at me. Guy sat on the periphery, as usual, rolling his cigarettes and drinking coffee between coughing fits. When the hacking got particularly bad, he'd light up a smoke, which invariably stopped the coughing. Ted was complaining about his bad back. Tom tried to one-up him with whines about his stiff body. Jay's nose was running but he didn't complain. He looked ill but he was assessing a small pile of treasures he'd rounded up on his walk to the coffee shop, which included Ken Kesey's *The Further Inquiry*, a rather appropriate find, I thought. I introduced Chuck to everyone, went inside the café and ordered a round of coffees from Elise.

"You pushover," she said.

Wisdom Man was giving his Truth Trumps Deception speech when I returned. "Conservative Christianity is still stuck in the Flat-Earth paradigm. The deceptions of that school were demonstrated centuries ago," he said as I distributed the caffeine.

"You are so right," Jay quipped. "Those Christians have been deceptive for a few thousand years. What's coming up next on the Christian calendar? Christmas? Ever hear where all those symbols come from – the tree, the candles, the Yule log, kissing under the mistletoe?"

"They come from the pagan tribes," I said. Jay gave me a look; this was supposed to be his subject matter but it was also a subject I knew a bit about. I might also have been showing off. "The oak tree was sacred to the Druids and the Celts," I said. "Mistletoe grows high up on the limbs of oak trees and it stays green year-round so the Druids considered it pretty special too, and magical with healing properties. People hung it over the door to ward off evil spirits. If enemies met under mistletoe, they would have to kiss and make up. What's that got to do with the Flat-Earth idea?"

"The pagans thought the world was flat?" Tom suggested.

"Before I was so rudely interrupted," Jay said tersely, but he smiled sweetly so I would know he was only kidding. He stroked his scraggly beard. "Before I was so rudely interrupted, I would have said the problem with all these Christians, conservative or not, is that they want to claim their saints for themselves but their saints, at least the early ones, were all Jews. Jesus was a Jew. John the Baptist was a Jew. And Moses was a Jew, the best of the lot."

"Moses wasn't a saint," Tom said.

Wisdom Man was feeling upstaged. "You mean the Roman Catholic Church hasn't ordained him as a saint. That alone is suspect, especially as the Eastern Orthodox Church has." Then he abruptly changed the subject. "Tell us, Jay, what's your middle name?"

Of course, Wisdom Man already knew Jay's middle name was Moses. It could have been J. Moses for all I knew, and it could all have been made up. Probably, it *was* made up. Wisdom Man and Jay had undoubtedly been through this Moses routine a few times before my meeting them, but I was winding the reel back through some of our previous scenarios there at the café, reviewing them for moments when Jay, who liked to spice his tales with Biblical references, might have been playing double entendre on me.

"Actually, you're wrong," Jay Moses said. "There are something like six Saint Moseses: Saint Moses of Balkim, Saint Moses the Black, Saint Moysetes who went by the name Moses."

Suddenly a car screeched to a stop at the intersection. A woman in the passenger's seat rolled down the window, leaned out, yelled "Fuck you," and hurled a bagel at us. It bounced on the sidewalk, rolled, stopped at Jay's feet.

Everyone was astonished, everyone but Jay. He was on his feet in half a second. He scooped the bagel off the sidewalk, held it out at arm's length and gave it a good inspection. He brushed it off. "Thirty second rule," he said, took a bite, turned to us and said, rather grandly, "Manna from heaven. Cinnamon raisin."

I snuck a quick glance Chuck's way.

"You planned that," I said. "You know that woman. You got her to throw that bagel at you at that very moment."

"Oh that would have been clever," Jay said, "but I never saw that woman before. It was just God bestowing his gifts upon me. I've experienced many miracles. Sometime I'll tell you about them."

But not that day. On that day, he announced, he was off to see what other gifts God had bestowed in the form of refuse and litter deposited on the streets of San Francisco. "The further inquiry," he said as he turned down Page and headed for Market Street.

Back home, Chuck looked at my mound of laundry. "Were you waiting for me?" he asked teasing, knowing that one of the many things I loved about our relationship was how nicely he did my laundry. Indeed, one of the hardships I'd brought upon myself with my bicoastal life was giving up Chuck's various gifts, which included morning coffee, dinner dishes and routine laundry. I told him the laundry room story, all the while thinking that, between Jay eating a stranger's tossed bagel and my building mates, Chuck must have thought I'd fallen into one strange existence.

"No, darling," he said when I expressed those thoughts. "I think you've found the perfect place for you. For you, this place is manna from heaven."

We put a desk and the kitchen table together to make a larger area for the Thanksgiving feast, then gathered around, Bonnie and Birdie, Denise and her boyfriend, Giuseppe, Chuck and I, each giving our gratitude. I was thankful for the way my lives at that moment seemed in synch. And for Denise's sweet potatoes. And for the stuffing; Mother would have approved. And for Bonnie's Brussels sprouts, which had been sautéed in olive oil and garlic, then doused with balsamic vinegar and hot mustard. The gravy was, let me brag, divine. The turkey is never the big thing for me. It's the rest of it. And cranberry sauce, made fresh, of course, full berried.

Later, after we had recuperated, I opened my door and invited the apartment house in for pie. I'd made four – mincemeat and pumpkin, my famous jam pie and pecan in memory of my friend Barbara, who had died that past summer. That was only the half of it. Denise had baked a small pastry shop of goodies: plum tarts, a tower of rugelach cookies, and an outrageous chocolate and raspberry cake.

Over the course of the evening, the neighbors wandered in: First Patrick, apologizing for his wife and offering to do my laundry; then Brendan, nursing a hang-over and hoping for leftovers, which we indulged him with; then Robin, ogling the spread with the keen eye of someone suffering from the munchies. Jul arrived without Mary who was worn out from her own Thanksgiving. Ann and Alexandra stumbled in, exhausted by the turkey serotonins but keen for sweets. Glenn arrived, bearing a sweet potato pie. We added it to the surfeit.

Alexandra was the center of our attention as any toddler should be. She played with Chuck, then Giuseppe, then Glenn, then Jul. With no man in her home, she glommed onto them. I was the voyeur listening to the conversations as people who had lived in the same building for years – Patrick and Glenn, for example – introduced themselves to one another. How was it that they hadn't talked before we brought them together over pumpkin pie and a cherubic adoptee from Vietnam?

Before it got too late, I put plates together for Mae and Noel. Mae had been with her church family but welcomed the turkey and mashed potatoes and gravy and seemed especially keen about the jam pie, which she said she'd eat for breakfast. "I never had jam pie. Where'd you come up with that?" she asked.

"Oh, it's just something I invented a few years ago when I had a lot of jam I'd made," I said, not going into it. I wanted to get to Noel's before it got too late but there was no answer at his door. For two days, I tried to bring Noel Thanksgiving leftovers. As it turned out, Noel had spent Thanksgiving in the hospital.

"He's coming home tomorrow," Gordon said a few days later. But in answer to the small hope I was letting in, he just lowered his head and walked upstairs.

Stretch got Noel's leftovers, welcoming them with the ardor of the hungry. Like Mae, he favored the jam pie, even though it was a couple of days old. As for Lance, we hadn't seen him in days and I wasn't inclined to wander up to the top floor to invite him down.

When people get really bad, when their apartment smells like something has died, when the landlord has to break in and make sure they're alive, that's when it's deep trouble. Keys are no good when someone has barricaded himself behind double bolts. When Jul finally got in, he found Lance nearly dead from booze and pills, food spoiled in the fridge, trash reeking, pizza boxes covered with flies. That was when Jul called an ambulance. He called Lance's parents again, made arrangements for Lance to go to the hospital again, to get dried out again, to get treatment again. Jul, who usually enjoyed the trading of information, was close-mouthed about Lance's condition. Somehow we learned of the shock treatments, so that when Lance returned, clutching a bag of prescription drugs and a bag overflowing with girlie magazines, we didn't know what to think. Was there a cure in those bottles and magazines?

Weeks passed. We found him by the mailboxes, staring. We found him in the laundry room, crying. We found him on the landing, lost. Trash piled outside his door again. We saw the liquor bottles again and the general decline of his hygiene. Jul called the parents and Lance's psychologist once more, but he didn't suggest another trip to Langley. Lance may have come back to us a more sober person but there was less of him there. And, as we watched him slide back into his dependencies, we couldn't imagine how little of him they would send back after more treatments.

In many ways, even though Lance had a roof over his head and a bed to sleep in, I thought that Stretch and some of the other street people I knew were better off. How far was Lance from homelessness? How many rescues did a person have?

It was surprisingly hard on me when Chuck returned to Vermont. In the weeks that he had been in San Francisco, we had slid easily into comfortable patterns: coffee in the morning at the café, long afternoon walks whenever our schedules allowed, making dinner together at night or eating at our favorite restaurants in the neighborhood, concerts, museums, and martinis at Martuni's, where the bartender claimed the martini had been invented.

How nice to emerge from the Muni station at Church Street after a day of teaching to find Chuck waiting to walk me home, his nutmeg eyes a reward, his smile so familiar there above his trim goatee. How nice to share my favorite adventures with him. The Muni, short for Municipal Railway, was a favorite form of free amusement; fortunately, Chuck also loved climbing aboard to watch the show. The F train, which I took to downtown, the Embarcadero and the Ferry Building, was my favorite line. It featured a fleet of restored historic streetcars, trolleys and trams from around the world. The trolley cars from Milan carried original advertisements in Italian while the Boston cars were just like ones I rode in my childhood. My favorite, the 1934 tram from Blackpool, England, looked like a cross between a gondola and a streetcar with its open body and nautical horn. Another favorite, a streetcar named Desire, had served New Orleans from 1923 until well into the 1990s. San Franciscans took these gems for granted, or lamented the slowness with which they traversed Market Street, but I was still new to city life and found them quaint. Which was a good thing because, without a car, we took public transportation everywhere, communicating through code words as the weirdoes of the world entertained us, whether intentional or not, from the ancient ballerina doing pliés while hanging from the bus strap to the fashionably dressed businessman sucking his thumb behind his briefcase as if no one could see.

Chuck also shared my love of walking. One of our favorite walks in San Francisco began with a ride on the F train along the Embarcadero to the Fog City Diner, where we hopped off, crossed Battery and Sansome, then climbed the Greenwich Steps up Telegraph Hill, enjoying the wild parrots as they careened through the trees and the wonderful views into gardens and homes, all so ingeniously tucked into the hillside. At the top, we always stepped into the Coit Tower to see the Labor Movement murals on its walls and then headed down the hill to North Beach where in Washington Square, ancient Chinese women practiced Tai Chi while couples snuggled on park benches. Mario's Bohemian Cigar Store and Best Cappuccino Café was situated across from the park. On damp days we sat inside the steamy café and drank cup after cup of luscious cappuccino and ate meatball sandwiches, but on sunny afternoons the café's sidewalk at the corner of Columbus and Union was the perfect place to watch the show with a nice glass of Chianti. From there, we usually meandered past the strip joints to City Lights

Bookstore, located at the nexus of North Beach and Chinatown. There, we gave ourselves over, losing hours in the bookstore's three floors of quirky, outraged, important, radical, ecstatic, heartbreaking words. Then we joined the masses on the bus ride home through Chinatown, so crowded, so exotic, so noisy. So wonderful to share all this, if only temporarily, with Chuck. The truth was that no matter how much I enjoyed my independence, some activities are just more enjoyable with the one you love.

I was consoled by the fact that I would be joining him soon in Vermont for my winter break.

風

I did my Christmas shopping in Chinatown, the largest Chinese neighborhood outside of China. Although close to San Francisco's famously upscale Union Square and the Financial District, Chinatown is a world of its own, so exotic, so foreign. Approximately 70,000 people of Chinese ancestry live in Chinatown's narrow blocks. After the original Chinatown was destroyed by fire following the 1906 earthquake, city officials tried to move the area's residents to less valuable land out in the Richmond District of San Francisco. But the Chinese benevolent societies and civic leaders were able to convince the city that rebuilding Chinatown with traditional architectural details such as pagoda roofs with curved eaves and authentic-looking dragon lampposts would bring tourists to the city. It worked. Beyond the red and gold paint and the brightly lit main streets, however, on the streets I explored, tenement buildings were jam-packed with elderly residents, exotic-smelling herb shops with open containers of oddly shaped ginseng and food markets where people bought live roosters, king pigeons and sea slugs. The sounds of Chinatown were deafening, chatter in Taiwanese and Cantonese, traditional Beijing opera vying with rap blaring from boom boxes for sale on the sidewalks, car horns and bicycle bells, mechanical tweetie birds chirping annoyingly, along with the commerce of daily life. It was delightfully chaotic.

Who could choose anything when cardboard boxes overflowing with plastic kitchen gadgets lined one storefront next to another rimmed with boxes of lacquered umbrellas, silk slippers, porcelain eggs, paper lanterns and wind-up China dolls, all cheap, cheap, cheap. Of course, just when I had purchased adorable silk purses for $1.99 each, I found another shop with the same item for thirty cents less. Silk shirts and jackets cost $100 or more in quiet, tastefully appointed shops while knock-offs sold next door for a third of that in stores jam-packed with a profusion that made choosing impossible. That's the thing about Chinatown: you can buy lots of little goodies for cheap – I was particularly fond of the cigarette lighters shaped like tubes of lipstick, pocketbooks, tape measures and slot machines – and really nice clothing, linens, porcelain and furniture in another couple dozen shops. There was so much to gawk at: junk shops selling cheap T-shirts and suitcases; restaurants with greasy ducks hanging in the window; the fourth-floor Kong Chow Temple, a Taoist shrine above the post office where seventeen gods are honored on differently colored altars, red for virility, green for longevity, gold for majesty. I loved to wander along tiny Ross Alley to the Golden Gate Fortune Cookie Factory where Chinese women made little pancake cookies into which paper fortunes were inserted, one by one, to be shipped to Chinese restaurants around the world. On the corner of Washington and Grant, J. J. Chin stood on a white plastic bucket, chanting "Happy, Happy, Happy," as he held a sign covered with Chinese characters, which roughly translated to, "Recognizing a thief as a father. Notoriety abides for two thousand years! Bian is an apocalyptic star. Tai island is out of luck! China reunify. Chinese people will enjoy glory, prestige, joy and unity!"

While Chuck was in San Francisco, I'd hinted obnoxiously often that all I wanted for Christmas was a puppy, something small and cuddly. A Maltese puppy would be nice but I'd take any cute little furry dog. I told my daughter Dawn several times that I wanted a puppy for Christmas. I knew she would pester Chuck to find one for me and hide it at her house until Christmas morning.

In most cities, Gavin Newsom, the Democrat who ran for mayor of San Francisco to follow the flamboyant and powerful Willie Brown, would be considered a liberal. But there he was labeled a corporate thug and centrist, in bed with the big developers, such dirty words in this fair city. The students and the liberals who called Newsom a capitalist pig favored Matt Gonzalez, the Green Party candidate for mayor.

Jul liked to promote Newsom as a rags-to-riches story, another example of his theory that hard work was the essential ingredient to success, but Newsom's story didn't fit the mold, certainly not as Angela Yvonne Davis might have defined those words. Newsom's father, William Newsom, a state appeals court judge, was connected to many of California's most powerful politicians, men like Pat Brown, the former governor of California, and, of course, Willie Brown.

During his tenure as mayor, Willie Brown had named Gavin Newsom to one vacated position after another, culminating with Newsom's appointment to the city board of supervisors in 1997, making him not just the youngest member in the board's history but also at one time the only straight male in its membership.

William Newsom was also close to the wealthy Getty family, especially Gordon Getty, one of oil tycoon J. Paul Getty's six sons by four wives. They'd gone to Catholic school together. Before his death, J. Paul Getty had locked up his millions in a trust so complex that his heirs couldn't get to the money until William Newsom, as executor of the estate, found legal ways to break the trust. William Newsom was the witness at Gordon Getty's wedding in Las Vegas in 1964.

The rags-to-riches story dated back to Gavin Newsom's teenage years, after his parents had divorced. According to the oft-told story, his mother had to work three jobs to cover expenses and once told the children there wasn't enough money for Christmas presents. Newsom worked throughout high school and college, cleaning bathrooms and selling podiatric orthotics. I wondered why the family was so strapped when the father seemed to have access to so much. Some said the hard times were a result of William Newsom's generosity, that he would give the shirt off his back, along with significant sums of money, to causes and people he believed in.

In 1992, Gavin launched a business called PlumpJack Wine with the generous backing of Gordon Getty. Within ten years, PlumpJack had grown into a $7 million business that included five restaurants, a winery in Napa Valley, a ski resort and a clothing line.

As supervisor, Gavin Newsom's voting record was fairly liberal except on development issues, when he often voted in favor of high-rise housing complexes and other projects that the more liberal supervisors opposed. The more progressive board members believed these development projects would further displace low and middle-income residents; they argued that what the city needed was more housing for middle and low-income residents.

In 2002, as supervisor, Gavin Newsom introduced a program called Care not Cash as an attempt to tackle the city's homeless problem. Care Not Cash reflected the common belief that San Francisco's excess of homeless people had two causes: Other cities sent their homeless to San Francisco, literally buying them one-way bus tickets there, and perhaps more essentially, a conviction that the city's generous system of handouts and support agencies, while well meaning in their inception, provided little incentive for the indigent to change their lifestyles. This was the position that Jul had posited the day we met.

Under Care Not Cash, San Francisco's homeless would receive substantially less financial assistance than they had for decades, roughly $59 rather than the $395 monthly allotment then given each person on general assistance. Instead of cash, they would be offered housing and other services if they enrolled in drug and mental health treatment programs and stayed clean and sober. Theoretically, the savings would pay outreach workers who would engage the homeless directly on the streets and encourage them to come into the shelters to get help. San Francisco voters approved the measure in November 2002. Newsom ran for mayor the next year.

His opponents, Angela Alioto and Matt Gonzalez, campaigned rigorously against Care Not Cash. Alioto was the daughter of longtime San Francisco Mayor Joseph Alioto, a popular Democrat who had supported the building of the Transamerica Pyramid and other large-scale city and transportation projects. Angela Alioto had served as president of the board of supervisors and was also well connected in state Democratic circles. She argued that Newsom's homeless plan didn't address the more urgent problem of the chronically homeless, people who were often mentally ill or addicted, and too damaged to take advantage of existing programs, never mind comply with more complex ones.

It was the Green Party's Matt Gonzalez, however, who articulated the opposition to Care Not Cash most eloquently. Care Not Cash was doomed to failure, he said, because it didn't address the underlying causes of homelessness: the disparity between the haves and have-nots; the high cost of living in San Francisco; the loss of many mid-level and higher-paying jobs during the dot-com bust; the failure of government to create a safety net for people with mental health or cognition problems after the process called deinstitutionalization went into effect;

the breakdown of the human family and society's code of responsibility for the less fortunate in our midst; the paucity of the educational system, which had failed to provide some of its graduates with even the most minimal of life skills; and the isolation of the individual who cannot function in a culture that emphasizes success, achievement, the getting and spending. The list went on, a list so long you knew Gonzalez knew there was no solution, only political posturing. I tended to agree with him.

Even though I was a newcomer to the city, I could see that these debates encapsulated the conflict between those still committed to the city's long history of progressive politics and the demands of a changing citizenry that wanted a more practical response to homelessness and other social ills. The city was experiencing a host of economic woes that stemmed from the dot-com bust; caring for the homeless often seemed like a bottomless hole into which the city's precious revenues would disappear with little measurable results. The problem, of course, had its roots in national movements that had aimed to correct other social problems, another example of unintended consequences.

In the 1950s and 60s, many institutions that had served the mentally ill and developmentally disabled were closed out of concern for their poor living conditions and the potential for abuse within these facilities, as well as a belief that these institutions maintained and even in some situations created greater dependencies, and restricted the ability of people to care for themselves. Activists, mental health counselors and public officials argued that community-based services would be cheaper and more effective than institutions, while allowing people with handicaps greater dignity. Those optimistic expectations about community-based services were never met, however, and as the safety nets that close-knit families and communities once offered eroded, many individuals who once would have been cared for at home or institutionalized were now homeless or imprisoned. California as the nation's most populous state suffered from the failures of deinstitutionalization at a level that seemed impossible to reverse – hundreds of thousands in prison; hundreds of thousands in shelters or living on the streets despite having the largest economy of any state in the nation.

In many ways, Gonzalez's story was a perfect narrative for San Francisco while also an example of that ethic Jul so admired, that of the self-made man. In contrast to Newsom, a native San Franciscan, Gonzalez resembled so many idealists who came to San Francisco from somewhere else, drawn to a place where they could espouse visionary but often impractical objectives. Gonzalez was born in McAllen, Texas, a border town where he identified as Mexican. After earning his undergraduate degree at Columbia University in New York, he came to California as a Stanford law student, was editor of the *Stanford Law Review* and worked on immigration issues in East Palo Alto, the neighboring city to Palo Alto and its economic opposite. He worked as a public defender for more than a decade and ran unsuccessfully for San Francisco District Attorney, campaigning to fight illegal evictions, political corruption and environmental crimes. In 1997, Gonzalez funded the publication of Beat poet Jack Michelin's *Sixty-Seven Poems for Downtrodden Saints.* He gave away his 1967 Mercedes-Benz and rode public transportation to show his concern about global warming.

Originally a Democrat, during the 2000 presidential campaign, Gonzalez became disillusioned with party leaders like Al Gore for not coming out aggressively against the death penalty and for not supporting same-sex marriage, and he joined the Green Party. Coincidentally, that year the city changed its system of electing supervisors, abandoning citywide district elections. Tom Ammiano, who had run for mayor against Willie Brown, encouraged Gonzalez to run in the new District 5. Gonzalez defeated Juanita Owens, who was supported by Brown and other leading Democrats, 66 to 34 percent, becoming the first Green Party member elected to office in San Francisco.

As supervisor, Gonzalez campaigned to raise the minimum wage to $8.50 an hour and helped write a ballot measure giving San Francisco control over its municipal electric utility system. The latter proposal failed. Later, as board president, he successfully shepherded an ordinance to prevent the San Francisco Zoo from keeping elephants. (This followed the death of two elephants in the zoo's care and questions as to whether the zoo's two remaining elephants should be removed to a larger sanctuary, away from San Francisco's foggy air.)

In opposing Newsom's Care Not Cash program, Gonzales campaigned for the renovation of the city's numerous SROs (which stood for "single resident occupancy," usually small single rooms with no kitchen and shared bathrooms) to provide emergency housing, and he lobbied hard for construction of more low-income and affordable housing.

Not surprisingly, the candidates presented differing physical images as well as ideological ones. Newsom was handsome in a self-aware way. His hair was perfectly coifed – that's the right word, coifed from the Latin, *cofia* or *cofea*, for helmet – while one suspected that Gonzalez's bad hair days, and there were many, were also intentional. As it turned out, no candidate for mayor received the required majority, resulting in a run-off between Newsom and Gonzalez, on Dec. 9, 2003. How thoughtful of the city to schedule the run-off in time for me to experience it before leaving for Vermont. Despite all the money and starlets who surrounded him – Clinton and Al Gore came to San Francisco to campaign for Newsom, who spent $4.5 million compared to Gonzalez's $850,000 – Newsom won by only six percent.

Some of my students were at my apartment the night of the run-off election, finishing up the last issue of the student magazine of the semester. No one actually thought Gonzalez would win. Still, when we'd finished our business, we ambled over to the Gonzalez consolation party, held under a big tent just a short distance away. There we found the Green Party celebrating with two rock bands, a feast of free gourmet food, organic and vegetarian, of course, lots of wine and a who's who of San Francisco liberals. The students consumed and schmoozed. We all danced together and had a riotously good time until one of the students downed too many drinks and began to take seriously the creepy leech offering her Brussels sprouts from the end of tiny plastic toothpicks.

After I helped the student home, I headed home myself. It was probably 3 in the morning by the time I rounded the corner and started up Octavia. As I looked up Waller, I could see Stretch sleeping in his alcove. I wondered if he'd take the care the new mayor was offering, get a room and give up the street. It didn't sound like a bad deal to me.

"No, not me," Stretch said when I inquired the next morning. "I'd take the room but I ain't talking to a bunch of shrinks or getting pissed every day. That's a violation of my unalienable American rights. I'd rather sleep on this here street than sit in no meeting and talk about what went wrong in my life. I like my life just fine."

"Wouldn't it be worth it to have a place of your own?"

"Nope, it's too late for that way, to have to report to anyone. I never was good at that," Stretch said, nervously fishing around his mouth with his tongue and stretching his neck oddly, perhaps addressing a crick caused by sleeping on cement, then picking up his blanket and straightening out the items in his shopping cart before heading off to work, trolling Market Street for recyclables.

A week before I left for Vermont for my five-week winter break, I distributed my holiday presents in the building. For Mae, a box of Godiva chocolates, which she insisted we open on the spot. "No soft centers so far," she said after the third round.

"Of course not, Mae," I said. "You are not a soft center woman."

Ann and Alexandra didn't celebrate Christmas but we exchanged holiday presents nonetheless. Ann gave me a pillow filled with beans that could be heated to relax sore neck muscles or provide neck support on the plane ride home. I gave Alexandra Hello Kitty stockings and child-sized sunglasses and Ann a jacket from Chinatown.

I had purchased a brilliant red silk scarf for Noel. I could hear the TV behind his door but he didn't answer my knock. He'd been home from the hospital for a few days, but I hadn't seen him. I put the scarf in a gift bag, hung it on his door along with a note that said I'd take him up on our dance date in the new year. I was counting on Gordon and Liya's prognosis, which went something like this: Their daughter Lydia would be home from college for the Christmas break. She always cheered Noel and would be the perfect antidote for what ailed him.

I threw one last party for my students complete with chicken parmigiana and cheesecake, celebrated an early Christmas with Bonnie and Birdie and stayed up for two nights before my flight packing, cleaning, correcting papers and drinking wine with various friends.

The day of my flight, I spent an extra hour on the sidewalk outside the Laguna Sidewalk Café, chatting with Wisdom Man and Jay and Guy about the knighting of Mick Jagger and George Clinton's arrest for cocaine possession. Jay did a king of funk cocaine dance on the sidewalk, singing an impromptu funkadelic Christmas blues before declaring Al Gore's endorsement of Howard Dean the kiss of death.

"Not even the kiss of life could save Dean," Wisdom Man said, then launched into a symposium on the phrase "the kiss of death," beginning with its origin as the kiss of Judas, followed by a recitation of the movies, TV shows and albums with the phrase as their title.

"I have recorded at least four in all three categories, not to mention Sonya Blade's preferred weapon, the kiss of death, in the Mortal Kombat games," he said, blowing a kiss my way.

"Great," I said. "That's how you bid me goodbye, the kiss of death."

"No, it's there to protect you," Wisdom Man said. "The kiss of death works both ways. Death to anyone who threatens our fair sidewalk companion, Master Bard of the San Francisco Uniterrans."

I canvassed the neighborhood for Stretch to no avail. Was he in jail, working the streets? I didn't know. I looked for Jack too but someone at the church said it was his day off. A minute before Bonnie and Birdie were scheduled to pick me up for the airport, I raced back upstairs to say a final goodbye to Ann and Alexandra. Ann completely dismantled me, turning blubbery as she engulfed me in her generous bosom, my face and my neck instantly wet with her tears.

"Six weeks is too long," she said, embarrassed by emotion.

"We can talk," I offered. "Besides, it's actually only five."

"Of course, we'll talk," she said. "That's not the same."

That good Jewish girl certainly knew how to make this good Catholic girl feel guilty. Finally, excited to see the children and grandkids, Chuck, my Vermont home and all my oldest friends, I climbed on board the red-eye to Vermont with no regrets. The plane, of course, was crammed. I was squished between two people whose bodies overlapped their seats. It was December so the flight was roller coaster turbulent and I was having hot flashes, so overheated and itchy in my seventeen inches of space that I never slept a minute on the first leg of my flight to Pittsburgh. The three Tylenol PMs I'd taken finally clicked in on the second leg of the journey and I awoke with a jolt as we landed in Albany, New York. I was fairly out of it as I stumbled from the plane, jet-lagged, discombobulated, but there was my daughter Dawn's beautiful face and the babies and Saint Michael, her husband, waiting for me in the main terminal. Minutes later, tooling down the interstate, grimy snow to left and right, I looked down at my left hand and realized there was no wedding ring on my finger. I had a vague memory of the prickly heat on the plane and of taking the ring off; the band was wide and my skin sometimes got irritated underneath. I must have put the ring in a pocket or my backpack for safekeeping but I couldn't remember the details of what I'd done.

"Mike, turn around; I don't have my wedding ring on," I yelled.

Dawn and Mike convinced me of the illogic of that maneuver. A phone call would be more efficient. And so, after I dug unsuccessfully through my pockets and my pocketbook, once, twice and then again, and came up literally empty-handed, I called the Albany airport; I called US Airways. I learned that the plane had turned back to Pittsburgh soon after it landed, that I wouldn't have been able to reboard to search for my ring even if we had turned around the moment I discovered it missing. The airline promised to search both planes but I knew it was either lost forever or belonged to someone else. Still, as soon as I arrived home, I searched my carry-on and clothing, over and over, again to no avail. I was really unhappy to have to tell Chuck I had lost my wedding ring when he got home from work. After the initial "How could you do that," we had a good laugh about my dizziness. And on Christmas Day when Chuck gave me a wedding ring much nicer than the original, and said, "I was going to look for a puppy but I knew you'd rather have a wedding ring," of course I lied. Of course I said a wedding ring was much better than a puppy.

On Christmas Day and throughout the holiday week, I passed out presents at the various gatherings with family and friends, the gifts from San Francisco, lacquered paper umbrellas, silk pajamas, embroidered linens, tiny purses, ginseng, fortune cookies, origami cranes, silly lighters, all big hits. Part of me remained a little disappointed not to have received a puppy for Christmas, inconvenient as *that* would have been. Smart Vermonters do not buy puppies for Christmas. How exactly do you train a puppy to pee outside when there were several feet of snow just beyond the door? I hadn't thought of that.

Snow is a lot more beautiful when you don't have to drive into the wilderness to talk to neighbors about the murder suicide next door or scrape an inch of ice off your window before heading off to the State House for a press conference on waste disposal. It snowed twenty-three of my thirty-four days in Vermont. I saw that beauty with new appreciation. Vermont was clean. Of course the trade-off for not having to negotiate around the bodies passed out on the sidewalks of my San Francisco neighborhood was having to negotiate this thing they call black ice, a mirror-like glaze that coats roadways and possesses the ability to send your car spinning at the first moment of distraction. But on days when the weather blew south from Canada, bringing crisp clear air and magnificently blue skies, when we donned snowshoes or cross-country skis and headed into the woods, following the trails of tiny paws made by winter creatures or startling a herd of does hunkered down in a sheltered deer yard, or when I climbed into bed with a load of books to read to some combination of my grandchildren or gathered my oldest friends around my Vermont hearth and served them dinner on my bird plates, each one a repository of the memory of its discovery, when so many conversations unfolded effortlessly, each built upon a common history that spanned decades, I felt blessed beyond words.

The best thing about going away was being missed. I had discovered this truth upon my return to Vermont and discovered it anew upon returning to San Francisco. I was unloading myself from the taxi when Stretch walked by. "You left without saying goodbye," he chastised. "I had to ask Jack where you were and he had to guess. You didn't say goodbye to him either."

I told him I'd looked for both of them before I left. Then I give him the little treat I'd brought from Vermont. Given his sweet tooth, I knew the maple candy leaves I'd carried three thousand miles across the country would be well received, but I was unprepared for the childish glee that spread across his face when I handed him the box containing nine individually wrapped maple sugar leaves.

"I'll eat one a night," he said as he bit into one, then kind of melted there on the sidewalk, a child stretched tall and lanky beside his loaded shopping wagon. "Well, maybe not. Maybe two a night," he said as I dragged my suitcase around the corner.

In the morning, there was a love fest of greetings in the hall. Alexandra, shy for way too long as if she'd forgotten me in the weeks I'd been gone. Ann with lots of building gossip, primarily stories of debauchery and pathos on the part of Robin, his entourage, and Lance, whose Christmas and New Year had been characterized by a fall down our stairs, an overflowing toilet and the usual clanging of bottles as he dragged his trash down four flights of stairs.

I gave Ann and Alexandra a box of maple candies as well. Ann knew better than to pretend: "They'll be gone by morning," she said, happy when Alexandra handed hers back to Ann, making a face.

"Too tweet," the child said

Another semester began, another round of classes. The winter rains were already overdue and the locals were talking about a possible drought. But the day after my arrival, when the temperature hovered near 60 and the sun was startlingly warm, I felt no guilt for the pure joy of going out without a winter coat or mittens. I made my way to the café early, hoping to see Elise and the guys, and I was not disappointed.

"Welcome home," Elise said as she steamed my milk and refused my money.

"Welcome home," Wisdom Man said as I sat beside him. "We've been looking forward to hearing your take on Screaming Dean, your fair-haired boy. How will he do in New Hampshire?" He was referring of course to Howard Dean, whose enthusiastic yelp after losing in Iowa was being referred to as "the scream heard 'round the world."

My latte was still too hot to drink and already I was lambasting the media for misrepresenting Dean's enthusiastic speech after Kerry pummeled him in the Iowa caucus. I felt compelled to explain that there was no guarantee Dean would do well in New Hampshire, even if it were Vermont's neighboring state, and then to explain that Vermont and New Hampshire weren't exactly palsy-walsy. I gave Wisdom Man and crew the quick-and-dirty story of the two states' historical animosity for one another, quoting liberally from former *Boston Globe* reporter Mike Barnicle who once wrote, "Vermont is a beautiful place, a postcard. New Hampshire looks like Arkansas with snow."

Silent Guy leaned back, balancing his chair on the two back legs. He looked from one of us to the other, rubbed his hands together like a kid about to get a treat, and grinned his semi-toothless grin. His body language was the best welcome back. I had a bad feeling about the New Hampshire primary. The press had been beating up on Dean over what they called his "I Have a Scream" speech for days. You could smell the blood. The establishment wanted Kerry, that stiff, and they'd make sure to get him. Not that I thought Dean could or should be president. It was just too embarrassing being a journalist these days, not to mention teaching the "profession." The reason Dean's scream had come across so loud was that he was yelling over the roar of the crowd and into a mike that blocked ambient noise so that his "scream" was literally taken out of context. But it made a better story without the details.

I had other things I'd rather talk about. I wanted to get back to Wisdom Man's school, to determine once and for all whether his school was real or, as I had begun to suspect, a figment of his imagination.

"How's your school going?" I asked, feigning innocence.

"Fine. We're studying journalists now. I understand the writer Dorothy Parker frequented Vermont. What do you say about her?"

I had just stepped right in it. I was fairly sure that Wisdom Man had been waiting for my return to ask me that question, that he had brought up Dorothy Parker, queen of acerbic wit and outlandish behavior, for the same reason that he had asked about Howard Dean, to egg me on or show off. After all, it's not like Parker was still a household name.

But I obliged. I knew a few things about Parker that he would find entertaining. And it sure beat talking about the primary election.

"Oh, yes," I said, "Dorothy Parker and the other members of the Algonquin Roundtable – Alexander Woollcott, the Marx Brothers, Tallulah Bankhead, what a name! – they made quite a scene when they visited an island in Lake Bomoseen near where I live. Woollcott owned the island and hosted great parties there, attended by the Algonquin group of intellectuals from New York City. The natives were perpetually enthralled. But remember, Parker and the other Algonquin Roundtable members were in Vermont only intermittently, mostly summer. Vermonters have a certain disdain for what they refer to as Summer People."

"Like you," he said, mockingly. "I knew you'd know that story. I just read about her and them."

I ignored his snide remark about my becoming one of those dreadful summer people. "What were you reading when Dorothy Parker's name came up?"

"Oh, just checking up on you Vermont writers, or people with a connection to Vermont. You're writing a book on Vermont writers, right? By the way, did you hear what Parker said when she was asked on some TV show to use the word 'horticulture' in a sentence?"

Then I understood. Wisdom Man didn't give a hoot about a book on Vermont authors, my latest project. Rather, I was quite sure that he had been awaiting my return to tell this joke. It was a little pitiful how he'd orchestrated the conversation to that purpose, to tell an arcane one-liner. I knew the answer to his question but I feigned ignorance. His cheeks were crimson, his eyes brilliant as he said, "Parker said, 'Horticulture: You can lead a whore to culture but you can't make her think.'"

He got a good yuk out of that, especially from Silent Guy. Yuk, yuk, yuk. But I had one or two Dorothy Parker zingers of my own.

"Did you hear what she said when someone told her that President Calvin Coolidge, Silent Cal the Vermonter, had died?" I asked.

Gotcha. He hadn't.

"She said, 'How can you tell?'"

It was good to be back.

Other treats greeted me upon my return – the Peruvian food and mintinis at Destino's restaurant, the Baja omelet with tomatoes and pesto at the Baghdad Café, the promise of a good show at the Fillmore, a full display of exotic orchids at Plant It Earth in the Castro. Most of all there were the city streets. I simply stepped out my door and headed off in any direction where adventure would find me. Besides my favorite trek up Telegraph Hill and down to North Beach, I loved to walk up Haight Street to Amoeba Records where I bought cheap CDs of folk singers who had died long before the CD was invented. From there, I often meandered through Golden Gate Park's botanical continents and that was where I ventured on my first Sunday back in the city, following paths that looped through giant tree ferns, gingko trees and ancient cycads growing huge in the park's Primitive Garden. Later that week, I took the N-Judah to Ocean Beach and walked for miles on boardwalks framed with beach grass and roses, and watched wet-suited surfers hoping for a wave in the frigid ocean. Still, the rain held off and, on yet another day, I headed to the Mission, where outside a Mexican restaurant I caught an impromptu rendition of "La Cucaracha" played by a Flamenco band wearing black sombreros decorated with pompoms. People who have lived in San Francisco for years said the Mission had been ruined, intruded upon (by people like me, whiteys, professionals), but when I shopped at La Chica Produce, buying key limes, dried ancho chilis and queso fresco for the tacos I planned to make that night, chatting with the woman at the cash register in my broken Spanish, I felt transported to another country, exotic and real.

Uphill and down I trekked, putting off work to relish the joy of walking outdoors in January and February. It was all there, just a few footsteps from my door: San Francisco, what a country.

The Primitive Garden in Golden Gate Park

But harsh absurdities also assailed me upon my return from Vermont to that rich and progressive city, none more painful than the irony of the Redemption Center, where the poor redeemed bottles for cash. I was struck anew with the logistical paradox of the Redemption Center being located next to the Safeway grocery store on Market Street in the shadow of the U.S. Mint, staggered again by how the mint loomed over the neighborhood, cold and impenetrable as a medieval castle. Ruth slept in the alley beneath the mint, not far from the Redemption Center. At least the woman I encountered there not long after my return to San Francisco said her name was Ruth. I wouldn't have provided my real name if I were she with her two babies, one about eighteen months old, the other an infant, six months old at most.

The baby slept in a Styrofoam cooler Ruth had rescued from the trash. I was coming back from the grocery store with two bags of groceries when I saw her there with her dirty-faced toddler. I offered her an orange, then my loaf of bread and jar of peanut butter. I nearly croaked when I heard the sound of crying coming from the cooler on the ground behind her, and looked inside to see a baby. I went home and got a blanket and some warm clothes for the woman. It was both nasty and protected in that alley, which served as a pedestrian and bicycle lane connecting Market Street to Duboce. People used it to cross to the N-Judah train line.

The wall that separated the Safeway shopping plaza from the alley had been painted with a colorful mural of bicyclists and trolley riders, its perspective skewed so that orange and fuchsia wildflowers dominated a bus or bicyclist on an adjacent panel. The city also ran a needle exchange program for drug addicts in the alley, providing users with clean needles, no questions asked. But it was not unusual to see old needles, broken bottles and condoms on the ground, and old and young men passed out or huddled together over something, talking or exchanging, bartering or killing themselves. The alley's high walls and its proximity to Safeway offered some advantages to a single woman with two children. I was sure I was not the only person who opened her pockets for Ruth. And the constant traffic of pedestrians and bicyclists offered some protection from the rougher elements, as well. Still, I was terrified for those children and for Ruth. I became protective, relieved if I saw a huddled mound of blankets installed just yards from the side of Jamba Juice when I walked by. I had seen Hudson Bay Blanket Man only once since the time I gave him some money and that had been months ago. He wasn't the only homeless person who frequented my streets for a month or two and then disappeared. Jul had a tarp in the basement and gave it to me without question. Ruth accepted it silently. No thank you, just a quiet calm as she added it to her belongings. The baby mewled from her cooler; the toddler said not a word.

The more I studied, the more I wanted a Maltese dog, especially after spending several afternoons with Patrick and Dale and their two Maltese at the landscape shop they ran on Market Street. Patrick told me Roman sailors found the breed living on the island of Malta and brought them home to keep their sweethearts company while the sailors spent months and years at sea. I could use a companion like that. But finding one was not easy. The breed does not reproduce easily, a plus in terms of over-breeding, but one that limits availability. I checked craigslist so often the computer search box went to "Maltese" as soon as I type "m."

Then I saw the ad with a photo of two dogs for sale:

An email revealed the following: the puppies' owner had purchased them after completing a big sales contract. She expected to be out of work for a few months so she bought the puppies. Then she got one of those offers you can't refuse, one so demanding she wouldn't be able to care for new puppies. Their owner lived in a penthouse apartment in San Francisco's Pacific Heights. The dogs were ridiculously expensive.

"I'm just going to look," I told Ann.

"Yeah, sure," she said.

As soon as the door opened, this blur of white fur came flying across two rooms, up my legs, up my chest, to my face where he whimpered and licked me like I was his long-lost mother. His name was Rome. The other dog sniffed with interest but not abandon. The owner wanted cash. I made the rounds to all the ATMs within walking distance and took out as much cash as my bank allowed in one 24-hour period, not nearly enough. Truthfully, the woman wanted more money for the puppy than I had in the bank. No, she wouldn't take a down payment until payday. And, besides, someone was coming later that afternoon to look at him. Rome's brother, Palmer, was already sold. Desperate, I called Ann, who just happened to have a handful of hundred-dollar bills stashed in her apartment. And after teasing me about "just looking," she offered it to me. All of it, enough to buy Rome, the pillow from his birth home, his toys, dishes and pee pads.

I could pay her back over time, she said. Ann wasn't worried; she knew where to find me.

It was unbelievable that someone who'd known me only six months – a single mother at that – would be so generous. But Ann convinced me it was a good way for Alexandra to have a dog to play with. She was actually talking me into it. "I keep telling you, you need a dog," she said for the umpteenth time. So, I rushed home to Ann, rushed back to Pacific Heights, handed over more cash than I'd ever held at one time, and, there I was, walking down Fillmore Street carrying my own adorable puppy.

"Who's that yapping?" Mae was standing by the door, awaiting a ride. It wasn't a Saturday so she wasn't going to temple, but Mae looked good enough to grace any holy place.

"It's my new puppy. Want to feel him?"

"Is he big? He sounds like a little dog. What's his name?"

"I don't know yet. I'm trying names out."

"Don't wait too long," she said as I lifted the puppy, all two pounds of him, for her to touch. He was a cartoon dog, walking on air to get at her. His little tongue was working overtime as he tried to lick her. I didn't think Mae would like that; I arranged him so he was licking me but close enough for her to touch.

"You sure that's a dog? Feels like silk. What color is she?"

"He's white, Mae, with big black eyes and a black nose. He's tiny. He'll probably weigh no more than four or five pounds when he's full grown."

"Now, girl," she said. "You got big responsibilities there. The smaller the dog, the bigger the responsibility. You pick him a good name. And don't let him bark too much. No one likes a yapper."

And off she went, wielding her cane like a sword of state as her car pulled up. Sometimes, you had to wonder whether she was really blind. Then she turned and shouted over her shoulder. "Take good care of that baby boy, now."

I couldn't call my puppy Rome. It was too close to Romeo, the name of the Himalayan cat I used to own, a disaster from the get-go. For the next few days, as he learned in record time to pee on the puppy pads and then outside on the deck, I tried on my favorite boy and dog names, silly names and studly names to see if the puppy liked any of them. I called him Atlas and Amigo, Gizmo and Galileo, Peter and Presto, Tang and Taz, Zip and Ziggy. He wagged his tail and came whatever I called him, his diminutive tongue sampling anything that came his way – except food, that was; he hardly ate anything. At Best in Show, the pet store in the Castro, a very muscular man with a shaved head and the biggest blackest plugs in each earlobe, tattoos climbing out of his T-shirt at neck and sleeves, came completely undone over my new puppy.

"Call him King," he suggested. "Okay, you don't like that. Give him a big name, though; he's so entirely himself, so adorable, so confident. Call him Rex or Prince or, no, I got it, call him Big Boy."

I couldn't quite picture myself yelling Big Boy to get my miniscule dog's attention, especially not in the Castro where some really big boys might come running, but I accepted the bags of dog food samples, ten options, he gave me to try. My puppy didn't like any of them. I called the vet in panic. Oh, a Maltese, the vet said. Fussy eaters. I hadn't reckoned on that. Cook him a chicken breast and mix a little, a very little, less than a quarter cup, in his food, the vet suggested. The puppy ate the chicken, picking it out carefully and leaving the dog food untouched. Back on the Internet to Maltese sites, all I got was commiseration and offers to stud out my new puppy.

Monday came and time to go to work but puppy still needed to go out every hour or so. So I carried him onto the Muni, tucked inside my coat, and brought him to my office. Before long word got out that Professor Daley had a puppy in her office and he was making the rounds of classes, king of the Humanities Building. Perhaps Prince was a good name. He danced around on his back legs and went to anyone, except an office employee who smoked.

On the way home I had him tucked into my jacket again, just his adorable little head with the black eyes and nose sticking out. I was sitting in one of the front seats of the train when three homeboys came on, walking funny – knees wide and toes turned in to keep their oversized pants from falling down. Their caps were on sideways; they wore the bling. Fuck this and fuck that, they said, taking up all the room at the front of the trolley. Suddenly, one of the homeboys saw me or, more correctly, saw the puppy peeking from my jacket. In a second, Homeboy was sitting next to me and talking baby talk. "Who's this?" he asked, gently tucking a finger under the puppy's chin. He was a boy now, not a wannabe gansta' showing off his underwear. "What's her name?" he cooed.

"I don't know yet. I just got –," I was saying when he interrupted.

"You mean you haven't given her a name? Dog needs a name."

"It's a him."

Quick again, Homeboy jumped to his feet and addressed the entire car. "This little guy needs a name. What should it be?" he asked.

Silence for just a moment but because everyone, especially those who looked like they weren't paying attention to us, was watching the drama, the riders started shouting out names:

"Powder Puff," someone yelled.

"Snowball," a woman nearby suggested.

"Or Snowflake," someone else amended.

Homeboy was irate. He was disgusted. "People," he said, his voice something you paid attention to. "He's a BOY. None of them pansy names for him. He needs a manly name."

And, then, I got it. Of course, that was it: Daniel. Just like my little Daniel in Carcès, just like that little puppy from the café in Provence, that cockapoo who gave me comfort when the Iraq war started. What was I thinking? Gizmo? Not on your life. My own sweet Danny Boy.

For several weeks, I saw Ruth regularly and gave her and the children a few dollars, a scarf, some diapers. She wouldn't let the toddler touch the puppy. She used the tarpaulin once that I know of; then it disappeared. The weather had been nasty and I feared for the baby. I tried to be gentle with my questions. In broken sentences, she told me she used to work cleaning rooms in a hotel until just before the baby was born. When she returned after the baby's birth, the job was gone. She'd been homeless for about four months. Ruth said she wouldn't sleep in the shelters, too much noise, and too many crazy people, too unsafe. The same with the SROs. Something bad had happened there, what I didn't know, but the only time I saw her agitated was when I mentioned the Care Not Cash program. I'd never seen her waiting outside the Baptist Church on free dinner night but she ate somewhere. She was not skinny, nor were the children. Ruth had an oddly shaped mouth and a speech impediment. She might have had a cleft palette; she had a crooked scar along her top lip. She was mentally challenged or let me think so.

What was the ethical thing to do? Should I call someone? Would they take her babies away? Should her babies be taken away?

Danny loved to walk the streets but he was ridiculously tiny and hadn't completed his shot regimen so I carried him in my backpack through the Castro where he'd be exposed to too many dogs. Not that the dogs in the Castro weren't the most healthy, pampered sweethearts. I was just so aware of how small he was. He had a big personality but he was tiny. I found out how tiny the first time I washed him. His poor little ribs stuck out, which the veterinarian said was a good thing. "He's not skinny; he's svelte," the vet said.

We were coming back from Danny's second-to-last batch of shots. I carried him in the backpack in front of me like a baby on the crowded 22 bus from the Fillmore. Danny occasionally unfurled himself from where he had snuggled into the curves of my body to give me a look, as if checking to make sure I was still there. When we got off, I went to maneuver the backpack and him to a more comfortable position when Daniel tumbled out of the pack, splat onto the sidewalk. His yelping transported every gay guy in San Francisco upon me in about two seconds flat. We melded into a cooing, crying, soothing, accusing puddle of concern there in front of Home restaurant. I was almost sick with self-reproach. The yelping went on for what seemed like twenty minutes. I was a really bad dog owner. A few of the guys stayed with me after Daniel had calmed down. We examined him from head to toe, moving limbs gingerly, putting him on the ground. Now that he was finished with his yelping, he wagged his tail like it was a pinwheel on a breezy day and went from one of the men to the other, licking and whipping his tail around with pleasure at all the attention. Two of the guys thought he was fine. One, however, insisted I take him to the animal emergency room and have him X-rayed. He was sure Daniel had injured his spleen and would die within a few hours. Daniel didn't look like he had injured his spleen. Eventually, with the dog jumping and barking and skipping about, I decided he'd survive. But the man's words stayed with me for days. Of course, he was fine -- other than that he had this habit of digging to China before lying down. He was part cat and part rabbit, too. About once a day, he'd race around the house like a loony, ears flapping behind him. When he was older and acted crazy, I would say, "He can't help it. I dropped him on his head when he was a baby."

It was not funny, but it was.

Weeks went by with no sign of Ruth and her children. I asked about her at the Redemption Center. No one copped to knowing her. The woman with the babies, I said to the man who seemed to run the place. I called him Navajo in my journal. He was a rugged looking fellow, with straight dark hair, chiseled features, his buttery-brown skin, his chest bared whenever the weather allowed. He turned dark, cold eyes upon me, said he didn't know any Ruth or any mothers with babies. Sure, you do, I said, the woman with the Styrofoam cooler. You must have seen her sleeping in the alley, the woman with the baby in the cooler. Another bare-chested man – he wore a skirt he had fashioned from colorful ties he'd cinched into his belt so that the ties flowed petal-like over ratty jeans as he roamed the smelly confines of the recycling center – looked at me like I was crazy. "Sister," he said. "Jesus may be late but he's right on time. You see a baby in a Styrofoam cooler, you need help. You better go talk to your Lord Jesus before you miss the bus."

So, of course I paid Ann back. And she borrowed money from me when she was strapped. And then she paid me back. We supplied each other with quarters for the Muni or laundry. With toilet paper, coffee, laundry detergent, the essentials of life. She walked Daniel when I was detained and I watched Alexandra. Alexandra and the buppy, as she called him, became our evening entertainment, racing though Ann's over-stocked rooms, him stealing her "baby," cleaning up Cheerios, her entranced by his tail, the snowdrift of his white hair, his quick tongue. Allie, as she had begun to call herself, wasn't sure she liked the licking.

With such trust – giving me hundreds so I could buy Daniel – Ann established between us a kind of allegiance that went beyond neighborliness. Wikipedia defines disambiguation as a path leading to different topics that share the same or a similar term or root. Ann and I were on dissimilar paths but we walked them together for some time. She was beginning her years as a mother; my maternal work had taken on a different form: as teacher, grandmother and mentor. She considered her apartment on Octavia a long-term, maybe forever, address; I was temporary and seasonal. I'd be there for two semesters each year, back to Vermont for the winter and summer breaks. I would be away from San Francisco almost as long as I was from Vermont. Yet, from the beginning, we had invested in each other's lives and in return garnered assets that couldn't be measured in dollars or calendars.

Alexandra and Daniel

Ann trusted me and I her. She could tell me about her problems with money. Like me, she sometimes spent more than she should. She was American, after all. "Remind me sometimes," she said, "that I need nothing."

"Me, too," I said.

Except that, because we were living in the dark time of war and hatred, because we were human, because we needed chocolate in the middle of the night, or some new item or entertainment, we helped each other make excuses and exceptions. After all, that was what friends were for. When life had given either one of us a swift, hard kick, we had our favorite Thai restaurant where we would order the eggplant dish, and lamb in curry sauce, and drink endless cups of green tea. Often we were the only people in the restaurant and the wait staff treated us like royalty, especially Alexandra who got free green tea ice cream after every meal. We would walk home slowly, the complaints we'd traded on our trek to the restaurant dispatched by the soft and sweet natures of our waiter and waitress, by coconut milk and chili peppers, by the sobering knowledge that we had nothing to complain about as Alexandra skipped beside us, and we pulled her closer as we passed the homeless men already bedding down on Market Street.

Jul painted a homemade bumper sticker on his truck to show his disdain for how business was conducted in San Francisco and beyond. It read, Nation of lawyers/Land of crooks. When I inquired about its origin, I got a half-hour summary of what he called nuisance lawsuits brought against him by tenants over the years. One tenant had tripped over a crack in the sidewalk and sued; other suits were filed by tenants who felt they'd been unfairly evicted even though they were months behind on their rent; another sued Jul when he removed an old furnace from the building, the tenant claiming he had been exposed to asbestos.

I wasn't paying attention to the details as he recited a litany of wrongs. Rather, I was tuned to his tone and mannerisms. It wasn't the first time that I had concluded that Jul was conflicted: He wanted to be liked by his tenants, he wanted to do good by them, but he suffered from a deep fear of being sued or taken advantage of.

It wasn't just the cost of lawyers and the time spent preparing for and appearing in civil hearings that he abhorred, I realized, but more so the anxiety he experienced in the months or years during which these suits ensued, anxiety that came from what he considered an unfair system.

"I'm always at a disadvantage in these things," he said, referring to tenant-landlord lawsuits. "If the city scheduled a negotiation or a hearing on behalf of a tenant, that indicates the city officials had found some merit to the tenant's complaint."

Beyond that, he explained, the tenant would be represented by the city while Jul would have to pay his own legal costs. If a case made it to the court system, again the tenant might have free representation while Jul would need to pay for his own attorney.

"I can't be friends with my tenants," he said one day during the latest dispute, one I'd succeeded in not learning the details about. "It's against the law."

"Well, we're friends," I said.

"One of us might regret that one day," he said, expressing an honesty I wasn't capable of, although I knew it might be true.

I came to think of the territory marking that dogs do as their equivalent to our email only the dogs were leaving their pee-mail. Danny was less than a foot high so he was like a midget at a urinal, definitely challenged in the area of pee-mail. He lifted his leg so high one day, attempting to leave his message on top of the previous dog's piss, that he flipped over. He gave me a look that said, don't you dare tell anyone I just did that. Danny had pride. Soon enough, he taught himself to lift his entire hind end up into the air and kind of pirouette around a pole or tree, peeing all the while, leaving his message as high as possible. Passersby marveled as Daniel essentially did a handstand, circling on his front paws while squeezing out a couple of drops of piss.

Whenever he saw another dog, he would get up on his back legs and hop forward, entirely submissive, his tiny penis exposed and totally trusting, as he tried to sniff the back end of every dog along our route, regardless of size or breed. As his owner, I was properly fearful of the jaws of Rottweilers and pit bulls. Daniel had no such fears. When an owner convinced me that his dog was safe, I let them greet one another, often causing a little traffic jam on Market or Castro Street as passersby took their pleasure in Danny's performances. Trust may be a hard commodity in today's society but Danny was giving it away for free. Within weeks, I knew the names of dozens of dogs in the neighborhood and Daniel was famous. Daniel was partial to Molly and Dolly, my neighbor Gail's Shih Tzus. We'd meet at the park for play dates.

"Watch out for that one. Don't talk to her. Not ever," Gail said one day, using a tone of voice I'd never heard from her. Gail was regal and soft-spoken. This new voice came from under her breath, adamant and fearful. It took a minute to figure out she was talking about the blonde woman dragging a garbage bag filled with cans down the street. I'd seen the woman on Market Street with her boyfriend. She was pretty – not skinny or sloppy like so many street people. But I'd already learned to avoid her. I didn't like the demanding tone in her voice when she asked for money. Or the snarled insult when I walked on by.

"My daughter used to help her out," Gail confided. "Every few months, that woman would catch her coming home from work and give her some Sad Sack story about just getting out of treatment or jail and needing money to buy clothes for a new job. Or she'd say she got the job but had no place to stay. My daughter gave her $10, $50, even $100 one time. Then one day last winter, she rang the doorbell and I answered. I told her to stop coming around, that she'd gotten enough from us. I was asleep a few nights later when my phone rang. I've got that program where they call you if your car's being broken into. The phone woke me up and then I realized someone was also ringing the doorbell. It was my neighbor telling me my car was on fire. Seems someone had pulled a dead Christmas tree into my driveway, shoved it under my car and set it on fire. The whole back of my house was on fire.

"My car was wrecked; my whole house could have burned down," Gail said. "Stay away from her. She's dangerous."

I watched as Ruth carried the bigger child and sort of kicked the cooler in front of her toward a small corner of the alley that was a bit more protected from the weather. When I asked Ruth where she'd been for the past few weeks, she said she had been picking grapes. It was not grape-picking season. Her sentence structure was rudimentary but her sense of protectiveness for those babies felt immense. Was she mocking me? The children looked healthy, although the older one had wet pants. I bought diapers for the infant and pull-ups for the older child but Ruth wouldn't take them. "No," she said. "All done."

I didn't want to scare her away with too many questions so I simply said, "We aren't done with winter. You should find shelter." Ruth kicked the cooler further away, trudging slowly down the alley with her toddler stuffed under her arm. It was the last time I saw her.

Feb. 19, 2004: The official voice shouted through the official bullhorn, "You have zero chance of getting married today. We have two hundred people waiting in City Hall. It will take most of the day to process their marriage licenses. You can wait in line out here if you want, but I need you to know your chances of getting married today are less than slim."

It was 7 a.m. Bonnie and Birdie had been in line for two hours already, along with hundreds of other same-sex couples who had come from all over the city, the state and, I quickly discovered, from all over the country and beyond to get married after Mayor Newsom had shocked those who had labeled him conservative by issuing a directive to the city clerk to issue marriage licenses to same-sex couples. Newsom was inspired to make the proclamation after he'd heard President Bush speak of the dangers of allowing same-sex marriage.

I'd just arrived at City Hall, bearing a bag full of pastries, coffee and juice and all the roses and baby's breath I could find at the grocery store, not much of a wedding breakfast and bouquet but better than nothing given the early hour.

Behind us, Chris and Rick announced they were not giving up. Ahead of us, Martine and Joe also vowed to wait it out. Bonnie and Birdie were willing to wait – they'd taken the day off from work – but within limits. After all, the city official had said zero chance. They had both taken the day off from work, but if they left they might never have another chance. Besides, this was a moment in civil rights history; we wanted to be part of it.

Bonnie is like a daughter to me. In the year that I had known Birdie, I'd come to love her as well. Anyone could see how perfectly matched they were, how their commitment to one another should be seen as affirming the sanctity of marriage rather than a threat. How could these two women who worked serving others, one as a teacher of ESL kids, the other as director of a house for adults with developmental disabilities, be seen as anything but a miracle? It was clear the city officials were doing all they could to process the thousands of applicants who had come to the city to marry since Gavin Newsom had married Del Martin, 83, and her partner of fifty-one years, Phyllis Lyon, 79, on February 12, 2004. But the city's resources – people, time, computers – were limited and the line just kept growing. In the end, the decision wasn't all that hard, really; we would stay and take our chances.

We camped out there on the sidewalk in front of San Francisco's spectacular city hall, trading stories with other couples. We met two women from New Mexico who had been in a committed relationship for thirty-four years and had brought their grandson with them as best man and two men from Colorado who had driven to San Francisco without stopping to publicly acknowledge their relationship of thirteen years. The stories sounded like the narratives of love and family that were at the heart of humanity, not tales of sex or its perversions. I heard no talk of promiscuity, no gay agenda, but rather of a desire to do what other couples in love can do: marry.

Meanwhile, the occasion had turned into a national event. A constant stream of people drove by, honking and shouting praise and congratulations. Every once in a while, a van from a local florist shop would drive up and out would pour a staff of workers laden with armfuls of bouquets that had been sent by supporters from all over the world. As newly married couples exited from City Hall with their marriage licenses and bouquets in hand, the crowd would erupt in cheers of congratulations. They clapped for the bearded men in their suits with bright rainbow ties. They clapped for the woman in the wheelchair, beaming as her partner pushed her and her oxygen tank by the cheering crowd. They clapped for couple after couple with straight parents, children, and friends in all colors and combinations in tow. Late in the morning, two mothers walked by with their four children, pulling a stroller laden with daffodils. One of the children, a boy of about three, walked up to Birdie. "Are you getting married today?" he asked, then handed her a daffodil and a paper scroll, tied with a pink ribbon. When she opened the scroll, she read:

> The moment I saw her
> Love
> Like a sudden breeze
> Tumbling on the oak-tree leaves
> Left my heart
> Trembling.
> > Sappho, *Fragment 23*.

Next to us, Scott Turner from LA, at San Francisco City Hall with his lover Michael Roberts, opened his scroll to read:

> I have run to you fluttering
> Like a little girl to her mother
> > Sappho, *Fragment 13*

Of course there were nay-sayers: the Asian man in a tattered suit, ranting about Gephardt and extra-terrestrials as he carried a huge sign with odd combinations of words on it, "God knows" and "Boycott Gap" among them. A large, black truck laden with tall wooden panels covered with slogans such as "Jesus died for your sins" and "The 10 commandments" circled City Hall hour after hour. TV camera crews showed up and recorded their footage but there was so little controversy going on that there wasn't much to document or ask about.

Every now and then, Joe Carruso, the city official in charge of the gay marriage procession, came out to reiterate the news. "Your chances of getting married today are zero," he'd repeat, apologize, and apologize again. But other city workers on lunch or coffee break were encouraging. "Hang in there," one with heart stickers pasted all over his shirt extolled. "We're moving right along. Don't give up."

Incrementally, we moved closer to the front of the line. And even though it would increase their chances of getting married, few couples celebrated when their neighbors gave up and left the queue. When a woman in a blue tuxedo below frosted hair and her partner in a blue velvet dress stepped out of line, nearby couples shouted, "You're not giving up, are you?"

"No way," the one in the tuxedo shouted, grabbing the hand of her beautiful mate. "I'm not leaving without my marriage license, damn it. I want to marry this woman. But we have GOT to pee. Save our space."

Martine and Joe weren't leaving either. They stood in suit jackets over jeans, handsome and affectionate, giving one another discreet kisses. Martine, who was from Madrid, said, "It's a long time before this will come to my country."

Finally, nearing mid-afternoon, Carruso announced they would take thirty-seven more couples that day. Birdie and Bonnie were lucky number thirteen.

The interior of San Francisco's City Hall is finished in marble, Indian sandstone and Manchurian oak. There are three acres of marble tile floors, giant historic photographs, a café, two glass-ceilinged side courts and a huge rotunda. The ceremonies would be held there, but first there would be more waiting in lines, starting with one in the long, high-ceilinged corridor that led to the city clerk's office. Again, we queued up, traded stories and gave advice to those planning to spend the night. All the while, city employees and volunteers came by to examine forms, answer questions, offer congratulations, expedite the process.

Suddenly a rush of young, handsome men sped by followed by a phalanx of TV cameramen and reporters. One of the reporters urged the others "Faster, faster," as the men darted through the queue of couples waiting to enter the clerk's office to have their paperwork recorded. When they reached the front of the line, the men broke into song. We thought some couple was being serenaded until the words reached us near the back of the line: "I have decided to follow Jesus," they sang. There was nothing wrong with that statement, of course; Jesus is one of the most loving people we know of throughout history, but those words were accompanied by hateful comments about homosexuality and terrorism and the destruction of America, at first sung but then hurled with such venom that I wondered how men so young had accumulated so much rancor and revulsion.

As if it were rehearsed, however, the hundred or so people in line waiting to get married and the people with them broke spontaneously into their own song, Our voices filled the grand corridor with its twenty-foot ceilings, culminating with the words, "O'er the land of the free and the home of the brave." Soon, the sheriffs were upon the protesters and led them away. And back came the city's Carruso to tell the crowd their singing was spectacular, their safety would be protected, and that they shouldn't throw rose petals and rice inside City Hall. As we waited another hour or so, the time quickly approaching 4 p.m. when the recorder's office would close, couples talked about how they'd never been all that fond of the national anthem but would think of it differently in the future.

Volunteers were waiting to marry the couples as they completed their paperwork. Finally it was Birdie and Bonnie's turn. Christmas Lubry, a middle-aged woman in turquoise and purple, introduced herself as a nurse at San Francisco General Hospital and a deputy marriage commissioner. There, in that lavish rotunda, she asked Bonnie and Birdie where they wanted the ceremony performed. By now, fatigue had set in and, as we looked around at the double balconies overlooking the rotunda, the sweeping staircase that opened up onto a glorious, light-filled balcony decorated with Greek statues, it was hard to decide. But time was literally of the essence. Bonnie and Birdie chose to be married in the wide space beneath those statues, two representatives of naked human perfection, light filtering around them.

They faced each other, holding the bouquets that filled their arms, Bonnie in a handsome loden green suit, Birdie in a black velvet jacket over trim pants, as Christmas Lubry read the familiar words except man and wife had been changed to spouse and spouse. Kisses, photos, then the rush to get to the recorder's office in ten minutes when it would close. A judge might rule the marriages illegal; indeed, the voters of California could. But, for Bonnie and Birdie, that public declaration and the physical record of it were enough.

Daniel's classmates were a Cavalier King Charles spaniel, two Chihuahuas, a dachshund, three Shih Tzus, a miniature schnauzer, a Brussels griffon and a Pomeranian-schipperke mix. It was the class of small, beautiful and odd dogs with Daniel fitting into the small and beautiful classifications. The Pomeranian-schipperke mix won the odd category; he had the hair of the Pom mixed with the silky black of the schipperke but its small round body looked all out of proportion on the long legs it inherited form the schipperke from whom it had also inherited the lack of tail. He was willful but Daniel took to him right off, making it clear that the dog, named Spirit, was his favorite in puppy class. He dissed the Cavalier King Charles spaniel that was, I had to admit, stunning. He was a mommy's boy, however, and spent class hiding behind his owner, a portly scuppie (the new term for socially responsible yuppie) oozing with the awareness that her dog was the most expensive in the group. The Brussels griffon on the other hand was a challenge. He came charging at Daniel the first day of class, a little toughie ready to compete for top man on campus. Daniel was half the size of EU, the name the lesbian couple had given their dog simply because Brussels was the capital of the European Union. You said it like it sounded, EeYou. EU was mischievous. He was used to being the center of attention and flung himself at whichever dog he felt was getting all the notice at any particular moment. Since these were among the most pampered pets on the West Coast, poor EU spent the class racing from one dog to another while the rest of us were trained. Puppy class is for the owners as much as the dogs.

Daniel was brilliant at everything except the command to come, which he did only if EU was charging, defusing the competition issue by rolling onto his back to show submission. Once EU had chilled, Daniel rolled back onto his feet and stood as poised as Napoleon.

"He thinks he's a big dog," I said to Zeus, our male trainer.

"No, he knows he's small," Chloe, the other trainer, corrected. "He's just confident."

Daniel got A+ in puppy class. A+ from Zeus is pretty impressive.

Daniel and I were walking to the café when I saw Dolly and Molly's photograph on a sheet of paper taped to a telephone pole. Big letters spelled "LOST DOG," followed by Dolly's description and Gail's phone number. Elise had pasted the posters all over the front counter. The story came out in pieces, first from Elise, then details and speculation from the guys on the sidewalk, and finally

Gail. She had taken the dogs to the park and come back into the house by the back door. She was sure she'd shut the back gate, but somehow Dolly must have gotten out. She didn't think it had been long before she noticed Dolly wasn't in the house, went running out the back door, which was open a crack, and saw that the back gate was open too. And now, a reward: $300 for the return of Dolly.

"It was the woman with the Christmas tree," Jay suggested.

"Wag the Dog was a Gnostic movie," Wisdom Man said.

We just groaned.

"Fine. Be ignorant," Wisdom Man said. "Dogma does that to people."

"Not funny," I said.

"Daniel Daley, no bark," Alexandra told Daniel, wagging her index finger at him while he wagged his little tail and danced around her, barking. She said his name like this, "Danyah Dayey," not saying the l's, and said the word bark the way I do with my Boston accent, "no bahk." Now, everyone in the building instructed Daniel the same way. Gordon would be outside my door, vacuuming and whistling, both of which drove Daniel crazy and so he'd start to bark. From the hall, Gordon would shout, "Danyah Dayey, no bahk." Jul might be at the door with some obsession to share and meowing to get Daniel going and he would say, "Danyah Dayey, no bahk." Daniel was an excitable boy. He loved people and he was often bored with just me. When someone came by, he'd greet him or her with the bark, the tail wagging, spinning around in sheer abandon. And we'd say, "Danyah Dayey, no bahk."

So the pundits were fooled and Mayor Newsom, on first blush anyway, appeared to be something of a radical himself. From February 12 to March 11, the city issued marriage licenses to 4,000 same-sex couples. A few days later a judge ruled that California statutes limiting marriage to opposite-sex couples were unconstitutional, but that ruling was overthrown by the California Supreme Court, which ruled on August 12, 2004, that the same-sex marriages were not valid.

Still, Bonnie and Birdie's license graced the mantle of their home in the Sunset. I was sure that many of the couples who came from far and wide considered their unions legal, whether the government did or not. Newsom may have ruined his chances for greater political power by sanctioning same-sex marriages. It was hard to tell, but some of the pundits were left wondering if Matt Gonzalez would have taken so bold a move.

Jay was singing "Danny Boy" to Daniel, who was twirling around in pleasure on his back paws. Guy was a little put out. Usually, he was the one Danny flirted with. That was because Guy fed him tiny bites of bologna or salami from the sandwiches he carried in his breast pocket -- his lunch, which he usually ate around 9 a.m., having left his halfway house after an early breakfast.

Howard Dean had ended his campaign for president the day before but I didn't bring it up. What astounded me the most about his campaign, beyond how well he did using the Internet as a campaign tool, was Dean's outspoken opposition to the war. In all the years I'd covered him as a reporter in Vermont, I'd never imagined Dean as a peacenik. I knew Wisdom Man would have a thing or two to say about Dean's unraveling and, just as I was getting ready to leave the café for work, he came rushing across the street from the mauve building.

"I was involved in a very engaging discovery," he said, out of breath. "But I wanted to offer you my condolence. Who do you think they'll pick? Kerry?"

"That cadaver," I said. "Probably. I don't think the pundits will be writing about a cult of personality there. What I want to know is, in this great country of ours, why can't we come up with a great candidate just once? I mean someone who ideologically appeals to most of us."

"You're dreaming, Yvonne, we've been polarized since the beginning of time. But the good news is that scientists discovered a black hole in the galaxy that tears apart and eats stars," Wisdom Man said apropos of nothing. "I saw photos of it on the NASA site. The black hole is one hundred million times bigger than the sun. Puts our petty worries in perspective."

"I don't get it. What's the good news in that?" I asked.

"The good news is that proves everything is relevant."

"Huh? I still don't get your point."

"The point is that once a black hole has formed, it continues to grow by absorbing additional matter. It will eventually self-destruct."

"If you say so, but how does that prove everything's relevant?"

"Just watch this election. You'll see. That Bush team is our own black hole. It's going to eat everything in its path but — and here's the good news — it will eventually self-destruct."

"How long do we have to wait for that to happen?"

"As long as it takes."

"And that's the good news?"

"Probably all the good news you're going to get for the next four years."

And still no Dolly.

My fascination with the homeless, hoboes, gypsies and the like was nothing new. The word vagabond – from the Latin vager, to wander, or vagus, wandering – sounded so romantic, so quixotic that I wouldn't mind if my obituary contained the line, "She was a vagabond in her later years." I also love the word wanderlust. It captures the Americans' need to be mobile, to begin anew, with the rebel's desire to be wholly independent of jobs and spouses and responsibility. There's a Vagabond Inn at the San Francisco airport. Perfect.

As a child, I read all about bums and beatniks, hoboes and tramps, the people living on the outskirts, and felt deep affection for the rascals in *Cannery Row* and the heroes in Charlie Chaplin's silent films, *Tramp* and *Vagabond*. The very idea of a gypsy camp enthralled me. I was prone to melodrama. Remember the old camp song, "The Happy Wanderer?"

> Oh may I go a-wandering
> Until the day I die
> And may I always laugh and sing
> Beneath a clear blue sky.

My *very* favorite song was the folk ballad, "The Gypsy Rover." I'd hike through the woods surrounding our house, so close to Boston and yet gloriously bucolic, and dream up little scenarios of me on the road with my hobo buddies. I'd sing in my horribly off-tune voice:

> She left her father's castle gate
> She left her own true lover
> She left her servants and her estate
> To follow her gypsy rover.

Such silly words and images for a girl growing up in the security of a Boston suburb under the roof of a father who wouldn't even let her go to a pajama party. Maybe that was why the wandering life intrigued me so much. It was forbidden. Mister Tambourine Man was just another version of the tale, the seduction. Oh come with me, leave the weary world behind. We'll have fun and freedom, tra-la-la. Yet, even as a child I recognized the inherent loneliness of the hobo and the wanderer, which of course made that life even more romantic. Did he choose this life or did it choose him?

But it wasn't just me; it was my generation. In that first year on Octavia, I pondered why so many of our songs, stories and films recalled the life of the person on the outside, the person who died alone, songs like Peter LaFarge's "Drunken Ira Hayes" and Bob Dylan's "Only a Hobo." I first heard LaFarge's song about 1964, sung by Johnny Cash in his cigarette-gravelly prison voice. Ira Hayes was a Pima Indian who was among the Americans who raised the flag on Iwo Jima only to come home to "no money, no crops, no chance … "

My favorite version of the song was by the Creek Indian Patrick Sky. So strange to recall sitting in a coffee house in Harvard Square and listening to Sky sing about how Ira Hayes died:

> … drunk one morning
> Alone in the land he'd fought to save.
> Two inches of water in a lonely ditch
> Was a grave for Ira Hayes.

And now, homeless men slept on the sidewalk outside my door, the door to a building where apartments rented for $1800 or more, at least to someone like me rather than a long-term tenant. I was thinking all this because I'd found myself singing Dylan's "Only a Hobo" as I walked home from work the previous night.

> As I was out walking on a corner one day,
> I spied an old hobo, in a doorway he lay.
> His face was all grounded in the cold sidewalk floor
> And I guess he'd been there for the whole night or more
>
> Only a hobo, but one more is gone
> Leavin' nobody to sing his sad song
> Leavin' nobody to carry him home
> Only a hobo, but one more is gone

I'd never really considered how many of my generation's songs glorified the hobo life and that of the outcast, the person loathe to make a commitment – Tom Rush's "Got the Urge for Going," Gordon Lightfoot's "That's What You Get for Loving Me," Mimi and Richard Farina's "Pack Up Your Sorrows," Eric Anderson's "Thirsty Boots." The road enchanted us more than love. We scorned possessiveness of the heart or of material objects. For a while, that is. Few generations have embraced capitalism and commercialism more than mine once the idealism of youth had passed, a realization that always made me sad and wondering whether the words and ideas of the Sixties had been mere fashion, another quickly fading trend, rather than a commitment to make the world a better place.

All those special interest and support groups, here, there, around the country, had fractured the populace into so many one-issue groups that the ideas and goals of that-now- long-ago time seemed quaint and unlikely. And what was I to do with that realization?

Talk about wanderers. Tom had not been in either Paris or Vermont the last few weeks, as we had surmised. As he explained the morning he reappeared at the cafe, he'd left San Francisco, intending to go to one or the other location but in the weeks that he'd been gone, he'd wandered instead to an old college roommate's house in Ohio, to a writers' retreat in the Rockies, then started east again, unsure as to his destination before he turned around in upstate New York and retraced his route west, back to his son's living room floor. In either location, there was a woman whom he loved, whom he'd left the other for. In either place, there was a woman who either did not wish to share him or did not want him back again, depending on the version of the story he felt like repeating.

Tom looked like you hoped Marlon Brando would have looked in middle age, instead of fat and sloppy and whatever the word was for what Brando had become by *Last Tango in Paris* – extinguished, maybe, ruined. Tom was not ruined but he was worn. He reminded me of Robin, a good person who had spent his talent and affections lavishly, with little regard to the future, a good person with a procession of interrupted lives now trailing behind him.

Outside the Laguna Sidewalk Café

Like Robin, Tom felt compelled to pour out his misadventures without censorship as he poured cups of green tea down his gullet. His mouth was feminine and petulant, the way Brando had looked in *On the Waterfront*, and his chin was quite actorly. He was proud of that chin; you could tell by the way he held it out and up, and the way he brought his teeth together, purposefully, when he smiled. It was the prep-school smile the boys of the Fifties learned from their parents. But his eyes revealed the aches he felt. He was, in a word, conflicted.

"Have you ever noticed that instead of going toward either one of your women friends, you flee in the opposite direction?" I asked. "You're just about as far away from Vermont as you can be right now and still be in the United States. And if you're on your way to Paris, you're sure taking the long way around." I hadn't wanted to respond to him. I didn't like men who strung themselves and their lovers along. He had worn me out with his angst. He loved that word. Why he directed so much of his struggle my way was beyond me except that I was the only one who actually responded to him. He loved my take on why he had returned to San Francisco – its distance from his women – but suggested his presence on the West Coast had more to do with it being March in Vermont, mud season, hardly an opportune time to return, and that March was one month too early for Paris. He'd be on his way again any day, he said.

In the meantime, Tom continued to torment me day after day with demands for writing tips and writing assignments. "You're the professor," he'd say, mimicking Wisdom Man. "Give us an assignment."

Finally, to shut him up, I suggested he write an imaginative piece describing each of our homes, based on the random bits of information we'd traded during our morning sessions.

"What do you mean, write about where each of us lives? What's that got to do with character development?"

"Well, we know you sleep on your son's floor rather than return home to your wife or the Parisian lover, so that tells us something about your character," I said. "And we know Ted lives with people he'd rather not associate with but that he sees his current living arrangement as a step toward stability. And we know that Wisdom Man lives in a mauve house across from a coffee shop and a Zen center and that tells us something about his character. And we know that Guy comes here each morning from the halfway house he lives in around the corner –"

"I don't live around the corner," Guy said, interrupting.

I raised my eyebrows his way. I'd half forgotten he was there.

"I live in a halfway house but it's way across town, in Visitacion Valley," he said, referring to a neighborhood miles across the city. As if I'd opened a duct, he volunteered that he took two buses each day to arrive at the Laguna Sidewalk Café, that he'd been traveling that route every day for almost two years since he got out of the alcohol treatment center.

"But why?" I asked. "Why here?"

"My mother's store was right down there," he said, pointing toward Market Street. "I used to work for her before, before …" and his voice trailed off. I tried to imagine taking two buses each morning, before coffee, simply to sit in a neighborhood that felt familiar. If I'd felt more generous toward Tom, if I had wanted to turn these conversations into teaching experiences rather than learning from them myself, I would have told Tom that the story we just heard from Silent Guy would make a wonderful writing assignment, that we could all write a story about our conceptions and misconceptions of one another. I would have had him try to turn those facts Silent Guy had just revealed into a story, how a boy growing up not far from this café had become this man staring straight ahead, mostly silent except for the hacking fits that came over him like a force of nature and the sound of that first drag on the cigarette that would stop the cough. That was a story I wanted for myself.

Daniel adored Stretch. Their morning ritual involved mutual smelling and rubbing as Stretch climbed out of his covers and Daniel clambered over him. They were a study in opposites. Daniel, clean and tiny; Stretch, filthy and long. His hands were as big as Daniel. Usually, as soon as he saw him, Stretch would get down on all fours and blow air at him, ruffle his hair, getting Daniel so excited he'd be jumping around on his back paws, his front ones batting the air. In response, Stretch would jump around, too, hands and feet on the sidewalk like a big, scrawny dog. "Danny Boy, Danny Boy," he sang in a kind of childish singsong. Daniel responded by barking and jumping some more until I broke it up because I either needed my coffee fix or had some other demand on my time.

"I had a dog once," Stretch said one morning. "I loved that dog but my father hated him. The dog did something bad one day. I can't remember exactly what, ate some trash or piddled on the floor. When I got home from school, that dog was gone. My father said he ran away but I know he got rid of him. I hated my father after that."

Days later, Elise was shopping downtown when she heard a familiar bark. She followed the sound until she came to a group of men lounging on a sidewalk, sharing a quart of beer.

"Where's the dog?" she asked.

"The dog? Arnie's dog? They're they go," one man said, pointing to where a chunky guy was walking away with Dolly leashed to a short rope. Elise was a formidable young woman with her Roller Derby body and she took off after them.

"I found this dog. Finder's keepers," the man said when she called out to Dolly and the dog turned and wagged her body. Elise knew where the closest police station was, ran there and got a cop. The problem was that Dolly wore no tags and the man swore she was his. It took another day for Gail to get Dolly's papers notarized and bring them to the precinct office, along with a recent photograph of Dolly and the story of the Christmas tree and the homeless woman. The weird thing was that when she and Elise and an officer went looking for Dolly, there she was, not far from where Elise had first heard her barking. And when the man saw the three of them coming, he just walked up and gave the dog to Gail.

"I got him as a gift from my homeboy's girlfriend. She said it was his," he said, giving yet another version of the story. And when Gail asked for a description of the woman who had given him Dolly, you know who it sounded like. But proving that a person had set your car on fire or stolen your dog was easier said than done. Within days, no one at the police station even remembered the incident, but at the Laguna Sidewalk Café, Elise was our heroine forever.

Now on Saturday mornings when Ann and I went to the Farmer's Market at the Ferry Building, we stopped foot traffic. There was the golden girl holding the handsome tiny white dog, the two of them in the stroller with Ann and me taking turns pushing and buying. We were a universal love machine, an antidote to the news. People didn't just stop and coo. They took photographs. They wanted to know the histories of both the girl and the puppy. Clearly, what the world needed was love, sweet love. Love in the form of a rescued orphan girl or a puppy also rescued, not from an orphanage but from life in a penthouse.

Daniel and Alexandra at the Farmers Market

On March 14 (That's 03.14) each year, the San Francisco Exploratorium has, since 1988, celebrated Pi Day in recognition of pi, the symbol for the number 3.14159265 – pi is actually a never-ending number; it actually goes on indefinitely. In Euclidean geometry, pi represents the ratio of any circle's circumference to its diameter. The Exploratorium hosts an "international geek holiday" on March 14 each year, complete with a parade that begins precisely at 1:59 p.m., the next numbers in the sequence after 3.14, followed by the throwing of pizza pie and the sharing of birthday cake for Albert Einstein, whose birthday happens to be March 14.

"Are you going?" Wisdom Man wanted to know. "It's one of the most important days of the year, even if the date has nothing to do with Euclid or pi or Einstein. Don't you just love living in a place that celebrates the man we refer to in our school as the Father of Geometry? What a wonderful world it would be if we Terrans paid homage to the value of Euclidian axioms and notions: A point is that which has no part. A line is a breadth-less length. Things equal to the same thing are also equal to one another."

Wisdom Man's pi dialogue was an improvement over his latest obsession, Dan Brown's book, *The DaVinci Code*, which he celebrated while also criticizing as superficial and historically inaccurate. Wisdom Man appreciated Brown's attack on the Catholic Church and the church's suppression of the Gnostic bibles. My problems with the church, as I explained to Wisdom Man, had more to do with its attitudes toward women, children and homosexuals than its dogma about faith.

"Precisely," he said. "It was the derision of women so that the men could assume power, it was the denial of the power of women to create life and of Jesus' true humanity that set the church on the road toward Christian fundamentalism. That is why in our school we welcome the criticism of those who feign Christianity but whose actions are so un-Christlike. How wonderful to be despised by the despicable!"

"Can I come to class some time? May I meet some of your students?"

"You're already in attendance," he said. "It's here. It's now. It's all the time. Haven't you known that all along?"

Tears wet my cheeks as I walked with thousands of other demonstrators on the first day of spring, protesting again, again, again another war. Last year, I marched with my daughter and son-in-law in New York and Washington in brutal cold, and later Chuck and I joined peace marches in Rome, Paris and Provence, each time hoping optimistically that our demonstrations could stop another war. Those Europeans (except the Brits – or perhaps just Tony Blair) certainly could see that the war in Iraq would turn into a quagmire. That hope was gone and we all knew it as we trudged down Market Street, our sluggish progress body language for the defeated. Yet I felt compelled to march, to say this is not the way to put an end to terrorism, to hate. The only pleasure I got came from the creativity of fellow protestors, the signs that read, "Impeach the Dim Son" and "Fermez La Bush." We were loud, I will say that. Sidewalks were jammed with tourists and shoppers who cheered us on or stared impassively as we brought business to a standstill along Market Street.

It was Daniel's first demonstration. He was too small to walk in the crowd and did not like the drums, so I carried him snuggled against my chest. I had made a button for him that read, "Puppies for Peace." Each time we stopped to listen to a speech or yell at the officers who clubbed demonstrators by the San Francisco Shopping Center, I tucked him into my zippered sweatshirt for protection. When things calmed down, he would come out from hiding and bestow kisses on fellow peaceniks. We were packed together, an unruly mass, as the police stopped the crowd to let traffic cross the intersection at Market and Montgomery when one officer stepped from the sidewalk and reached out to pet Daniel.

San Francisco Police at an Anti-War Demonstration

The officer's movement startled Daniel and he snapped then growled at the cop. Within an instant, the cop was giving me a hard time. Daniel weighed less than three pounds. His teeth were tiny triangles of porcelain. He had never snapped at anyone before. Indeed, he'd let himself be manhandled by dozens of people over the course of the past few months. I should have apologized and moved on. But I didn't. I said, "Good boy, Daniel" in reference to his little growl. After all, he was protecting me. That was when the officer got testy and ordered me to the sidewalk as if Daniel were a public menace.

The cop was actually threatening to arrest me, to take Daniel away. But as one, the crowd of demonstrators surrounded us and I stepped back and away from the cop, folded into the mass of bystanders and just kept walking.

"Good boy, Daniel," I said again as we left the march behind.

I couldn't find anyone to go with me to the Fillmore to see Joan Baez but I couldn't miss it. Baez was as beautiful as ever with her silver hair and sun-kissed skin. Her voice was an old friend, more perfect with age, as she opened the concert singing "Finlandia" a cappella:

> This is my song, oh God of all the nations
> A song of peace for their land and for mine …

I called Chuck periodically and held my cell phone out so he could hear Baez singing. I wanted to share the experience with him, although he couldn't see the tears that ran down my cheeks as she sang the union song "Joe Hill" and Woody Guthrie's "Deportee." How many times had I heard those songs? How many times have they been sung and still laborers got screwed, immigrants got deported and wars were waged?

"What are you doing?" a woman standing next to me asked, nodding her head toward the phone.

"I'm letting my husband hear her," I said. "He's in Vermont."

Within a second, she was dialing her cell phone. Her husband was dying of cancer; she had come to the concert without him but was feeling his absence profoundly. Now I had given her a way to include him in the experience. We stood together all evening, cried together, sang together, laughed together as we held our phones up for our husbands to hear the music. Baez talked of her old friend Bob Dylan, "the genius of our generation," her voice full of awful certainty as she sang his "It's All Over Now Baby Blue" with its damming lines:

> The vagabond who's rapping at your door
> Is standing in the clothes that you once wore.
> Strike another match, go start anew
> And it's all over now, Baby Blue.

Around 2 a.m., after listening to noisy revelry from Robin's apartment for hours, I knocked loudly on his door and then more loudly. Robin was lounging on the mattress on his front room floor, a giant hookah nestled in his crotch. Half a dozen bodies were arranged in varying positions around him and sprawled about the rest of the room. Robin was singing along to Lynyrd Skynyrd's "That Smell" and obviously having a great time as *that* smell filled the air. I had meant to tell him to tune it down. But after all, it was only 2 a.m., why should I interrupt the fun? Just as I was about to slip back out, the song ended and I heard, "Hey, look who's here." It didn't really take much to talk me into joining the group, although I sat on the edge of the bed.

"We're remembering Ronnie Van Zant," Robin said, waving his arms around inclusively. "We planned this party for October 20, the day Skynyrd's plane crashed and most of the band died but we couldn't get it together." More laughter. More drinking and passing of the hookah.

"Most of us were at Winterland when Skynyrd played there in '75 or '6, can't remember which, right before the plane crash that killed most of them. We partied down with those southern boys. It was weird because they always toured with the Allman Brothers Band and I remember Billy Powell being so pissed about Duane Allman dying in a motorcycle accident. Then he goes and dies, too. Shit head."

The rest of the group seemed too loaded to follow the conversation. "Artimus Pyle, remember him?" I asked. "Couldn't forget that name. He was the band member who crawled out of the wreckage and went looking for help, then got shot by some farmer who thought he was an escaped convict."

"Nah, that's not true," someone hunkered down in the corner said. "Artimus just said that to make the story better."

"You would know, Ragu," Robin said to the greasy haired guy.

We plundered the cache of stories about our favorite dead rock and folk singers, a treasure trove of misfortune and stupidity, for a half hour or so. Robin had met many of those dead singers in his years before, during and after he owned the Paradise Lounge; there was a commonality to the tales and that was excess. I guessed the party was a sleepover because nearly everyone had fallen asleep and I was getting ready to leave when the fellow Robin called Ragu told the weirdest story of the night, claiming to have been among the fans who tried to steal Van Zant's casket from a Florida graveyard. I figured he was just trying to scandalize me but the story creeped me out, especially when I realized Robin had passed out and Ragu and I were the only ones still awake.

I got up to make a quick exit. Ragu moved then, too, and when he tried to follow me into the hall, I had a moment of unease until from his blankets I heard Robin bark out, "Hey, asshole, don't you hassle her, you grave robber, you."

Even before I bolted from the bed, I knew something disgusting was going on in the bathroom and, as I blinked into the brash light I'd just turned on, black gunk spurted from the overflow drain. It looked like sewer water or something equally vile although there was no odor from the slime now filling my tub. Jul's answering machine said he was in LA and gave the usual list of people to call if he was away, useless at 2 a.m. One thing I knew: there was no going back to sleep.

I finally tracked Jul down at sunrise.

"What's it look like?" he asked.

"Coffee grounds."

"Do you think it actually is coffee grounds?" he asked hopefully.

He kept giving me mini-plumbing lessons, trying to convince me that it was impossible for sewer water to come up in my tub. The last thing I wanted was plumbing lessons at 5 in the morning. I just wanted it out of there, even if it did look like coffee grounds.

"No, I'm not going to pick some up and smell it," I yelled into the phone. "Just tell me how to get rid of it."

I did what he suggested, turned the shower on hot and prayed the goop would go down the drain. When it did, I poured a bunch of bleach into the tub, ran the water some more, and eventually went back to bed.

I cleaned the tub again. I took a shower. I forgot about it. But Jul didn't. When he returned to the city, he called to ask how the drain was working. Fine, I said, then suggested that the problem might be the ficus trees planted by the Friends of the Urban Forest in front of the building, since ficus trees send out monster roots that reach for water and so notoriously clog drains and sewer lines that some towns in Florida have banned them. The next day, Jul was outside hacking at the trees with a handsaw. There was something else about ficus trees he hadn't taken into consideration. It's next to impossible to kill them. Amputate them like he was doing and they would retaliate by sending out more roots. I pointed this out to Jul but he was on a mission. He'd kill every new sprout that dared to grow, he said, until he learned something else about ficus trees. Their wood is quite dense. That was when he came up with plan number two. Wait for the city to cut them down when work started on the new boulevard. I'd almost forgotten that promise of a new boulevard, now long overdue.

Rent day came and Jul was on the phone again. "I got your rent," he said.

"And?"

"Well, I was half expecting you would have deducted money for the coffee grounds."

"You mean the gunk in my tub?" I asked, refusing to concede it was coffee grounds.

"Another tenant might have threatened suit, demanded a reduction in rent."

"Jul," I said. "This building is a hundred years old; it's probably got hundred-year-old plumbing. I knew that when I moved in. But have you ever heard of Roto Rooter?"

Another day went by and he was on the phone again.

"Yvonne, here's the deal. Chuck's coming back to San Francisco next week, right? I want to do something nice for you for not making a fuss about the coffee grounds. I'm going to send you two to Mendocino. I'll pay for a stay on the coast for the weekend, have you meet a friend of mine I know you'll like. You can take my truck so you won't have to rent a car."

So, of course I was wondering what the catch was. But there wasn't one. He had this friend, Eleanor, a writer, and she had a cabin on her property in Mendocino where we could stay and get to know her, etc., etc. He had the whole thing figured out, except that Eleanor had rented the cabin to someone else. Fortunately, Eleanor knew of a cheap but lovely place where we could stay and made the arrangements, $45 a night. Jul liked that.

The cost-effective place was the lower level of a house tucked into the redwoods along the Mendocino coast. We had a kitchen, a bedroom/sitting room, bathroom and entranceway, and our own little deck. It was Mendocino in March, so it was about as damp as the inside of a well when we arrived. But a small wall heater made the place snugly warm and Chuck and I climbed into bed with Danny and a stack of books and fell immediately asleep.

The owners of our rental were almost as adorable as their place. They charged just $45 a night because they were appalled by the jacked-up prices at the swanker places along the coast. The husband of the couple was a retired children's dentist from Malibu who was about eighty years old. We spent a morning ga-gaing over their house, which was essentially two circles of glass connected by a glass greenhouse, all of it looking onto redwood, laurel and dogwood trees, just then in bloom, lamenting the state of politics, talking about art and nature, and realizing we had a lot of opinions and interests in common. Their son had just moved to Vermont. Chuck and I were reading the same book as the couple – another TC Boyle offering. And they loved Danny.

The next day we met Eleanor and her partner Mitch and instantly loved their house, their cats, their stories, their food and wine, their Mendocino green, and had a great visit all around. Sunday morning, we were packing up to go home, a little hung over from our feast with Eleanor and Mitch. I was hauling stuff onto the deck and Chuck was schlepping it up to the truck. I had books, Danny's crate, food, my clothes and my computer, way too much for a two-night stay one hundred miles from home. So much for the vagabond life. I was thinking this and laughing at myself when a plank beneath my left leg gave way and I fell hard through the deck, catching myself in the crotch with my left leg extended down roughly into the hole beneath me. I cried out for help, screamed really, because it hurt so bad I thought I might have broken my leg. Chuck and our hosts managed to get me out of the hole and I went back inside our lodging to assess the damage. I pulled down my pants and saw the beginning of a bruise purpling the outside of my thigh while another bloomed on the inside of my leg right into my crotch.

"Did they give you back your money?" Eleanor asked when I told her the story.

"No, I didn't ask for it," I said.

"And they didn't offer?"

"No, we left in a rush."

"Are you going to sue? You should. Definitely. They've got to make sure that deck is secure if they want to rent to people."

"But they're such nice people," I argued. "They only ask $45 a night because they think that's a fair amount. Why would I want to sue such nice people? It wasn't their fault."

"That's what people have insurance for," she said.

I wasn't home ten minutes before the phone rang.

"How are you?" Jul asked.

"Sore," I said.

"Remember the tenant who sued me when he tripped on the sidewalk? Unlike him, you have a legitimate injury. You should sue. Well, maybe not sue but there should be some compensation for your injuries."

I went through my arguments against asking for recompense, explaining that I hate people who sue over every little thing. It was just a bruise, I said. (Actually, it hurt like a bitch, but a bruised crotch was no one's business but my own.)

When he insisted that I deserved some damages, I said, "Jul, are you listening to yourself? Doesn't your homemade bumper sticker say, 'Nation of lawyers/Land of crooks'? Aren't you the most lawyer-phobic person I know?"

"No. Some of my best friends are lawyers. What I object to is nuisance suits. You're not a fraud. You wouldn't need a lawyer, though. This is obvious neglect. Besides, how long is Chuck in town for, just another week? And you haven't seen each other in months? And I send you to Mendocino for a little romantic getaway and now he can't even have his conjugal rights. That ought to be worth something."

I got off the phone.

Ten minutes later, there was Jul on the phone again. What was the name of the people we stayed with? Describe my injuries, etc., etc. Half an hour later, he called again. He'd been talking "about my case" with his brother and the two had figured out that the dentist we'd rented from was the very same dentist they'd gone to when they were kids living in Malibu.

He said Malibu like it was a code word for rich.

An hour later he called again. This time he had talked to an injury lawyer friend in New York who just happened to be best friends with the son of the retired dentist and his wife, the son who just moved to Vermont. I was beginning to think that saying about six degrees of separation was a vast overstatement. And, by the way, Jul added, while he was catching up with his lawyer friend, he just happened to ask what it would be worth to a homeowner to avoid a lawsuit from someone like me for the kind of injuries I had sustained.

"Jul," I said for what I hoped might be the last time. "You forgot something. I'm not suing."

"Of course you're not," he said.

An hour later Jul called again, this time to tell me to keep an eye on my mailbox. There might be a little something coming my way from Mendocino. Probably Wednesday.

And, lo and behold, Wednesday arrived as did a lovely note of apology from Mendocino with a check for $1,000. Jul had called the retired dentist and his wife on my behalf. "Not to threaten suit. Of course not," he said. "Nothing that base. I just introduced myself and pointed out that I'd been in the rental business for more than twenty years and it was always better to invest in making things right than risk things escalating into an uncomfortable situation."

There was a moral to the story: Don't bitch; don't sue. But do cash the check. And I did.

Chuck and I spent the rest of his month on the West Coast closer to home. We watched trumpeter Chris Botti perform on Nob Hill and took our favorite walk up and over Telegraph Hill, then down to North Beach where we lunched at an outdoor table – Caesar salad and popcorn calamari and wine – before wandering over to City Lights Bookstore for our lost afternoon among the stacks. Talk about a Coney Island of the Mind.

One of the gems I discovered there was Adah Bakalinsky's book, *Stairway Walks in San Francisco*, which provides detailed directions, historical, cultural and botanical data on more than two dozen public staircases in San Francisco, which in turn provide intriguing entry into the city's neighborhoods, intimate views of homes and gardens, aerobic exercise and million-dollar views of the city, all for free. Every few days, we set off on foot to explore one of these staircases, following Bakalinsky's directions, discovering new coffee shops and bookstores, artists' studios and hidden parks while marveling at the creativity of San Franciscans in carving out private niches and snuggling domiciles into the most unlikely places. Among these, the Sanchez steps soon became a favorite. Sanchez Street is so steep that it's interrupted with a double flight of steps that is part of a walk that Bakalinsky compares to Dutch painter Pieter Mondrian's configurations. Heart-stomping inclines take you above the city with views in all directions, past homes of a former mayor and innovative architects, and along streets lined with Art Deco, Queen Anne and Victorian homes. Up there in Dolores Heights and Noe Valley, the neighborhoods melded city and suburban living with small corner stores, ice cream and coffee shops, tiny bookstores and a sense of comfort I found quite attractive, even though I probably could never afford to live in the area.

When the fog finally lifted, we rented a car and drove down the coast to hike our favorite beach in Pescadero, bird-watch in the estuary, and eat artichoke soup and boysenberry pie at Duarte's. While I taught, Chuck and Daniel traipsed far and wide. Chuck loved Daniel so much I wondered who he was going to miss more when he returned to Vermont, Danny Boy or me. At the end of my day, I would telephone them when I got on the Muni and there they would be, waiting for me when I came up from the Church Street underground station. Daniel always gave me the proper greeting, turning inside out and doing his cartoon stunt, literally walking on air as he propelled himself from Chuck's arms toward me. Chuck was just a bit more restrained in his greeting.

This is what I loved most, walking home as the evening settled in, stopping together to give our regards to Yanni at the dry cleaners, to Stretch taking his place at the Baptist Church, to Gordon finishing his vacuuming or setting off on bicycle, to Ann and Alexandra performing their nightly ritual by the mailboxes. I loved sharing my life on Octavia with my husband. We each enjoyed our time alone and our time together. Indeed, we had discovered a formula for a successful marriage.

In the wink of an eye, the last three weeks of spring semester melted like soft-serve ice cream so that April disappeared into May in a flourish of school work and meetings and writing assignments, parties, museum shows, mintinis at Destino's and the work to get my apartment ready for the couple to whom I had sublet it for the summer.

And then my first year of city living was over and it was time for me to return to Vermont for my long summer break. I had my last coffee with Silent Guy and Wisdom Man at the Laguna Sidewalk Café – the others had scattered to Paris or elsewhere -- and made one last stab at nailing down the specifics of Wisdom Man's school.

"Say I'm at my house," he said, pointing to the mauve Victorian across the way. "If I send out a signal to you, it might bounce off the top of that telephone wire over there." He pointed to the telephone pole in front of the Zen Center. "Then, it might rebound over here and bounce off this window right here. And if you have your receiver on, if you are attuned, so to speak, to the wisdom in the air, there it is. It's not the telephone pole or the window that matters. They are insignificant. It's you, whether your neural system, the interconnecting structure of nerve cells that makes your brain function, is adjusted to receive the signal that determines whether you and I can commune."

With that, he bid goodbye and headed off to the library.

I turned to Silent Guy and uttered what I had been unwilling to voice until then. "Guy," I said, "do you think this school is all in his head?"

He sucked on his cigarette, then in a voice that conveyed a hint of mockery, a tone I'd never heard from him before, Silent Guy said, "You think?"

Later in the day, I gave Stretch a $10 bill so he wouldn't forget me. A year ago I might have told him what to spend it on, cautioned him to be good; I knew better than that now. He was good.

At home on Octavia, we had our last potluck dinner. Maybe they would have potlucks over the summer while I was away; I didn't want to think of that. I made two pies just to tell Glenn, Gordon and Liya, and Ann and Alexandra how much I would miss them. I stopped to visit Mae, who could not understand my comings and goings, and warned she might not be there when I got back.

"I'm an old lady," she said. "Don't take me for granted."

Of course I told Mae she was the last person I would take for granted. Of course she got three pieces of pie. Of course I promised to bring her back some maple syrup.

"Those maple leaves you brought the last time will do just fine," she said, then changed the subject. "You taking that Daniel with you?"

"Of course, Mae. What else would I do with my sweet Danny Boy?"

"You could leave him with me."

I sat with Noel on the sofa in his crowded apartment. To get to the sofa you had to weave your way between boxes of newspapers and magazines and the general detritus of a packrat. Now that he had been homebound, his need to have more than one of the essentials in life, tissues and Ajax and cherry lozenges, for example, and to hoard reading material had created even more of an obstacle. He was shy but assured me we'd go dancing upon my return.

"It's a promise," he said.

Ann didn't cry this time. Perhaps she was a little upset at me, upset perhaps that I was excited to be returning to my Vermont house, to the gardens, the grandchildren, my own true bed, my husband. I could understand her annoyance with me. I had been a single mom. I had needed my friends, especially my women friends, relied on them for comfort and companionship and help. She and I had developed our little routines of TV and to-go food in the evening or trips to the farmer's market on Saturday. She and I had come to rely on one another for quarters for the laundry or chocolate on a bluesy night. And of course, I always said yes when I could baby-sit. Then I'd leave for weeks or months at a time and expect that, when I returned, we'd just pick up our routines as if I'd never been away.

"Hey, Allie, I'll miss you," I said to Alexandra but she wouldn't look at me. Was she old enough to be upset with me, too? Was she just picking up on her mother's vibe? Or was she just a kid, embarrassed by the intensity of the moment?

The truth was that when Bonnie and Birdie arrived to take me to the airport, I was so psyched by the prospect of not seeing any homeless people on the corner of my street for months, no glass on my sidewalks, and by the thrill of going home to Vermont for the summer that it wasn't until the plane was high in the sky that I thought of Ruth and wondered what had happened to her and her children. Perhaps it was better not to know.

First there was the love fest at the airport. Daniel and Chuck and I hugging and licking our way to baggage claim, then the drive home from Burlington where, outside the car window, nature had dressed up in spring green, a soft chartreuse that lasts for just a few weeks in early May. Chuck drove the back roads home so I could survey the countryside and take in the marsh marigolds, skunk cabbage, trilliums and dogtooth violets vying for attention along the roadsides. It was the in-between season, the season between winter's flagging brutality and full-on spring, when one day it might be 80 and the next 30 degrees. The woods and fields along the route home were all so familiar to me, so deliciously fertile, that I felt a great rush of emotion, a relief. I first drove through those woods with my old friend Lois after my first winter in Vermont thirty-five years previously. I'd nearly lost my mind that winter – closed up in a huge old house with a new baby, the never-ending snow, the beauty and harshness of winter, a mud season that swallowed cars whole. But, as Lois drove us down from the mountain town of Goshen where we lived to Middlebury, which back then meant civilization, taking what was essentially a logging road through the Green Mountain National Forest, and I saw my first swaths of marsh marigolds, yellow as egg yolks, and fists of skunk cabbage literally thrusting themselves out of the thawing ground, I found myself sobbing for the sheer beauty of it all and marveling at nature's endurance.

That first winter returned to me as we drove home from the airport, arriving as I was at the very beginning of Vermont's time of resurrection, and I felt that same combination of guilt and gratitude. Spring green is the reward Vermonters deserve for outlasting what must be one of the longest winters on the planet. And here was I, undeserving because I had escaped from it, yet nonetheless welcomed back and replenished as if I'd been penned up all winter in that old farmhouse.

My gardens had waited for my return to unfold in fern and daffodil and tulip. The two magnolias that were not supposed to grow in Vermont's climate zone were bursting with buds as was the forsythia that grows along our property. There were scilla and jonquils and grape hyacinths, as perky and fresh as if they had been equipped with underground springs that the melting snow had released. And Chuck and I, we were like young lovers again even though it had been just a few weeks since we were last together. Perhaps it was the spring green that had flooded our car windows on the drive home, that filled the bedroom windows when we awoke from our lovemaking, something about the season and being home together that made us young again.

Daniel loved Vermont. He loved the big back lawn. He loved chasing squirrels. He loved watching the cardinals in the cedar hedge. He loved running without a leash. He loved the grandchildren and quickly taught them how to play hide-and-go-seek with him. He raced around lawn chairs, hid behind the chaise lounge, the shed, the woodpile, then rushed out to sprint past us.

Yes, summer. Summer is the time to have grandchildren, to go to the lake, to make picnics and mud pies, to celebrate birthdays and throw garden parties. That June, we hosted a party for Bonnie and Birdie, married in San Francisco, joined together in civil union in Vermont. I was proud of my two states.

The oldest grandchild Philip, eleven then and still under the influence of his mother's Baptist ideology, told Bonnie and Birdie he liked them well enough, but that when he grew up, he wanted to marry a girl. "Just like us," Bonnie said.

Yet when I went to the farmers market in downtown Rutland, it wasn't simply that it was held in the parking lot of the downtown shopping center, home to Vermont's first Walmart, rather than on San Francisco Bay. It wasn't just the paucity of choices that saddened me but more so the whiteness of the place. There are many wonderful and quirky things one can say about Vermont. No other state, for example, has a capital city as small in population as Montpelier or its largest city as small as Vermont's Burlington. The state has the lowest gross domestic product, the term applied to income from industry and other sources. As a result, Vermont has only experienced moderate growth during flush times nationally, but it has had far less of a fall during times of serious recession. This makes residents careful with their money but also resourceful. Vermonters are the original recyclers. They have the lowest credit card delinquency rate in the country. All these are wonderful traits that California with its constant budget woes could learn from.

Beyond all that, I would rate Vermont and California as two of the most beautiful states in the country. California has the largest population of any state in the nation; Vermont has the second smallest. More than 98 percent of Vermont's residents are white. In the time that I had lived in San Francisco, where roughly half the residents are not white, I'd come to take for granted the panoply of faces, the wealth of diversity, the richness of culture, all those brown and black and yellow and white faces, so beautiful when they were mixed together. I was now vividly aware of Vermont's whiteness but while one might be inclined to draw some conclusions from that statistic, consider this other statistic: While Vermont has the highest percentage of people in the nation who attend no church whatsoever, the state has the highest concentration per capita of westerners who have converted to Buddhism.

No place is perfect. I had two worlds that I loved, and they were 3,000 miles apart. It was precisely because of my job in California, one that paid me full-time for working roughly thirty weeks a year, that I could have this time off in Vermont. And it was precisely because San Francisco was so expensive and so difficult for someone to find temporary housing that I could rent out my apartment when I was gone for long periods of time, providing the necessary income to pay for two homes. One life was dependent upon the other. And so, I concluded within a few days of being back in Vermont, was I.

Then sadness came calling. First were the emails and phone calls from former students, bringing the inconceivable news that one of my favorite students, Adam B, six feet seven with his dreadlocks, piercings and bell bottom pants, the skateboard king of the Journalism department, was dead. Adam had been in the first class I had taught at SF State in 1998, one of the students who came into the Journalism program the same year that I had started teaching. I had loved those students as no other, not just because they taught me how to teach but also because they were a cast of unforgettable characters. Adam actually thought that journalism mattered. His aura of self-confidence was misleading, however. In the class in which the students cover the neighborhoods of San Francisco, Adam drew Bayview-Hunters Point. I realized he was reluctant to go to the neighborhood when his first few stories contained scarcely any environmental details. They were full of information he was getting off the phone or the Internet. When I quizzed him on the matter, he confessed that his van was dead and said he wouldn't be caught in Hunters Point without a car. Adam worked as a bouncer at a fairly sketchy dance club in North Beach; he was gregarious, charming and daring within his areas of comfort but clearly uncomfortable in Hunters Point, populated primarily by African Americans. Did I mention that Adam was white? Frankly, I felt the strip club where Adam worked posed more danger than a bus trip to Hunters Point. It was my job as his instructor to help him get beyond his biases and teach him and my other students strategies for keeping themselves safe when covering rough neighborhoods and dangerous issues. Knowing that Hunters Point was relatively safe in daylight, I assigned him, despite much protest, to take the bus there on Election Day to explore what issues the residents wanted their elected officials to address.

The day after the election he told me and the whole class how he had sat at the back of the bus with "some old grammas," feeling rather naked with the sterling silver lightning bolt that jutted from the space between his bottom lip and chin, not to mention the rainbow suspenders he wore over a Hawaiian shirt. His natural politeness, however, had led him to help one of the grandmothers onto the bus with her bundles and soon he found himself telling them how his mean professor was making him talk to people about the local election, twenty people or more, and write a story about their concerns. Within minutes, the grammas were sitting on either side of Adam and brainstorming between themselves about who he should talk to and then taking him to the precinct house and to polling places and telling him stories about the neighborhood and introducing him around. Before the day was over, he was going home with them for a cup of coffee. None of this surprised me. Adam's optimism was contagious. I knew he'd be fine once he got over his initial discomfort. He aced the course with one great story after another. The best was a profile he wrote of three brothers, one in jail on drug and gun charges, one in a gang, one going to college.

Over the years, Adam had kept in touch with me and proudly announced not too long before his death that he had returned to campus to earn a graduate degree in TV journalism. He planned to cut those astonishing dreadlocks when he graduated and hoped his experiences, from working as a bouncer at a strip club to covering gang warfare in one of the city's more notorious neighborhoods, would help him get a job. That never happened. He was shot in the head over the night receipts from the club where he worked. Followed home and shot dead in his own apartment. I was just devastated by the news.

Then, more bad reports: Just as it was impossible to believe that Adam could be dead, so too was it incomprehensible that Torri M., a fellow teacher who looked as healthy and energetic as one of my students when I last saw her at the copy machine a few months previously, had died. Incredulity doesn't keep death away; incomprehension is no antidote to an obituary. Diagnosed with cancer in April, although she'd not shared that information with me, Torri was dead by early August. I hadn't even heard she'd been sick.

When I'd left San Francisco for Vermont in May, the months ahead had seemed large and luxurious and carefree. But misery kept coming from the West Coast. Ann called to say that Noel was back in the hospital. Jul called to say that Lance was bad again. And then, two weeks before my return to San Francisco, it was my turn.

I was driving down a country road on a flawless summer day in Vermont. Daniel had been on my lap when I started out, but the sun kept getting in his eyes so he had jumped down into the well on the passenger side floor. Suddenly, a big red truck came barreling over the hill in front of me, right down the middle of the road. I tried getting out of the way but the road was narrow and rutted and the truck was traveling at a terrific speed. I yanked the car further to the right, trying desperately to get out of its path when the rear wheel on the passenger's side caught in a ditch and threw my car back onto the road. The last thing I saw before the collision was the face of the old Vermonter behind the wheel, his eyes startled as he finally looked up and saw me.

For the first few moments after the crash, I'd been deep down in a bright sphere of light. Daniel licked me awake. Later, I realized that if he had been on my lap or on the passenger seat, he would have been crushed by the airbag. I had three broken ribs, plastic shrapnel from the dashboard buried in both knees, a fractured pelvis, a broken pinkie, a bruised chest, lungs and spleen, and the airbag had burned my face. The doctors and Chuck and everyone else who knew me wanted me to take the fall semester off to recuperate, but for reasons I couldn't articulate I was determined to return to San Francisco and to work, which I did a week after the semester began with a reduced class load.

Why did I return? A sense of obligation, perhaps, or the need to be with my colleagues after all our losses, or the drive to see Noel before it was too late. It may have been in the airport as I struggled toward the boarding gate with a small carry-on and Daniel in his crate that I began to realize that I was not equipped either emotionally or physically for the tasks ahead. I had a support system in San Francisco but it was not the same as the one I had in Vermont where there was the husband and the children and the old, old friends. But if I said I was fine, I would be fine.

Of course, it wasn't that simple. I had gone to look at my car after the accident. No one should, after the fact, view the car they nearly died in. There was something about the crushed metal frame, the broken windshield, my blood on the dashboard and the scattered belongings resting in odd places that lodged in my brain to reappear when the lights were off. My dreams were bad.

I had also seen that bright light. It was probably just the after-affect of being whapped in the face by the airbag; I'm not claiming a near-death experience. I just know that, unlike all the stories you hear in which dying or injured people are drawn to the light and feel comforted by it, I was neither attracted to it nor did I feel comforted. I felt as if I were drowning in it. I pushed against it frantically, compelling myself away from that bright place way down deep and simultaneously outside of myself where I had gone. The only thing I took from that accident was the realization that it was quite easy to disappear. That memory, that fear of vanishing, traveled back to San Francisco with me.

PART TWO
2004 - 2005

I carry a horn to blow in all these streets
A solo riff outside my head
How could you ever know I feel
So high on life and feet and ass and legs and thighs
That I can rise and dance with all the stars
And I can eat the moon and laugh and I can cry
The dark caves of cities hungry streets
The tired faces dark and dreary bent
And all the death it dies
I let it die …
                    Jack Micheline, "Blues Poem"

Jul picked me up at the San Francisco airport, which was a blessing because by the time my plane landed, there wasn't an ounce of energy left in me. I was screwed up in ways I hadn't acknowledged in Vermont. I had to close my eyes on the freeway. I couldn't stand it when Jul zipped in and out of traffic. I had to ask him to slow down. And, later, when I took Daniel for a walk, I purposefully walked in the direction away from the church and Stretch. I wasn't ready to see that. But Daniel was a dog high on pee mail, high on discovering the barest whiffs of himself and all his old dog friends lingering on light poles and tree trunks. If that dog had any piss left in him after a twenty-minute walk, he must have been saving it up all summer.

The apartment, which I had rented to a law student through craigslist, looked almost the same as when I'd left. I needed to buy some new orchids and scrub the tub to make it mine but when I opened the door I found a homemade card from Gordon saying, "Hey, #3, welcome home. You were missed."

We slept like the proverbial timber until we heard Ann and Alexandra in the morning and, when I limped from the bedroom, stiff from the flight and the accident and middle age, Ann's hug – "careful," I warned -- was as genuine as rain and Alexandra, peeking from between Ann's legs, looked like a remedy to misery.

There were poems etched into the cement at the bus stops all along Market Street. I had read the one nearest Octavia dozens of times but, as I stood waiting for the bus that first morning back in San Francisco after my accident, I understood it at an entirely new level:

> not to see anymore
> but inward
> not to know anymore
> your own self
> > Etel adnan

My reason for returning was evident as soon as I arrived on campus. There were my students, their eager faces on me as we began the task again of creating story, of asking questions and seeking the truth, of bringing people alive on the page. Their belief buoyed me, their optimism was a blessing and I welcomed it as I'd never before.

Because I was injured and sad, Ann forgave my absence. She and Alexandra were my anchors. Ann announced that two or three nights a week I was to have dinner with them and then ordered Chinese. She controlled the TV clicker. I was obsessed with the war in Iraq, the mess in Fallujah where seventeen civilians, including three children, were the latest victims of an unnecessary war, and simultaneously the ongoing mess between the Israelis and the Palestinians. Normally, Ann would have also seized unto the unfolding dramas of hostages and rescues, but she was trying to save me from further harm. "You shouldn't watch the news," she said. "It's bad for you. Watch *American Idol* or *Survivor*. The last thing you need is more bad news."

Perhaps because I was hobbling about and quieter than I used to be, perhaps because I felt a little tentative, Alexandra was extra sweet to Daniel and me. When Daniel became enamored with one of her Teddy bears, a brown bear half his size, perfectly made for dominating and humping, Alexandra took no offense. She gave the bear to him and he carried it around the house and slept with it. When we returned from our walks, the first thing he would do would be to grab that bear by the back of its neck and toss it around a bit more roughly than I would have liked and try to hump it. It was hysterical. We discouraged Daniel from humping the bear in front of Alexandra, of course. When I told Chuck about it, he made a little joke about me raising Daniel too close to the Castro. And then, the next week, when it was Bear Weekend in the Castro, I made my own jokes about Daniel and the bears, anything to lift my spirits.

"Bears" are a subculture of San Francisco's gay world. You knew there was a bear event in town when the streets were packed with muscled, bearded guys in flannel and leather. Men who identify as bears have a code by which they define themselves and their preferences with numbered ratings as well as plusses and minuses. Using the bear code, I came up with this ranking for Danny: B5 C++ D- F+ G+ K+ M Q-- R+ T--W--, which broke down into:

B (for the beard factor) 5 = full beard, though not very bushy;

C (for the cub factor) ++ = a total Daddy's boy;

D (for the daddy factor) - = looks like a daddy but isn't one (yet);

F (for the fur factor) + = above average fur;

G (for the grope factor) + = likes to be touched;

K (for the kinky factor) + = open minded about trying something new but not slutty;

M (for the muscle factor) = average brawn;

Q (for the queer factor)-- = looks like a bear but when he opens his mouth yards of chiffon fall out;

R (for the rugged factor) + = loves the out-of-doors;

T (for the tall factor) -- = shorter than your average bear;

W (for the weight factor) -- = a bony bear.

I'd been looking forward to one of Wisdom Man's lectures but no sooner had I sat down with my latte than he stood and prepared to return his glass to Elise before heading across the street to the Zen Center. It was a Saturday and I had forgotten that Wisdom Man often spent Saturday mornings at the Zen Center, which hosted a public talk, open meditation and simple repast on Saturday mornings. From his vantage point, Wisdom Man noticed my bandaged finger and the burns upon my cheeks, and perhaps the disappointment I felt with his abrupt departure.

"What happened to you?" he asked and I gave a very short synopsis of my accident. I didn't mention the deaths of my student and colleague, but Wisdom Man was wise; he could see my anguish or at least I thought he could because he said, "You should come with me. A little meditation might prove helpful."

I was in no hurry to spend any time inside my brain, which had been dishing up fairly morose thoughts of late. And besides, Daniel was still collecting his accolades. Silent Guy gave him especially generous bits of salami from the sandwich he retrieved from the inside pocket of his jean jacket. Tom was gone – to Paris or Vermont, no one seemed to know – he'd been gone for weeks apparently. As usual, Jay looked ill. He was thinner than ever and oddly subdued. Ted fussed over me, comparing pains and traumas, loving up Daniel like a long-lost child. Meanwhile, Wisdom Man nervously shifted from one foot to the other.

"Come on," he said. "Leave Daniel with Guy. You'll find the sit calming but at the same time, it will awaken you. It's quite curative."

"I'm awake enough," I said quietly. "I want something else – not to sleep necessarily but to shut my mind off."

"That's what awakening does. Shuts off the static. Turns on the bliss. Come on," he said again.

"I haven't figured out how all these various elements of your teaching and worshipping work together," I said, turning my full attention to Wisdom Man. "I kept thinking about it over the summer. How does the Wisdom School and Gnosticism and Zen Buddhism and Uniterranism, how does all that fit together?"

"I don't know why you should worry about my lives fitting together," Wisdom Man said wisely. "You're the one who comes and goes. Do your lives fit together? But since you ask, it's not that complicated. The Wisdom School is for learning. Gnosticism is for experiencing truth. Uniterranism is for living on the planet. And Zen is for refuge. We need all the refuge we can get on this planet. We take refuge in Buddha, in dharma. I tell my students, this is not something you will learn from books; it is something you learn by listening to your inner voice."

He looked at his watch. "You coming or not?"

It was precisely my inner voice – accompanied by images of dead soldiers, eyes behind the windshield, my dead student – that I wanted to shut off. I knew

Wisdom Man was talking about another voice, the voice that was not afraid of death or failure.

"Okay, I'll go but I'll take Daniel home first," I said and, moving as quickly as I could, walked Daniel home, then traced my way back to the Zen center where Wisdom Man waited on the steps. I wanted some of that refuge he was advertising.

The San Francisco Zen Center is a handsome three-story brick building designed in 1922 by the architect Julia Morgan as a home for single Jewish women. During World War II, the Emanu-El Sisterhood Residence, as the center was then called, offered sanctuary to Jewish women escaping from Nazism. The building was sold to the Zen Center in the late 1960s. I followed Wisdom Man into the meditation room where the zazen or sit was going to be held. When other practitioners entered, they bowed to the statues of Buddha and other worshipers already seated or kneeling about the room, some directly on the hardwood floor, some on small cushions. Wisdom Man didn't bow nor sit on the floor. He took a seat on one of the chairs lining the back wall of the room. I sat beside him.

I knew the shutting off of the mind was supposed to happen next, that I was supposed to quiet myself, but there was so much to observe – the exotic statues of Buddha and other divinities scattered throughout the room; the people and the various postures they had assumed, their degree of attention or inattention; and the preparations for our talk, which was going to be led by someone highly respected in the Zen community, a woman named Christine who had been ordained a Buddhist priest. There was a lot of silence in the room, which I liked, and I let it wash over me so my thoughts did not quite disappear but they were calmed, as Wisdom Man had promised. When I ventured a look, Wisdom Man's eyes were closed. He had gone inside. It was so unusual for him to be quiet when on the corner he rarely shut up. And, with his eyes closed and sitting close to him as I was, I saw for the first time the small lines etched on his forehead, a few strands of gray in his blond hair. He was older than I had thought.

After the flowers had been arranged and the golden cloth draped over a table and the microphone adjusted, then adjusted again, the woman called Christine entered, wearing a dark robe with a small, square bag hanging from around her neck. That mind of mine immediately put forth questions: What's the bag for? What's in it? Is it a symbol for something spiritual or does it have a practical use? I shut off the questions and turned my attention to her words as she addressed the issues of mindfulness and body awareness, of living in the moment. "Look around you for lessons on how to live," her voice slow water in the hushed room. I was the only one who looked around. "The trees and bushes do not ask where they are. They do not ask why. They and you are just here. That is the secret to compassion for self, to just be here."

I wished I could "just be here" but I found it impossible to empty my mind, to live in the moment. I felt conflicted. I fretted about small things. And for the first time since I had begun my bicoastal life, I wondered if I had made a mistake. It was not that I didn't love my job or my students or my apartment or my friends on Octavia. It was that once I had gotten myself back to the city with my bruised body and mind, I missed the comfort of family, the presence of my one true love. My sense of self seemed false.

In the quiet that followed her talk, as I meditated with strangers over the words, "They and you are just here," I realized I was not the strong, independent person I had thought I was.

Stretch was shoeless. He had stashed his boots by his side the previous night. When he awoke, they were gone. Daniel and I came upon him as he sat on the sidewalk, head in hands, high-water pants pulled up over skinny calves, dirty socks pitiful in the morning light. He just sat there, not angry but rather dumbfounded that he'd slept through being robbed.

"What will you do?" I asked, then stated the obvious. "Size eighteen shoes are not easy to come by."

"I'll call my ex," he said. "He'll find me some."

That was a revelation, that Stretch had an ex, that he was gay.

"He likes to buy me things. He got me this here hat," he said, tugging on his Giants cap, the latest addition to his wardrobe. "I got a good excuse this time. It weren't my fault I lost them boots. I just woke up and they was gone. He'll love that. 'You slept through someone stealing your boots. You're really slipping,' he'll say."

"Your lover? Your ex?" I was kind of stammering.

"He's a salesman for a pharmaceutical company, has clients all over the country. He just got back from Texas, which is good for me. He goes to Texas a lot. They must buy a lot of drugs there. He brought me a whole cowboy outfit on one of them trips. I keep it at his place so it'll stay nice. I'll show it to you sometime."

"Cowboy outfit?"

"Yeah, what you call them things? Spurs? I got them. Chaps too. He likes to see me in them."

"Well, what are you doing out here on the street? How come you don't live with him?"

"Oh we broke up. I been on the street too long. And I took some drugs from his kit. That pissed him off. But it's okay. I'm better by myself. Sometimes I use his shower and let him buy me a steak. Shit, what time is it? I gotta' go make my call. Got to catch him before he goes to work. You can't live my life without shoes."

With that, Stretch headed down Market Street in his stocking feet. Where he was going to make a call, I could not say, maybe at Safeway. If I'd thought of it, he could have used my cell phone. I was too flabbergasted by the idea of Stretch in chaps, an occasional kept man, to think of the phone. He'd seemed so entirely asexual, all these months and now to learn that he too had a San Francisco story to tell, one that didn't involve sleeping on the street, was something to ponder.

I think it was then that I realized Jul was right. He had been urging me to write some of this down, to catalogue my San Francisco experience. I had had a life-changing experience. My accident was not the first time that I'd been smacked in the face with my own mortality. I had something I wanted to say before I died, something that I couldn't articulate in a linear way. I wanted to let my story unfold in vignettes, a story that would take place primarily in San Francisco, in this city that embodied all that was wondrous about America and the West, a city that had always represented daring and experimentation, optimism and hope, but one that also flaunted the extremes of capitalism, of commercialism, the disparity between the haves and have-nots, a place that embraced the freedom to do whatever one wanted with the body and the mind but one that also displayed the results, for good and bad, of self-indulgence. Peace and justice and equality were more than slogans here, I knew, but gangs were fighting it out at Hunters Point, the neighborhood my student Adam had been afraid to cover. He'd come to love the people who lived there, to understand how poverty and racism and neglect fueled violence only to be shot inside his own safe apartment after thugs followed him home from work.

It wasn't just his death and Torri's or my accident that led me to examine and record what was happening all around me. I had been in San Francisco long enough to see that the city was being transformed once again, that money changed everything. We had begun hearing this new term, super-capitalism, in which making money was the supreme goal, and super capitalists, multibillionaires, were buying up San Francisco at an unprecedented rate. People like me, middle class, we would soon be priced out.

Something about Stretch's acceptance of his fate had made me realize I wanted to write about the homeless *and* the super-rich, the precious ones eating their $48 roasted chicken dinners at Zuni's restaurant while Stretch was content with a Twinkie for supper. But not just that ... I also wanted to explore my own absurdities and hypocrisies, paying nearly $2000 a month for a four-room apartment on a street that was about to be torn up. And also the beauty of the little families that random people could construct at a corner café or in an old apartment building, the richness that came of acceptance and personal freedom – and the pain and personal tragedies that self-determination and free will can also bring into individuals' lives and to those who love them. We had Lance to remind us of that. I'd seen and heard him the last few days as he stumbled about the building, loaded, lost, but I'd avoided him, as they say, like the plague.

I was under contract to finish a book about Vermont and Vermont writers, a project I'd been working on for the past year. It seemed appropriate to follow a Vermont book with a San Francisco story, one that was mine but not mine.

I already had my title: *Octavia Boulevard*. It was optimistic to name it that, to believe that a four-lane, tree-lined boulevard equipped with kaleidoscopes would become a reality, but I was snatching optimism wherever I could find it.

The city was empty on Labor Day. They'd all gone to Burning Man, which Jul had again tried to talk me into attending. What I had in mind was a stroll through the city, a slow stroll as I was still recuperating. On my way out, I ran into Ann and Alexandra. Alexandra had on her Hello Kitty dress, red with Hello Kitties all over it. She was more precious than the Hope Diamond as she stood on the sidewalk and practiced my name, "E-bonne! E-bonne," and generally tormented Danny, whom she had by his leash.

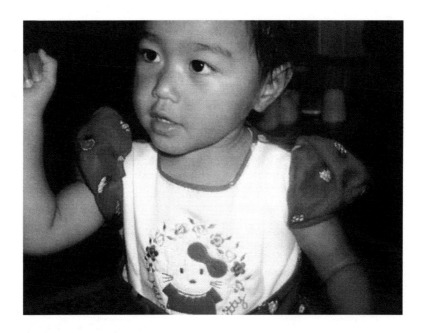

Alexandra in her Hello Kitty Dress

Alexandra was the first to notice the old woman walking toward us. She was only two and a half, so she didn't know not to stare. The woman was talking to herself in a singsong voice, electrical in its shrillness. It was hot out; Ann and Alexandra and I were in minimal clothing but the woman looked like she was wearing all the clothing she owned, and still there was no substance to her. Suddenly Danny spied the woman and ran toward her, barking protectively, with Alexandra racing close behind, attached to the end of the leash. They were a whirl of white dog and golden brown girl in red. The woman's hair was a dirty gray, but she wore blue sneakers, so spotless they must have been new that day. Clearly Danny did not like her. He lifted his leg to pee on her new sneakers and the woman pulled away, more quickly than seemed possible, her whine now so high-pitched it seemed stereophonic.

"He wouldn't pee on you," I said.

"Yes, he would, Ebonne," Alexandra said.

There is no preparing yourself for more bad news. When you are the most vulnerable, someone might rush in to your classroom to report that another student had died, this time in a freak car accident. Stacy D, a gifted photographer whom I had taught in two classes and had in Publication Lab, was dead. Dead. A word that sounded like its meaning.

I had responsibilities. I put on the professional face. I held the students as they cried. I sent them to the counselor. I called Stacy's parents and told them how she had helped an exchange student from Sweden, coaching him with his English grammar twice a week, how she had taken on a complicated story in North Beach because she'd seen an injustice and wanted to set things right. Her father told me things I didn't know about Stacy, how she had come home to San Francisco from college in another state to help care for her sick mother.

I was a mess. I found myself crying in front of class as we discussed the proper words to use when writing about suicide bombers, the Israelis attacking the Palestinians, the Palestinians attacking back, as we talked of the Iraq War and the war dead, as we talked of gang wars in Hunters Point and across the bay in Oakland and Richmond. Stacy's photos were displayed in a case outside my classroom, a daily reminder of loss.

"Where have you been?" Mae had her hands on her hips and was blocking my entrance, reminding me of the first time we met. "How long you been home, you and Daniel, and you haven't been up to see me?" she said.

Oh, Mae West, what could I say? I couldn't tell her about my dead students, my dead colleague, my car accident, the war, the election, the world. I felt protective of the dead as if gaining others' sympathy by talking about them would cheapen their lives. I had a similar feeling about my accident, that I would be exploiting it or being overly dramatic to bring it up. I hadn't visited Noel yet either. I was afraid that he would wear a mask of illness or even death. I felt unprepared for that, too. But Mae was a presence not to be ignored.

"Mae," I said, surprised by my candor. "I had a bad car accident right before I returned. My students are dying all around me. And I hate this war. I didn't think I'd be much company. That's why you haven't seen me. It's not you. It's me."

"Girl, you think I ain't got time for your misery? I got all the time in the universe. You come see me tonight when I get home. In the meantime, I'll ask my Yashua for some guidance. You bring the chocolates."

Mae was in a housecoat, the lipstick gone, her head wrapped in an old turban, the TV sound in the background when I arrived. "You know you can bring your question to the house of Yahweh. You might find some comfort there," she said by way of greeting.

Her Yahweh? I could have used a little faith but I couldn't even articulate the hollow fear I carried around with me, a fear that the world we knew was at risk, a fear I felt for my students and my grandchildren and myself, a fear that something else bad was about to happen, that I couldn't stop the bad things from happening.

I didn't tell Mae any of that as we sat in her darkened apartment. Instead I told her about the U-2 song, "Yahweh." I recited lines from U-2's album, *Joshua Tree*:

> Take this soul
> Stranded in some skin and bones
> Take this soul
> And make it sing

"Would you like to hear the song?" I asked, then retrieved my Walkman from my apartment. Mae ordered books on tape from the Lighthouse for the Blind and was adept at listening on headphones. She put the buds in her ears.

"Again," she said, and I started the song again.

"Good," she said after the third hearing. Then – and it spooked me more than almost anything I'd ever experienced – she took those dark glasses off and fixed unblinking eyes on me, and she repeated those lines from Bono, her voice deep and throaty:

> Take this heart

And make it pray
Take this heart
And make it pray

Then she said these words: "It don't matter if you believe in prayer. Just ask for what you need. You'll see. You don't need to know if it's Yahweh coming to your service or some quirk of fate. But you'll know the answer. Just ask for a little peace of mind and I'll be praying for the same thing for you myself."

How had I been so fortunate as to have found that old Angela Davis pin more than a year ago and to have wandered into that sandwich shop in the Castro at precisely the same moment that Jul and Mary had decided to take their lunch so that I would live there on Octavia Street where an old blind woman would help me see that it didn't matter what you called it, that faith was hope and that hope was the antidote I needed at that precise moment, not painkillers? I left her apartment that night and threw away the prescription medicine I'd been taking the past month. Maybe it was the OxyContin the doctor had prescribed that had made me so blue. But as I wandered off to sleep, I remembered the Paul Auster line, "Just because you wander in the desert, it does not mean there is a promised land."

Two weeks later, I was helping the students complete the first issue of the three magazines they published each semester. Several stories were late coming together, nothing unusual. The students liked hanging out all weekend, sleeping in shifts and working late into the night, then hitting the bars for last call. As their advisor, I had a limited role in the actual production of the magazine, and that was as it should be. I had pulled one story due to its libelous content and provided comment and advice on several others, but as I reminded myself often, it was their magazine.

The final holdup was with a student named Shawn who had written an engaging profile of a local baseball player who was being courted by the major leagues. In the days since Shawn's last interview, the ball player had been invited to join the Oakland A's. The official announcement hadn't been made yet, but one of the players had tipped Shawn off. I wanted Shawn to update his story but he politely yet resolutely refused. He wouldn't change a word. It didn't make sense, especially as Shawn might have an exclusive if we met our deadline and it was his story that was holding up production. I was urging the editors, Katy and Michelle, to hold out for the update and, when he declined again, they sent Shawn my way for a chat.

"Professor Daley, I love those words," he said when I strongly urged him to update his original story. Later that day, he seemed to acquiesce, but when final proofs were ready for the printer, I asked to see Shawn's revision. The editors were surprised by my request. Shawn had been gone for hours; before leaving, he had told them that I'd agreed with him that the original version was fine. I was shocked. Why did he lie? But I let it go.

I was sleeping when my phone rang. Michelle and Katy were on the line and they were crying. Michelle said something about Shawn being dead. Was I awake? Could they come over? Hadn't he been in my office just a few hours previously? What did she mean, dead?

Katy and Michelle and I had plenty of opportunity for tears as the story unfolded in the torturous days that followed. Shawn had driven from magazine production to his parents' home, several hours away. There, he'd gone into his parents' garage and hung himself. I tormented myself as I went over every word I'd said to him in my office, as I worried that I'd been too harsh in my insistence that he revise his story. How insignificant that story must have seemed, how burdensome to a young man intent on killing himself.

At first, I wanted to keep the more gruesome facts from my students, to protect them from the pain and guilt and confusion I felt. But these were journalism students; they would want to know the cause of Shawn's death. I'd had no trouble getting the details from the medical examiner. Death certificates were public information. In the days before class met again, I fretted over what to say.

Finally, it became clear to my colleagues and me that none of us were equipped to deal with the situation. Several other faculty members, Katy, Michelle and I decided to seek the professional help of the campus counseling services before we met with our students. We felt paralyzed, afraid that whatever we said could backfire. Suicide is like that. It is both shocking and seductive. We wanted to make sure, or as sure as possible, that Shawn's death would be mourned not glorified. And we wanted to put it in perspective with the other deaths the students had just experienced. Willie, the university psychologist, may have been the answer to the prayer that Mae had urged me to say. He volunteered to speak to the students, to tell them that Shawn's death was a suicide, but also to tell them in very unemotional language that he was not authorized by the university to discuss the details of how Shawn had died. He would lead the discussion in class and create a process for students to talk to him and other counselors after class. We were unanimously relieved and grateful for his guidance.

As we stood to leave, Willie called out to me, "Yvonne, stay a minute, won't you?" After the door had closed behind the others in our group, he said these words to me: "I can see from your face and hear in your voice that you're having a difficult time. Would you like to stay and talk to me about it?"

Thus it was that Willie came into my life, that on Wednesday afternoons we began to take it apart, that I learned the words for the thoughts and images that kept me awake at night or caused me to cry at inappropriate moments. Intrusive thoughts, he called the images of my son's dead body upon the water, the thing I never talked about, the old Vermonter's face above his steering wheel, Shawn smiling at me from his usual place in the magazine lab. Intrusive thoughts, he called the images of my dead brother swelling behind the door of the cheap apartment where he had lived and died, dead three days before his body was discovered. The image of my boyfriend, a child, really, dead in war all those years ago; of Dad in his hospice bed and Mom, shrunken to 90 pounds and talking nonsense the last time I saw her alive. Intrusive thoughts, he called the images of Mai Lai, or Shock and Awe, or Adam, shot in the head, and, over and over again, of Shawn, dead by his own hand, his handsome face, his words, "Professor Daley, I love those words," the thought of his parents finding him, the worst of it all. It was all mixed up together in my head. Mixed up with Stretch and Bush and the trash on the sidewalk. I wasn't able to talk about any of it to anyone else.

Of course, I'd told Chuck and Ann and Bonnie and lots of other people about my students' deaths, about my accident. But I told no one but Willie how images from my past and present haunted my dreams, accompanied me on the MUNI bus, followed me down Octavia, how Shawn's death had been the coup de grace that had pierced the shield I'd been constructing for decades, the shield that all of us must construct to protect ourselves from the desolation of loss and human failure that we accumulate in a lifetime, from the guilt I felt that Shawn was dead and I, so many decades his senior, had survived an accident no one should have walked away from. That thought was there among the other damning emotions.

I rarely talk about my son Asa's death, that another child had pushed him into a canal during the brief time after my first marriage ended when I lived in Florida, a senseless death during a senseless time. There were few people in California who knew I was the mother of a dead child. Two decades previously, I had vowed for the sake of my other children not to be defined by the worst tragedy of my life, to carry it with me but not be paralyzed by it.

But, as I told Willie that day, somehow my inability to save Shawn had become entangled in my mind with my inability to save my own sweet Asa, my last-born, dead then for twenty-eight years. In the days and weeks that followed Shawn's death, I learned that what I was experiencing was not unusual, that a sudden trauma can make past shocks reverberate, causing waves of emotions that break into the sufferer's thoughts without warning and at the most inappropriate times.

Later, I learned from Willie that, after a bit of training, Daniel could be registered as an assistance animal. Willie would provide a prescription and a letter designating me as a person permitted to have a service animal. And as an assistance animal, Daniel could accompany me on public transportation and into most businesses and travel for free on the airplane. What a brilliant man that Willie was. Because it was true, I needed all the comfort I could get.

When Alexandra returned from trips to the museum with her grandfather, she would discuss some of the paintings she had viewed with astonishing recall. After a retrospective of Impressionist painters, she talked about how the light on the water in one of Monet's paintings looked "broke up, like sun dancing." If you used a word she was unfamiliar with, she would ask what it meant, then ask for a sentence with the word in it like her teacher did. I used the word "musicality" one day and after I explained its meaning, she said, "rhythm's when your feet know what to do."

Ann found a preschool that would nourish Alexandra's natural interests and instincts, her creativity and curiosity, but the tuition required a second fulltime job. Now she worked six days a week and our Saturday morning ventures through the farmers market were replaced by breakfast on Sunday at "the red café," as Alexandra called the crimson, ever-so-chic deli we frequented that sold meatloaf and chocolate by the pound.

Ann and I were perpetually on diets but on Sunday mornings we splurged. I got the bacon and eggs croissant. Ann had the double-dipped French toast and bacon. Alexandra lived on carbohydrates as far as I could tell, but at the red café she often asked for a soft-cooked egg, which cracked me up. There was something wise and all grown up about that girl.

"I can't stand the smoke from Robin's apartment," Ann said one morning. "It comes right up the stairs and into my apartment. It can't be good for Alexandra. And with Noel so sick … I've spoken to Robin but he just blows me off. "

"Noel's sick again?" I interrupted.

"You haven't heard? Noel's got cancer. I don't know the details but he's going in the hospital again next week. Can't you tell Robin to smoke outside?"

It was what I had feared.

"Ann, I've talked to Robin a zillion times about smoking outside but frankly I don't see Robin or the other vagrants hanging out there getting it together enough to get up and go outside with their cigarettes. But what about Noel? Tell me. How sick is he?"

"You're taking his side?"

"No, I just think that it's a waste of energy, asking him to smoke outside. What about Noel? How bad is it?"

"Well, I'm going to talk to Jul about it."

"About Noel?"

"No. Robin. I might get up a petition to have the building designated smoke-free. Will you sign it?"

I was simultaneously imagining Jul, the self-proclaimed greater-good libertarian, reacting to a petition to make the building smoke-free while the other part of my brain was fixated on Noel. I am inclined to mind my own business when it comes to rules and regulations. While the smoke from Robin's apartment was quite pervasive and Ann was my good friend and I certainly wouldn't want anything to harm Alexandra, I didn't think Robin's smoke had anything to do with Noel being sick and I didn't think it was making Alexandra sick either. More important, I was of the opinion that there was enough monitoring going on. If our building were to become smoke-free, who would do the monitoring?

Big surprise, Jul supported the petition. He couldn't believe I wouldn't sign the damn thing. "Ann's your friend," he said.

"I told Ann I didn't want to sign. I can't believe I'm the one telling *you* there are enough laws in the world. Maybe we need an ordinance to keep Gordon from using so much bleach in his laundry or prohibit Lance from stumbling around the building. All those might be good ideas but I don't want them delegated by other people. Do you?"

As it turned out, no one signed Ann's petition but Ann. That was why I was surprised when Jul posted a notice stating that the terms of tenancy for the building had changed; smoking would no longer be allowed in the building, it would be a smoke-free zone. Robin proved Jul's paranoia right. He immediately submitted a petition to the city's residential rent stabilization and arbitration board for a $200 monthly reduction in his rent, claiming "loss of services."

Jul was in a tizzy the day he received notice that he would have to appear before the board to respond to Robin's grievance. "Here I am, just looking out for the welfare of my tenants," he grumbled, "and what do I get for it?"

"Don't say I didn't warn you," I said.

I put on a good show. I taught my classes. I went to meetings. I did my union work. I counseled students. I went to breakfast at the red café with Ann and Alexandra, ate the Chinese take-out Ann ordered and watched whatever she had on TV. I worked on my book. I cared for Daniel or, more precisely, Daniel cared for me. I sat through the lessons Wisdom Man extolled outside the Laguna Sidewalk Café. I jabbed with Jul and chatted with Chuck on the phone. I listened to Robin's sideways conversations and tried to talk him into smoking outside.

And week after week, Willie and I made lists. On one large sheet of paper, we recorded the pros and cons of staying with the bi-coastal life. On another, we'd do the same for my return to Vermont where I'd been offered a teaching job.

Although my worlds were opposites in so many ways, the pros and cons seemed to balance one another out so there was no clear path ahead. I could stay or go. Neither path would comfort me.

I couldn't believe how frail Noel looked. He was rail thin and shuffling his feet in hospital slippers; his daughter was beside him, helping him along the corridor and up the stairs that he'd sauntered up just a year previously.

"Just a little cancer. No big deal," Noel said, avoiding my questions. The reason I hadn't seen him the last few weeks, he explained, was that he'd had a "little trip to the hospital, a little procedure. No biggie," the expression sounding so odd with his slight Latin accent, his polished manners.

"But I voted today. That's where we been, slippers and all. A little cancer didn't stop me there," he said. "You?"

"Vote? Of course, Noel. You don't know me well enough yet but I am a political nut. I'm obsessed. May I ask?"

"Oh, if you have to ask then you haven't been paying attention. Where I come from, from Guatemala, a man's word is his honor. A man does not pick fights unnecessarily, unless of course he is a politician or the military. In the main square in Guatemala City, we have a national palace that took many centuries to be built. Time after time, obstacles, juntas."

His daughter tried to interrupt, to urge her father upstairs, but Noel seemed to have been carrying his thoughts with him for days and looking for an opportunity to speak them aloud. "Our presidencies were corrupt," he said, flicking his daughter's hand from his arm. "You know the company, United Fruit. They owned our presidencies. Just as your George Bush is owned. I did not vote for him."

"I did not vote for him either," I said. "But we already know who won, don't we?"

"It is almost always so," Noel said as his daughter led him slowly upstairs.

The next day, it was just Wisdom Man and Silent Guy and me, depressed together on the sidewalk, watching the world with its buses and barking dogs and pigeons, rap-blaring cars and mothers pushing strollers, the world itself, going on as if nothing bad had happened. We didn't talk about the election.

We sipped our coffees, traded neighborhood gossip, fed crumbs to Danny, and watched the monks go to and fro from the Zen center. No one had seen Jay in weeks; we worried about him aloud. We worried about Ted the Politico, too. Ted had been ill, he needed a back operation and had told us he'd have to move if he had it; no way could he climb three flights of stairs after that. I was glad he wasn't there, glad not to talk about the mess we were in now for sure.

Abruptly, Silent Guy retrieved a wrinkled newspaper from an inside jacket pocket. "Almost forgot what I wanted to show you two," he said. "Says it all."

He must have attended the Wisdom School.

The Daily Mirror, Nov. 4, 2004

My desire to not talk about the election was quickly thwarted. "Fascism anyone?" Jul asked as he burst through the door later that morning, carrying a ream of printouts describing the basic tenets of fascism, the characteristics of a fascist regime, the origin of the word fascist and a picture of the fasces, a bundle of birch sticks tied around an ax, the symbol of the fascist movement. Italian fascists had used the fasces much as the Germans had used the swastika.

"You're the journalist," he said. I'd noted that both Jul and Wisdom Man used that line when they were particularly worked up about the world at large. It may be that they mistook my position as a journalism professor and small-time journalist to mean that I might be able to expose our emperor. Yet our emperor wasn't naked; he and his puppeteer, Cheney, they were clothed in Teflon. You could catch them in a thousand deceptions but nothing stuck. In Florida, fifty thousand absentee ballots had gone missing; nearly two thousand names and addresses of largely African-American voters had been purged from the voters' lists in Jacksonville alone, many of them Democrats. Yet, one of the best tools our democracy had developed to expose chicanery was in its death throes. Across the country, newspaper owners were cutting their staffs and asking the public to write the news. The blogosphere and Fox news made me gag. And I was under doctor's orders not to obsess about the news, to give it a break, as if that were possible.

Graffiti stenciled around the corner on Market Street

Jul, however, was still operating under the misconception that the American people could somehow be made to pay attention, and even more absurdly that I could get them to listen up. Lately, I couldn't get more than a scattering of my students to pay attention to the political news. They wanted to write about pocketbooks and products that made your lips fat and sexy like Beyonce's. And it was clear to me, if not to him, that I was far left of the mainstream, long out of style and, even if Willie never said so, a bit nuts.

But when Jul got on to an issue, he was a one-man weapon of mass destruction. "You've got to get the word out that Bush is a fascist, that we're living in a fascist regime," he commanded as he waved a document called the "Fourteen Points of Fascism" in my face. "Listen to this: Fascists hide behind the flag; they're jingoists. Sound like anyone you know? Do the American people know about *this*?" From his fistful of papers, he extracted a photo of the gravestones for the Iraqi War dead at the Arlington Cemetery. Each grave had been engraved with the name of a fallen soldier or Marine, followed by one of those slogans, "Operation Enduring Freedom" or "Operation Iraqi Freedom," that the military had adopted for a phase of the campaign. "This is classic fascist propaganda, using the graves – *the graves* – of the dead soldiers for advertisements," he railed.

I was surprised I hadn't heard about those inscriptions on the graves, that some parents hadn't made a fuss about the military's self-serving promotional slogan carved onto their dead kid's headstone. He was right; it was obscene. But it was nothing new. The military had used slogans like this in every war. In Vietnam, there was Operation Shenandoah, Operation Daniel Boone, Operation Yorktown; Operation Overlord, Paperclip and Doomsday in World War II, and so on. Had these terms been inscribed on the graves before or was this something new?

As Jul recited from the "Fourteen Points of Fascism" – the linking of religion and government, the use of fear to mobilize the masses, the widespread acceptance of sexism and homophobia, increased government protection for corporate power, rampant cronyism and corruption, manipulation of elections – it was easy enough to see Jul's point about the Bush regime. On this, we could agree. But, truly, had it been any different under Clinton, under Johnson. It was all a matter of degree, but wasn't politics inherently corrupted on both sides, in all countries? I was sick of the lot of them.

My book on Vermont writers included a notation about Sinclair Lewis and his book, *It Can't Happen Here*, a fictional tale of a fascist president who used gimmicky slogans and scare tactics to take away Americans' civil liberties and shut down the media. The book was published in 1935 while Lewis was living in Vermont. Nothing new.

But like everything else Jul tackled, that was not the end of it. Over the next few days, in person and by email, he shared his and Mary's discoveries: the fasces engraved on the back of the Mercury dime; the fasces on the armrests of the Lincoln Memorial, the fasces in a frieze on the Supreme Court building. Of course, we both knew that a symbol, whether a fasces, a swastika or some other representation, has many meanings and that symbols only get their power from the ways in which humans use or misuse them.

"It's true," Jul said after a week of obsession, "people get the government they deserve."

And then he moved on to his next fixation, cryonics.

Yes, cryonics. As illogical as it seemed, within days of Jul abandoning the subject of fascism, he had taken up the cause of cryonics. He was considering signing up for the procedure upon his own death. "By then, they'll have it down," he said. "After all, wood frogs can survive for months in a partially frozen state."

"Yes, but you are not a wood frog," I said.

"Neither is Ted Williams."

"You really think they'll figure out how to bring bodies back from deep freeze?"

"Sure, don't you?"

"Just don't have your head separated from your body, Jul," I said.

"Oh no, my head and body are quite fond of one another."

He was kidding, of course. He liked to goof on people, to tease, to pester. He attacked issues with a vengeance, and then moved on. He had printed business cards for a spoof organization he called "Save the Baby" that he would bring to Right to Life conferences and demonstrations. He'd wander around until someone would attempt to engage him in dialogue, bring him into the cause, then Jul would hand the person one of his cards. "Surely, you'll join *our* cause. Surely, you'd like to help one of our children. We have some crack babies in desperate need of a good home like yours. Or, perhaps an HIV-infected child, suffering through no harm of his own? With your prayers and guidance and the medical care you could afford to give this child of God, not to mention the upright blessings of your good Christian home…."

Invariably, the person found someone else to preach to.

"You know this fellow?" the mailman asked. "Is he away?"

Noel's mailbox overflowed.

"I haven't seen him in more than a week," I said. "I'll have Gordon call Noel's daughter to get the mail."

Three days later, Gordon came by. "Bad news," was all he would say.

Wisdom Man was drinking glass after glass of black coffee and regaling all who would listen with his latest obsessions, that British intelligence had killed Lady Di and that the CIA had brought JFK Jr.'s plane down. Diana because she was dating an Arab; John-John because he could have been the second coming. Wisdom Man loved a good conspiracy. We could spend hours trading magic bullet theories and speculating over who killed JFK or whether the CIA had used Jonestown as an experiment in mind control. On this day, he was arguing that it was their deaths, their "martyrdoms" that made Lady Diana, John Kennedy Jr., President Kennedy and Martin Luther King significant.

"Do you mean that these people wouldn't be remembered years later, revered or worshipped if they hadn't died in some shocking way?" I asked. "Isn't a martyr someone who is willing to sacrifice his or her life or personal freedom for a cause or belief? Are you saying these people were martyrs?"

"I think so. I'm not entirely sure but it seems like their willingness to place themselves at risk, to expose themselves in the public arena, to give witness to what they believed was exactly what made them both vulnerable and somehow invincible. They live on because of their sudden deaths," Wisdom Man said. "Actually, the word martyr has been completely corrupted by religions and politicians. The Greek word *martus* simply means a witness, someone willing to testify to a fact or event that they have experienced personally. It is entirely Gnostic. The idea of dying or being willing to die for what you believe came later."

"So is the suicide bomber a martyr?" I asked.

"I don't know if it applies to those who take their own lives or those who take other lives while giving up their own for a cause. I will have to bring that question to our network for discussion," Wisdom Man said.

"Can I get in on that discussion?" I asked.

Silent Guy cleared his throat. "Did you forget?" he said. "You already are." And then he winked, he actually winked.

"Actually, the first Muslim martyr was a woman," Wisdom Man said, "stabbed in her private parts for simply being Muslim." Fortunately, he didn't get the opportunity to explore the idea further because within a few moments of one another both Jay and Tom joined us, each walking from a different direction.

"You're back," I said to Tom.

"You're observant," he said. "Actually, I was on retreat, trying to decide what to do with the rest of my life."

"And?"

"Still deciding." He looked the worse for wear. I wasn't overly worried about Tom, but Jay looked seriously sick. He had a prescription for medical marijuana, which didn't necessarily mean he had a life-threatening disease. While he'd been quite open about the prescription, he had never offered any details about his condition.

"What are you guys talking about?" Jay asked. "Did I hear the word martyr? I am definitely a martyr, a martyr to what I should have done, a martyr to lost love, like the Warren Zevon song, you know," and he began to sing,

> We made mad love, shadow love
> Random love and abandoned love
> Accidentally like a martyr
> The hurt gets worse and the heart gets harder

"I love that song," I said, so glad Jay had come along to rescue us. Jay was often the perfect foil for Wisdom Man, making quick word associations off Wisdom Man's prognostications or, as he had just done, taking the conversation down an entirely unexpected route.

While all this was going on, Danny was making the rounds, trying to get the men to pay attention to him, failing miserably as they quickly moved from martyrdom to exchange quips about Cheney and his gangster mouth and Bush and his calloused knees.

"I have an idea," Tom said. "I've asked the professor here countless times for a writing assignment. Since she won't oblige, I suggest we all write a story about lost love. I certainly have an encyclopedia of tales of heartache."

Oh shit, here we go, Mister Self-Indulgent back on the Story of His Life. Of course, *I* was recording snippets from my sidewalk talks and snapshots of life in the apartment building. Wasn't that rather self-indulgent, the idea that someone might find these events and thoughts of mine interesting if I were to put them together in a book? Why not indulge him and use that as a way to learn more about my sidewalk chums, I thought.

Before I could respond, however, a man came down the street with a very large and muscular golden brown pit bull that Daniel was just about turning inside out to get to; everyone's attention went to Daniel, then the other dog. The owner tied the handsome dog to a parking meter while he went inside for coffee. Danny was beside himself with desire, whining and carrying on like a big baby while I restrained him on my lap. I have a proper fear of the jaws of the pit bull. Yet the dog was so well behaved, waiting patiently for his owner while Daniel was a poster child for Ritalin, that when the man came out of the café and sat behind us with his coffee, I asked if his dog was friendly and could Danny greet him. It's too bad pit bulls have been bred to be fighters. This one let Danny go nosey-nosey, kiss snout and sniff dick, smell all around.

"What's his name," I asked, and the owner said, "Courage. His name is Courage."

"There's our writing assignment," I announced without a moment's hesitation, rather dramatically I must confess. "Courage. Let's all write about courage."

And then we were off, the five of us – Courage's master, Wisdom Man, Jay, Tom and me -- debating and discussing the true meaning of courage. Jay defined courage as action after overcoming fear; I countered with the opinion that courage was action in the face of fear. Wisdom Man wanted to know the difference between courage and foolhardiness. Are women more courageous than men, Jay asked. Wisdom Man opined that it took more courage to give birth than to kill. Logically therefore, he said, women were more courageous than men. Being the only woman in the group, the guys eventually turned to ask if I had any children. Five, I answered, I have given birth to five children.

They all looked at me as if they were seeing me for the first time, as if I had just sprouted wings, rivulets of snake hair, a halo and other signs of magical, superhuman or diabolical ability.

"Five children?" Jay was astonished. "No one has five children today."

My café friends proceeded to show their ignorance on the subject. They all knew women who hadn't had the courage to have a second child after giving birth to the first. Wisdom Man moved his chair a little away from mine, sputtering something about how his ex-wife had gone nuts after the birth of their twins. I didn't say anything about Californians and their self-entitlement I didn't say people have been giving birth for eons without it being the drama to end all dramas. I didn't try to explain the hippie days in Vermont when we popped babies out like strings of pearls, nursed and toted them around in Snuglis, no car seats, no bras, no stranger danger, oblivious to the burdens that awaited us, blissed out and free, tuned out and deluded, depending on your perspective, then and now. Were we courageous? Were we foolhardy? We were both. I didn't tell my café friends any of that. I did tell them I had one child for every form of failed birth control. They could think I was courageous for having five children. I wasn't. I was stupid, the kind of stupidity that comes from a false sense of immunity, my faith that nothing bad would happen to me or mine until the sudden death of my son. But I didn't articulate that either. I wasn't going down that road.

"The rhythm method's the best," Jay said, beating on the table like a drum and singing, "I got rhythm. I got music. Who could ask for anything more?"

Wisdom Man went off on Catholics for a while and I reminded him that I was a recovering Catholic and he said we were all recovering Catholics deep down inside, that the word catholic actually means all-inclusive. "You should have recovered sooner," he suggested.

"Moses, now he had courage," Jay said, bringing up his namesake, "and he wasn't any Catholic. He was the archetype of courage in the face of overwhelming odds. What did he say? 'Let my people go.' Now, nuns and monks, people who give up sex, are they courageous?"

Wisdom Man said it depended. Some were courageous while others were cowards, hiding from life. We all looked at the Zen center across the street. We were silent for a minute while we each contemplated whether the Buddhist monks and nuns who lived there were courageous or not. Was Zen a courageous approach to life or that of the person who had decided to live outside such concerns?

Jay interrupted the individual reveries to ask, quite seriously, "Have I missed something? Are you a real writing group? Are you all really going to write about courage? Can I join?"

Tom was already at work on a monologue by the cuckolded husband willing to love again. "Now that's courage," he said.

"I thought you were the one doing the cuckolding," I said.

"Can I do my piece orally?" Wisdom Man wanted to know.

"Sure," I said, "This is a democratic writing group. And he" – and here I turned to Silent Guy – "can do a silent reading."

Silent Guy turned to me, ever so slowly, smiling over his glasses as he stubbed his cigarette on the bottom of his boot.

"Me?" he asked shyly. "I don't have a thing to say about courage."

When I got home, I had another revelation: Here I'd been trying to gain information about my sidewalk companions' lives away from the café, their back stories, and yet I'd known them for over a year and none of them apparently had known I was a mother. What did that say about my own willingness to reveal myself, and the way I'd separated my own two lives?

Willie taught me to say to a cab driver, "I have post-traumatic stress disorder. If you drive sanely, I'll give you a nice tip. If not, I'll ride with someone else, please."

It worked, but he had no cure for bad dreams, for the grief I felt when I looked up from my notes to see Shawn in his old seat in the classroom, all these public and private failures imposing themselves into my life at the most inappropriate moments.

"Time," he said every week. "Give it time."

What else was there?

"Hey, stuck-up, thanks for not signing that petition against me."

"How'd you know about that?"

"Jul asked *me* to sign it," Robin said, grinning. He was coming in or going out, I didn't think he knew which. "Equal opportunity, I guess."

"That's funny … but don't go thinking it's okay with me that you and yours are always smelling up the joint."

"Play on words?" Robin asked. "You didn't mind the time you came to my party."

"Hey, a little pot or cigarettes is one thing, Robin, but you get ten people in there, smoking butts and who knows what else, the whole building smells like an ashtray. But I never got to see you before I left for Vermont. I wanted to thank you for rescuing me from that Ragu fellow. He was one weird dude."

"You don't know the half of it. He's not a friend of mine, just another hanger-on living in the past. I know a lot of them."

"But did he actually help dig up Van Zant's casket? I went and read about it the day after your party. I never heard about people doing that or if I did I'd forgotten it. What's the point? Dance on Van Zant's bones? Were they emulating the people who stole Graham Parson's body and burned it in Joshua Tree?"

"Hey, give it up; he's just some weird guy. I'm glad I ran into you. How come I haven't seen you?"

I wasn't going into it. Talking about dead poets and rock stars was one thing; I just couldn't repeat any of the sad tales from my past few months, the list of deaths and losses. I didn't have the energy. I just told Robin I'd been busy, finishing my book on Vermont writers.

"That's exactly why I wanted to see you," he said. "I need your help with *my* book. I'm writing my memoirs. You'll help, won't you?"

I thought of Tom from the cafe, trying to glue his life back together by putting it into words. Why did these characters think I could help them? I was having enough trouble getting my own words down. Still, Robin's tale was one I might like to read.

"Robin," I said, "you get a hundred pages written and I'll look at them. That's all I'll promise."

"Well, I wrote a little thing already," he said.

The story Robin wrote was a bit convoluted and fragmented but it proved that my instincts were right. Robin had been part of San Francisco history in more ways than I knew, and the losses he had suffered in those years explained why he now seemed broken, why he felt he owed much to his daughters and why, years later, he still longed for resurrection. To understand him and his story, I had to do a bit of research oddly enough into the era of leather bars and the years in which they dominated San Francisco's South of Market neighborhood, from the 1960s into the 80s. Back then, SOMA was a low-rent district of mixed uses, with abandoned warehouses, residential hotels and corner bars lining its less than posh streets, establishments frequented by Merchant Marines, longshoremen, bohemian artists and immigrants. Long ignored by the powers that be, the neighborhood also provided cover for the leather, S&M and biker community of strong, cocky men who emphasized their masculinity so as to contrast with the effeminate gay men found in other areas of the city. The SOMA bars had names like the Stud, the Slot, Ramrod, Boot Camp, Folsom Prison, The Tool Box, and Febe's, which opened on Folsom Street in 1965 and soon became a favorite with the motorcycle crowd. It was famous for its "Leather David," a small plaster reproduction of Michelangelo's David, the body manipulated slightly to resemble a cruiser or a biker with a big package in his crotch. One columnists of the time called SOMA the Valley of the Kings to differentiate the neighborhood from what he referred to as the Valley of the Queens around Polk Street where the old gays were sovereign and the Valley of the Dolls, the Castro, where the young pretty boys ruled.

Curiously, the demise of the Valley of the Kings began with the murder of the city's first openly gay politician, Harvey Milk, and his ally, Mayor George Moscone, in 1978 and the rise of Muscone's successor, Diane Feinstein. As mayor, Feinstein made redevelopment her priority, rehabilitating parts of SOMA with the construction of the Moscone Convention Center and the Yerba Buena complex, which led in turn to the construction of upscale shopping and office buildings, and brought hordes of residents and tourists into the neighborhood. Almost overnight, SOMA was discovered. Soon, not only were the new developments encroaching on the Kings' territory, but also cops and Alcohol Beverage Commission inspectors were raiding the leather bars.

Enter Robin.

In 1980, his marriage a disaster, he moved from northern California to San Francisco and began looking for a place to relocate a metal foundry and gold refinery that he had operated for years outside the city. Freed from the constraints of domesticity, he spent his days in SOMA, canvassing dilapidated warehouses and hanging out in the neighborhood bars. After one particular night of heavy drinking, he decided to sleep it off in his parked Cadillac Seville. The first thing he saw in the morning was a sign on a building that read The Museum of Unnatural Acts under which had been posted a For Lease sign.

"That's the place for my foundry," he thought immediately, loving the idea of relocating into the former museum for unnatural acts. As he wrote in his story, Robin eventually contacted the owners of the building, they hit it off and Robin moved into the building and hired several of the museum's previous owners to help him run his business. The building was next door to Febe's. Soon, Robin was hanging out there, drinking with its Leather David and a cast of characters out of a hard-core film. He hired some Febeites, as he called the bar frequenters, to work at his foundry and he'd spend the night playing dice with the men, listening to their stories.

"It would have gone on for much longer but the AIDS plague deforested the Febes population. AIDS and the ABC inspectors," he wrote in the piece he'd given me to read. Robin annotated the story, explaining that he "wasn't gay but they didn't care about that and I didn't either. I just loved playing dice with those guys and listening to their stories around the bar. ... Such nonsense. Such good times. Lies and gambling. Humor and genuine male perceptions not hammered from a female perspective. I found it refreshing and insightful."

Must have been some marriage he'd been in, I thought. But on further reflection, I understood. I often prefer the company of only women; it's just easier especially after a hard time such as a divorce.

And here I come to the part that made me happy I knew Robin, the part where I began to understand his burden: "As people started dying, so fast back then, so horribly," he wrote, "I donated big sums to address the needs for hospice and short-term care. Short term was all they needed. They died that fast. That's how Coming Home started."

In those days when few understood HIV and AIDS, when the number of people getting sick and dying was overwhelming to the people who knew and loved them, there was no affordable yet comfortable place in San Francisco for sufferers to spend their last weeks and months. Robin wanted to do something to return the love and acceptance that the regulars at Febe's had extended to him. He talked to bankers, musicians, anyone he could, soliciting money for a free hospice, which he and others founded and located in the Castro. Robin also spent many hours there, keeping those who were ill and dying company.

About that time Febe's closed, the victim of all those deaths coupled with the fear and grief felt by those left behind. In 1987, Robin bought Febe's and turned it into the Paradise Lounge, hoping to create a new club, he wrote, "out of that sadness, but also to celebrate the memory of my lost friends, so many dead. The Paradise wasn't a gay bar, it was open to anyone. But I tried to keep the open atmosphere I'd discovered at Febe's. I wanted to keep that spirit alive, that sense of freedom and escape from society's restrictions that I'd experienced there. It was all I could do after I learned my greatest gift was the ability to hold their hands as they were dying."

That last phrase of his – "after I discovered my greatest gift was the ability to hold their hands as they were dying" – what could you say after that? It also explained why Robin wanted to reach out to his own daughters who, while visiting him as girls, had seen the best and the worst of the decade's offerings.

While Robin's club was successful, other forces were at play, ones that might have seemed like a blessing at first but inadvertently led to the next round of problems for the SOMA district. With many of the Leather Davids gone from the area, a new wave of revelers who relished the neighborhood's seedy history and its distance from the more civilized parts of the city moved in and began partying there. These included punks, both gay and straight, and others who liked living on the edge. Overnight, the neighborhood became recognized as the most exhilarating and influential music district in town with Robin's Paradise Lounge hosting some of the hottest bands. About the same time, the city of San Francisco passed ordinances aimed at making SOMA more affordable, hoping to attract artists and others who could work from home to live there. To do so, supervisors voted to alter zoning regulations in the former industrialized district to allow a mix of residential and industrial uses. The live/work zone soon attracted artists and musicians, who moved into the neighborhood by the dozens, renting or buying cheap lofts in old warehouses. The SOMA dance and music clubs and the artists cohabitated the neighborhood without much difficulty. Indeed, many of the artists were regulars at the clubs.

But then came the 1990s and the dot-com boom. Overnight all those newly wealthy techies wanted their own cool loft in the coolest neighborhood in San Francisco. In the wink of an eye, they started competing for those hip lofts and warehouse spaces. The city tried to create a definition of "artist" as a way of ensuring that the people living in those live/work units were actually artists but that move was resisted by the artists themselves. In defying classification, they essentially spelled their doom. Soon, SOMA warehouses were being renovated not for the artists to rent but for the dot-comers to inhabit. By the mid-1990s, live/work units that a few years previously had rented for $800 or so a month were selling for $250,000 and new units were going for $500,000 and more. Out went the artists and musicians. And those new people who moved into SOMA? Well, many of them actually had to go to work in the morning – and work often involved a commute to Silicon Valley, forty or so miles away. Hip was cool but it had its limits. Those new SOMA residents didn't want to be kept awake by the music and revelry going on all night in the SOMA clubs. They took their complaints to City Hall.

Now enter the Noise Abatement Team, city employees whose job it was to measure decibels emanating from the nightclubs and determine if nearby residents could hear the clubs inside their lofts. Of course they could. Robin's club and many others were fined repeatedly for being too loud. Many closed. After fifteen years of operation, the last six or seven spent in constant haggling over one ordinance or infraction after another, in 2001, just a few years before I met him, the Paradise Lounge closed.

Hearing all this, I suffered new waves of self-reproach. I had been so hasty in my dismissal of Robin, so critical, so quick to accept what others had said about him, so absorbed in my own miseries. And, as I thought of him, of Lance on the top floor, of Stretch on his sidewalk, of war in so many places around the world, I thought again of what the Buddhist nun had said: To be human is to suffer. The rest of it, the just being here now part, the acceptance part, seemed beyond my ability. I was not good at acceptance.

In the evenings in Ann's apartment, Liya gave Noel reports. I wanted to visit him but Liya said he slept most of the time; his daughter didn't want him disturbed until he was better. At least he was home in his cozy apartment with people who loved him nearby. Still I wondered about his beautiful Latina. I hadn't seen her in months.

"His daughter chased her away," Liya said when I inquired. "No sex for that old guy for a while."

"Maybe that's a mistake," I said. "Could be just what he needs. Or at least his sweetheart's companionship."

"You try telling her that," Liya said.

Liya was shyer than Guy. The idea of her discussing sex with Noel's daughter, the two with their different versions of English, was laughable. I recalled that sweet night when I met Noel and thought it sad that his lover had been excluded from his recovery. That of course led me to thoughts of my own recovery and I excused myself to go downstairs and call my husband just to tell him how much I missed him. That of course led to another sleepless night in which I went back and forth between giving up San Francisco life and moving back to Vermont.

I did not discuss my dilemma with Ann. I needed her too much to let her know I was considering leaving. Thus it was *my* fingers that plunged into the pumpkin's depths and pulled out the icky goo clinging to the inside of Alexandra's first jack-o'-lantern, which we were carving the week before Halloween. Ann professed not to know how to carve a pumpkin and, because I came from Vermont and had five children, she assumed pumpkin carving was among my skills.

So, there we were, snuggled together into her little kitchen under the hanging Chinese lanterns, beautiful, golden Alexandra on and off my lap, onto the next chair, into the living room to attend to her menagerie of stuffed animals and Daniel, then back into the kitchen and onto my lap, black eyes upon my face, watching intently as I made that face you make when the pumpkin gunk was particularly yucky.

"Ebonne," she said. "Ebonne, what's it feel like?"

"Like guts."

"Yuck. I don't know how you can do that," Ann said, elongating the word *that* so I almost questioned my ability to paw the slimy seeds and connective tissue.

Alexandra looked from her mother to me.

"Can I feel it? Yewee. Gross," she said, sounding so grown up. By then, I had chiseled a mouth, eyes and nose out of the pumpkin's flesh. We shut off the lights. We put a candle inside the pumpkin and the face glowed a little scary, a little funny.

"Ebonne, that's magic," she said.

"Oh, you think so? Watch this." And I took the candle from the pumpkin and held it under my chin so my face was eerily lit orange from below and my nostrils looked like black holes and I made the ghost sound OOOoooooooooowhoooooo!!!

And Alexandra screamed and ran away, feigning fright, then ran back.

"Can I try?"

When I left for my apartment, Alexandra was in the living room saying to her dollies, "It feels yucky but you have to get the gunky stuff out. Ebonne says so."

Jay had added another layer of clothes to ward off the chill but his eyes were rheumy. His breath and clothes smelled skunky, but he exuded the sweetest joyfulness as he pulled a chair up to our table and reached into the bottom layer of his clothing to pull a ratty scrap of paper out of his pocket.

"I've got my assignment. Remember? To write about courage ..." he announced excitedly. "It's a poem. Well, sort of a poem, a found poem. Do you know what that is?" He gently pressed the torn paper onto the table, ironing out the wrinkles with his hands. It was a flyer that read "Parking Garage Needed In Hayes Valley," with a drawing of a car and phone number underneath.

Jay's Found Poem

"Get it?" he asked, wrinkling it back up a little, the way he had found it. "I'm walking down the street, looking for stuff, and I see it, all wrinkled like that. I thought it said, 'Karage Needed In Hayes Valley.' Fucking A, I thought. Courage Needed in Hayes Valley. Lying there right on the sidewalk, my assignment. You see that, don't you? 'Karage Needed In Hayes Valley.'"

We were all clapping and laughing, even Silent Guy.

"Is it okay? "Jay asked.

"Okay? It's terrific," I said. "You get an A."

"A plus," Silent Guy said.

Overnight at least four cars had been broken into on our block alone, blue glass on the sidewalk, someone's misery or anger or just plain meanness translated into an expensive, annoying present for someone else to clean up. Jul kept saying the neighborhood was on the verge of improvement, but someone was mugged down the street a week previously. If anything, it seemed things were getting worse. And yet, the world went on. Movies, concerts, museum exhibits, marches, food, window-shopping, the farmer's market. We spent and they begged. The city was broke. The Muni was late. The money flowed.

These quirky moments at the coffee shop and my evenings with Ann and Alexandra grounded me. And when you needed brain numbing, there were the students' papers to correct. While I was still occasionally ambushed by memory at school, I also and primarily needed my students, the greater the challenge they presented, the more they had attitude, the better. Especially when they could write. I held on to their promise; how could I leave them? Yet, there was always something back there in Vermont, something I was missing: a grandson's first tooth or first lost tooth, Chuck's kiss (and laundering), my old friends, my home. I was torn and conflicted. And so I wrote lists with Willie.

At home on Octavia, there was Noel to worry about. I had this notion that I would read to him in the afternoons as I had to my mother near her end, but he was often too sleepy or dopey to listen. We'd talk for a while; he'd wander off, eyes open but clearly somewhere else until I'd feel uncomfortable, as if I was intruding, and I'd tiptoe out.

Truth be told, I hadn't communicated the more embarrassing details of my mental state with Chuck. I kept telling myself I would talk when I saw him in person. I am not a person who likes to need help, even the help of my mate. Yet, for days after Chuck arrived for his fall visit, I kept my mania to myself. That became a new concern. Why could I talk to Willie and not my husband?

I am not a naturally gloomy person, and there were many days without pessimism, days when my conversations with Stretch didn't send me into depression, when I relished living in a city with terrific food and drink, astonishing weather not to mention stuff like the girl who came to school wearing a tutu, leg warmers and UGGs. Cute. Other days, the memory of Shawn or Adam or Stacy would assault me and with them the death of my son. I would be sad if Noel died but he had lived a long, full life. The other deaths, they were just plain wrong.

I both wanted to talk to Chuck about all this, and didn't. It was a strange time, a time in which I almost felt protective of my feelings, afraid that he wouldn't understand or worse think I was being melodramatic, self-indulgent. Indeed, I felt self-indulgent.

One day we took our favorite walk up and over Telegraph Hill and down to North Beach. We were sitting outside Mario's Bohemian Cigar Store and Best Cappuccino Café when a street musician carrying a guitar ambled by and asked if we wanted a song. I'd been withdrawn all day and Chuck, perhaps hoping to draw me out, gave the street musician a couple of bucks to play my favorite Bob Marley tune, "No Woman No Cry." I was just so struck by the choice that I started crying, there at the outside cafe with Daniel nestled in my lap and Chuck holding my hand.

"What, honey?" he asked, surprised. " This song? I'm sorry …"

I said nothing as the fellow finished singing, "Everything's gonna be alright. Everything's gonna be alright." But I was thinking, I don't think so.

But then Chuck pulled his chair around close to mine. He put his arm around me. He looked me in the eye. He said, "Yvonne, you have got to trust me. Everything *is* going to be alright. Look at me. I'm telling you. Shawn's death wasn't your fault. I know you don't want to accept that, but you can't control what other people do. You can't stop accidents. Life is full of terrible occurrences we can't control. It also gives us these wonderful experiences. After all, we have each other. Think of all the people who don't have that."

It was one of those moments that define a relationship. Because Chuck really saw me then and he didn't think I was some weak, hysterical woman. He knew. I didn't have to tell him. And he'd also articulated words I needed to hear, words of hope and comfort. Words of reason.

Then he paid the guy to play my favorite Leonard Cohen offering, "Bird on a Wire":

> I saw a beggar leaning on his wooden crutch,
> He said to me, "You must not ask for so much."
> And a pretty woman leaning in her darkened door,
> She cried to me, "Hey, why not ask for more?"

I can't explain why that was the perfect tune for the moment. Like so many of Leonard Cohen's songs, the words were dark and honest, yet there on the sidewalk, with my dog in my lap and my husband by my side, I believed. There was a world of hurt out there. It would be wrong to ignore it. But it would also be wrong not to celebrate the good things in life, not to appreciate all the wonderful gifts that we'd been given. Life, that is.

And, yes, why not ask for more?

On the way home, we saw this poem scrawled on a wall near Broadway in North Beach:

> THIS IS NOT THE BEAT MUSEUM
> GO-GO-GO EAST ON BROADWAY (DOWN)
> ALL YE FREEDOM SEEKERS

And when we went to the Beat Museum, this was what we saw:

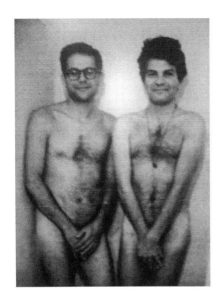 

Photo and Poster in the Beat Museum

Chuck in North Beach

An Artistic Tribute to North Beach History

City Lights Bookstore

Noel's daughter's answers didn't match my questions. I'd hear her at the mailboxes and rush into the hall to ask how her father was doing.

"His mail, not yet," she answered.

"No, his health. His cancer."

"We give him soup to last the week. He likes seeing the young women," she said, and smiled.

"You mean I should go up and visit. Is it okay? Would he mind?"

"Back to the hospital next week."

"He's going back to the hospital?"

"Gordon. You ask him."

"Tio isn't well," Gordon said when we met outside Noel's room. I could see by Gordon's face that those words were an understatement. "No visit tonight."

"Is he dying?" I had to know.

"He's a tough old geezer, but no books today. He just fell asleep."

Tomorrow maybe.

Mae was banging at my door with her cane. I rushed to open it, fearing bad news of Noel. But no, she just wanted me to come upstairs and help her count her skirts and suits. "Gordon thinks I'm crazy but I know something's missing from my closet. I know them by the feel and the way I had everything organized but now they're all mixed up and I can't find a thing. I told you someone fat's been wearing my things. Let me feel you? You ain't fat, are you?"

"No, Mae, I am not fat. I'm not exactly skinny either. But I haven't been wearing your clothes."

"I know you isn't. Let's just go up and you help me with them, get them in the proper order, will you?"

This was how I learned that Mae had long worked for Saks Fifth Avenue as a dress fitter, why clothes were important to her, how she came to have such nice outfits, all color coordinated. Twenty-six years as a dress fitter before age and blindness ended that career. Now her life was circumscribed by the walls of her apartment, the books on tape she ordered from the Lighthouse for the Blind, her great nephews who came to visit, her Jewesses and her temple.

"Let's start with the reds," she said. "They're my favorites."

We spent that afternoon arranging her clothes by red and black and white and gray – no pastels, she wouldn't hear of it – with the matching skirts and jackets and blouses hung together, shoes lined up under each coordinated outfit and her hats nicely arranged on the shelf above. She had a little stool that she used to get up to the hats and I worried aloud about her falling.

"Girl, you don't know about the mind. The mind and the senses, they are Yashua's golden gifts. I can see with the tips of my fingers. I can see with my nose. I can see with my ears. All my senses work together now to show me the world. Here, I'll show you." And with that she reached into the closet, pulled out a sleeve, rubbed it and smelled it, then said, "The red suit with the coin buttons. You see my scarf anywhere, the one with the anchors on it? It's made by some famous designer, can't remember his name but all the rich ladies have one. What's his name? Hermes, that's it. It's blue with gold. You see it? Put that with that suit, will you, girl? I'll wear that on the Sabbath and say a prayer for you for helping an old lady."

When Willie had first mentioned I could license Daniel as an assistance animal, I latched onto the idea as much to save on plane fare as anything else. But it had turned out to be true. He was a comfort. That was particularly evident to me when Chuck left for Vermont. During his month in San Francisco we had reviewed the lists of pros and cons that I'd constructed with Willie's help, but came to no conclusion. Chuck pointed out that, much as he'd like to have me in Vermont full time, I'd come to hate the winter. How would six months of freezing weather help my mental state, he asked. In the end, we concluded that I should continue to explore the job offer I'd received from a college in Vermont but also gauge how I felt about staying there during the upcoming winter break. The new job would mean traveling an hour or more a day in the winter, and it would mean giving up San Francisco.

In the weeks until the semester's end, I tried to very consciously look at my life in the city with a clear eye, assessing what was pleasant and what was not. It seemed to work. At school, I took fresh pleasure in the diversity of my students, their quirky stories and lives, and the genuine commitment of my colleagues. When I visited Ann or went out with Mary and Jul or took my coffee at the café with the guys, I tried to be wholly there, the way the Buddhist Christine had suggested, to fully appreciate my friends and their generosity to me.

I visited Mae on Tuesday afternoons and tried to visit Noel on Thursday's. Mae was always home, especially delighted when I remembered to bring raspberry turnovers or her favorite See's Chocolates. As often as not, though, Noel was either asleep when I knocked or unable to come to the door. But when he was awake and called for me to come in, I'd sit by the old man's chair and read a short story from the books I'd gathered, Agatha Christie mysteries primarily. Our favorites were the ones in which justice is meted not by the court but by fate, especially "Witness for the Prosecution" and "Death on the Nile." Noel sometimes nodded off as I read, or so I thought, but if I stood to leave, he'd come awake. "What happened?" he'd ask. "What happened next?"

I spent Wednesday afternoon in Willie's office. He saw improvement but warned there was no escape from life's disappointments; you just learn to live with the wisdom they bestow.

One of the city supervisors proposed a ban on smoking in all parks, public squares and other outdoor spaces owned by the city, an ordinance that Jul hoped might help him when the city mediation board heard Robin's complaint about the no-smoking ban in our building.

No such luck. The board ruled in favor of Robin and to avoid having to reduce Robin's rent, Jul had to rescind the no-smoking order. In return, Robin withdrew his petition for a rent reduction. The two shook hands and went their separate ways.

It really pissed Jul off that the city was promulgating a ban on smoking in public places – with fines of $100 for first offense, $200 for second, and $500 for subsequent violations – yet wouldn't support a building owner's effort to make his own building smoke-free. It became a crusade. He launched a blitzkrieg of antismoking propaganda at the supervisors and lobbied several in person. He sought the support of the San Francisco building owners' organization he belonged to. When these efforts failed, he called the local newspapers trying to interest some journalist into writing about his campaign.

Frankly I thought the city's no-smoking ban was for show. I don't smoke cigarettes and I've certainly lectured enough students about doing so, but I was tired of all the PC-legislation in the world. Besides, was there a culture anywhere on the planet that hadn't produced something that the experts considered harmful to the body or mind, some altering substance, whether coffee or tequila or absinthe or laudanum? The human put things into his body that felt good at the time, even if later there was a price to pay. And wasn't that what San Francisco was all about -- the place where permissiveness was celebrated, the embodiment of self-determination, the refuge for the self-indulgent? It was the city ban on smoking in Golden Gate Park that didn't compute, not the supervisors' failure to take up Jul's cause. I could just imagine the city trying to enforce the law. Walking past the drum circle, you inadvertently got a lungful of pot mixed with a generous helping of good old-fashioned nicotine. They'd need a fulltime cop to police that.

I put together a small package for Stretch for Christmas but he had disappeared again. Jack hadn't seen him in days and, night after night, two men I started calling the readers inhabited Stretch's alcove. They showed up in the late afternoon, spread their blankets and backpacks in Stretch's dry alcove and, supporting one another, sat back to back in the dim winter light to read. One of them had a bicycle headlamp he employed late at night while the other one slept; maybe they rotated later in the evening. I asked for Stretch at the Redemption Center but, as with Ruth, the employees and customers denied knowing Stretch, even though he was a regular. I asked for him at Orbit, where Stretch sometimes worked. They hadn't seen him. Then, right before my departure, the readers were gone and Stretch sat in his alcove eating Pringles.

"Wait here," I told him and ran to the apartment building where I grabbed the paper bag into which I'd put two pairs of wool socks, a long-sleeve undershirt I'd bought at Out of the Closet, the second-hand store on Duboce, and an Almond Joy candy bar.

"You gave me shit for leaving last year without saying goodbye, then you disappear. I'll be gone for a few weeks." I handed him the bag. "Where you been?"

"Oh, I got me a room in an SRO," he said.

"Oh, that's great, but what are you doing here again?"

"See that cart full of bottles? I missed the redemption center. They were closing when I got there but that mother fu ... – oops, sorry – he wouldn't let me in. Can't take my cart in the SRO and I ain't gonna waste a whole day's worth of hard work. So, here I am for the night."

"Well, I'm glad you got a place for the winter," I said.

"Winter?" he said. "I don't know about that. It ain't so great. They got rules at those SROs. I already told you they weren't perfect. I got to tell them if I have overnight guests. I got to show my ID every time I come back even if I was gone just a few minutes. Like the guy at the window don't know me. It's bullshit. If you pay for your room, it should be yours to do what you want with it. Besides, this sidewalk ain't any more comfortable than that lumpy stained mattress I'm paying $160 a week for. And they got roaches and bed bugs. First thing I did was spray my room down but those bugs'll be back."

I did the math. Nearly $700 a month, give or take, for a room with roaches and bedbugs and a smelly old mattress. No wonder Stretch slept on the street.

"Well, if it's so bad, why'd you take it?"

"Oh, I dunno. I sold some metal I scavenged and put it toward the room for a month. I like that I can store my things somewhere rather than cart them around all day, especially in the rain. But it ain't me, you know. Whole place smells like shit."

"Well, I hope you're inside for Christmas, or until the rain stops," I said. "I'll be thinking of you."

Days before the semester ended, the phone rang. It was the chair of my department with more bad news. Beverly Keys, a longtime journalist who had taught in our department for years, a lovely, soft-spoken woman, was the latest victim. Beverly had been walking an ailing friend's ailing dog when an eighteen-wheel truck turned right on a red light. He never saw her. She was yards from her own front door and crossing on the green light when she was run over. The dog survived. I had two more classes to teach before the semester ended.

"John," I said, "I'm going to bed. I'm not going anywhere until it's time to fly home. The students will have to finish the magazine without me. I give up."

We all felt that way – as if the department had a black cloud over it, a jinx. But of course, you can't just take to your bed. You have to put on your game face. You have to be the one to tell the students the bad news, to try to make sense of the senseless, to shepherd them through another loss, to see the work done. And it was. Despite our losses, the students produced three top-notch magazines that semester. Each explored a different issue or theme. The subject of the last magazine that semester said it all. It was Death.

Then, quite unceremoniously and with great relief, I bade my fellow apartment dwellers goodbye until the next year, quite sure that I would be delighted to see that year end. With Daniel designated as a service animal, he could stay out of his crate and sit on my lap on the plane, which he did, other than an occasional passing of the puppy, even the stewards taking turns carrying him around, feeding him cashews and talking baby talk. And when I strolled past the security gate and into the terminal, there was Chuck waiting with a winter jacket, boots and mittens for me, and a purple ski sweater for Daniel.

Two days later, Noel died. Ann called with the news. I'd feared the worst when I had left and now I was thousands of miles away, unable to commiserate in person with my Octavia apartment dwellers, especially Mae, Gordon and Liya, who were as close to Noel as family, with Noel's kind daughter, unable to be say a last goodbye.

For more than a week, Noel was in my head, his soft voice teasing, flirting, promising to take me dancing – and that memory of the first time when I saw him dressed to the nines. Just for diversion, I looked up the phrase "to the nines" in the dictionary, which said the exact derivation of the phrase was unclear. But among its first uses I found this: William Hamilton's *Epistle to Ramsay*, 1719: "How to the nines he did content me."

Noel would have liked that. I'd not heard content used as a verb before and when I looked it up, I learned it meant, "accept as adequate, despite wanting more or better." Amen to that.

Normally nothing got by Gordon, who was as conscientious around our building as a housemother with a dorm full of coeds. But Gordon was down four flights of stairs and around the corner in the laundry room, deep into his cleanliness ritual when the fire alarms went off. Noel had been with him for days, Gordon told me later, eleven days exactly, his handsome black face and sweet laugh, his gentle good mornings and his stories. Oh those stories, they had filled Gordon's brain ever since Noel's daughter had called with the news. He was thinking how fortunate it had been that his daughter Lydia was home from college when her Tio had died, that they had been together for that dark passing.

When the beeping finally penetrated, Gordon realized that it was the sound of not one, but at least two fire alarms blaring. He raced upstairs, red hair flaring behind him, all the way to the top floor, to Lance's apartment. Patrick was already in the hall, banging on Lance's door while his wife crouched in the crack of their doorway next door, hugging their Italian greyhound.

Gordon could hear Lance moving around inside his apartment, coughing. Then he heard something crash to the floor. He joined in the banging. When they got no response, Patrick and Gordon raced through Patrick's apartment and onto the fire escape to look in Lance's front windows. Only smoke. Patrick called 911 while Gordon ran downstairs and yelled to Lydia to evacuate the building, especially Mae and Ann and Alexandra. Then he ran back upstairs to bang on Lance's door again, to try to jimmy the lock. Finally, he simply ripped and kicked at the 1904 door until he was able to loosen one of the panels, stick his freckled fist inside and undo the lock.

Lance's apartment was filled with three kinds of thick smoke. There was the smoke from where Lance had fallen asleep smoking and set his clothes, bedding and the papers he'd been reading on fire. There was the smoke from the little fires that smoldered along the apartment's hallway, caused when Lance woke up on fire and tried to get to the bathroom, dropping burning clothes and papers onto the carpet along the way. That carpet gave off a horrid stench as it melted and burned. Then there was the smoke from the vinyl shower curtain, set on fire by the last armful of burning material Lance managed to toss into the tub. That was the smoke that nearly killed both him and Gordon.

Once inside, Gordon could hear Lance coughing but there was so much acrid smoke in the flat that he decided to wet a cloth to cover his face. The kitchen was a mess of plastic bags, booze bottles and pizza boxes and the smoke at counter height, where Gordon was fishing around for a rag, was a killer. He got back on his hands and knees, crawled outside and down the hallway, smashed the glass door to the fire extinguisher on the wall, and dragged it down the hall. By then Patrick had wet a rag and held it out to Gordon but Gordon needed both hands to manage the heavy extinguisher and crawl at the same time. Gordon managed to crawl to the bathroom and blast two separate fires blazing there, one in the tub, the other on the floor next to Lance. Then Gordon passed out.

It was at that moment that Noel came to him, just Noel's face, close and serious. No sound, just that handsome face. It jolted Gordon awake. Eyes burning, Gordon crawled to where Lance was sprawled now unconscious on the floor. He screamed in Lance's ear, over and over, until Lance came to enough that, with Gordon's help, the two could edge backwards down the hall and out of the apartment where Patrick helped Gordon get Lance down the stairs.

While all this was going on, Lydia was knocking on doors, getting everyone out of the building: Ann, Alexandra and Mae first; Robin and the various misfits, daughters and ex-wives who had flopped in his pad. Glenn was out at a movie and no one thought to rescue Zipper. Nearly everyone else was out for the night.

The firemen rushed into the building with a limp hose as Gordon staggered out. They helped Lance into the medic's van. Gordon was covered with smoky grit and hacking something awful but he went back into the building and helped the firemen up the stairs with the hose, nearly falling over when the water rushed in with a powerful force. It was then that one of the firemen noticed his condition and helped Gordon down to the medics. Before he sat down to be examined, Gordon did a little head count and asked for a group hug. He was corny that way.

Ann had been in the shower when Lydia pounded on her door; she threw her green plaid robe over her voluptuous nakedness. There she stood, clutching the robe to her ample self, Alexandra big eyed with all the lights and firemen and the acrid smell. Everyone was more concerned about Mae than Ann or Alexandra, however, and they tried to get her to go inside Robin's apartment for shelter. No way was she going in "that den of iniquity," she informed them all. Mae might have been blind but the words streaming from her mouth – "YHWH Eloheem, you be with us now. You take good care of us, you hear, and bless those poor boys" – sounded more like a command to God than fear.

Weird thing was, just then Jul pulled up to the building with Mary and Glenn. Consider this coincidence: earlier that evening Jul and Mary had run into Glenn at a movie theater across town. After the movie, he'd joined them for dinner then accepted their offer of a ride home. As they approached Octavia, Jul had to pull over to let several fire trucks pass. He made a joke about someone leaving a pot on the stove, a joke he regretted as he followed the fire trucks to his own building.

Thanks to Gordon, the only damage to our building was to Lance's apartment. The next day when my email and phone carried the various renditions of the story across the country, all the odd coincidences kept growing in significance with each telling, especially that momentary visitation from Noel. I'm not one to believe in ghosts or messages from the other side, but I took Gordon's word for it, that Noel came back to save our building and Lance and, of course, our hero, Gordon.

The fire, however, took a toll on Gordon. "It's not just Noel's death," Ann said in an email. "Gordon is sick. He can't eat. He has lung damage. That's expected, but I'm worried about his head. He seems kind of fuzzy. And Jul's being a jerk about the whole thing."

Instead of praising Gordon, Jul harrumphed on his end of the phone line when we discussed the fire. Jul thought it had been just plain stupid for Gordon to enter a burning apartment. He said he couldn't help him out in any way or he would be setting himself up for a lawsuit, that offering help would essentially be assuming liability for Gordon's injuries.

"Well, you did help get Lance back into the building," I said. "In a way, it is your responsibility. Besides, it's your building."

Jul was literally blubbering on the other line. "I didn't help him come back. I just didn't stop him from coming back. Under San Francisco's tenant laws …" and he was off again, casting blame upon the tenants' union and the liberals who made it next to impossible for a landlord to evict a tenant, even someone who would set a building on fire. As for Gordon, Jul's line, repeated again, was simply that "he shouldn't have gone in that apartment. I wouldn't have."

"Don't tell me that," I shouted into the phone. "Don't tell me you wouldn't help me or Ann or Gordon or any of us if we were trapped in a burning apartment."

"No, I wouldn't go into a burning apartment," Jul said with conviction, his voice somber. "I'm serious. There could have been two dead men in that apartment. It was a very dangerous situation. Gordon was very lucky. I can't condone my tenants going into burning apartments even to save another tenant's life. That's the job of the trained firefighter. I have the fire report: It took the fire department precisely two minutes and ten seconds to get to the building. There was no need for Gordon to have put himself at risk."

"But he did. That's the point. He didn't stop to think how long the fire department might take to get there. He just acted. Why not recognize that?"

"How would you feel if he hadn't woken up, if he'd inhaled even more smoke and died?" Jul asked.

"I would have been very, very sad," I said.

All the while, as I worried about Lance and Gordon, the snow blasted the windows, I thought back to the lists Willie and I had spent much of the fall and early winter refining, comparing the pros and cons of my two lives. The snow piled high in the driveway; the car was an igloo. I'll be old soon, I thought. I'll have to retire somewhere I can afford. It probably wouldn't be San Francisco. Better get it while you can, I reasoned, cancelled the appointment I had with the Vermont college that had offered me a job, and made my plans to return to San Francisco. My neighbors on Octavia had buoyed me during my semester of losses; now I hoped to help them with theirs.

The Vermont House After a Snowstorm

I expected to see evidence of the losses and disasters that had occurred in my absence, but the building on Octavia looked exactly as when I had left. No smell of smoke, no sign that one of our own had died, just Gordon, pale and thin. He hadn't seen a doctor nor had he returned to work since the fire.

"Don't worry. I'll be okay. Mind over matter," he said when we met in the hall. Lance had spent a few days in the hospital and then was transferred back to Langley. Here was something else to feel conflicted about. While my sympathies went out to Lance, I felt he was a danger to himself and to the rest of us. Nonetheless, it was also clear that he would return home to our building eventually. Over that, Jul told us, he had little control.

"Can't you evict him on the grounds that he started a fire in his apartment, that he passed out or fell asleep smoking?" one of us would ask, only to be reminded that we had refused to sign Ann's petition. The street construction was about to start – at least, that's what the city officials said. A letter to that effect had been in my mailbox upon my arrival. Once Octavia was torn up, a fire truck would have no easy access to our building.

"Causing a fire is not grounds for eviction in this city," Jul informed. "A terrorist is treated better than a landlord here."

The whole situation made Mary quite uncomfortable. She chastised me for my generosity and sympathy toward the homeless while I apparently had little consideration for Lance's wellbeing. And she was right. The truth of the matter was that it's a good deal easier to be sympathetic to people from a distance.

I was walking home from work, dressed in a black wool coat, tuxedo shirt and black slacks when I heard, "Whoa, look who's back in town. You look good." Stretch was pulling a shopping cart filled with returnable bottles up Market Street.

"You look good," he said again. "I don't usually see you dressed up like that when you're out walking Danny."

"Right," I said. "You usually see me in my pajamas."

"I never saw you in your pajamas," he said, throwing his head back and laughing at the very idea of that.

"Sure you have. My old white sweatpants. They're my pajamas."

"Well, I like that outfit you got on now."

I asked how he had been doing while I was gone and if he still had his room in the SRO.

"Jeez, I'm glad you asked. I'm trying to get two dollars together by 7. I went to collect my pay from the guy down there where I worked yesterday." Stretch pointed vaguely down Market Street. "But he weren't there. If I don't pay $12 at the hotel, I'll have to move out. With these bottles, all I need is $2."

His hands were filthy. I wanted to ask if the SRO had a bathroom, if he got to take a shower for the price of his room, if he had running water. I didn't. "You need just two bucks?" I said and dug out my wallet. I handed him a five.

"Now don't spend it all in one place," I said, using the old cliché.

"Don't worry. I don't do drugs no more. It's been ..." he tried to do the math. "One hundred and forty days left and I'm off probation," he said, strapping the rope attached to his shopping cart around his hand and turning back down Market

Street. "Gotta get to the Redemption Center before they close. I'll have money for a burger now."

The next morning, I saw Stretch in front of Orbit. "Everything go okay?" I asked.

"Yeah, I kept my room for another week."

As I turned away with Daniel, Stretch yelled out, "Nice pajamas."

And it was true. I was wearing my old white sweatpants.

"God gave me a strong body. I'll be fine," Gordon said when I worried aloud about his weight loss and persistent dizziness, the headaches and burning in his lungs. Hr had returned to work but not without difficulty. Before the fire, he could do complicated math problems in his head; after the fire, he struggled with the computations needed in his job as dispatcher at a cab company. Apparently, his boss was less than understanding and had given him a warning when he'd miscalculated a day's receipts. Liya was so worried about him. Finally, giving in to our collective concerns and the threat of losing his job, Gordon went to a doctor who confirmed that the smoke he had inhaled had caused severe carbon monoxide poisoning and injured the lining of his lungs. The doctor felt his lungs would heal; he couldn't say how long the mental haziness would last, not knowing exactly what toxins Gordon had inhaled. He recommended Gordon take a month off from work and avoid exposure to chemicals such as gasoline and exhaust fumes in the future, but it would be impossible to avoid petroleum-based contaminants in his line of work. "A month off and I won't have a job," Gordon said. "No way am I doing anything that would result in Lydia having to leave college."

A few weeks later, Mae called Gordon at work, frantic. Someone was in her apartment. Would Gordon come check? It was probably just Mae's old paranoia but she had been so distressed since Noel's death that Gordon was genuinely worried about her. During his lunch hour, he drove a cab home and, of course, ascertained that there was no one in Mae's apartment. When Gordon returned to work, the supervisor fired him on the spot, saying he had taken a cab without permission. Apparently, doing so was nothing unusual. He and other senior employees at the cab company did that routinely. It had never been a problem before. Whose permission was he supposed to ask anyhow? His own, since he was the dispatcher?

Poor Mae. It wasn't her fault but she felt responsible. "I love that family. And now look what I've done with an old woman's foolishness," Mae cried to me later that day. "Everyone probably thinks this old lady is losing her mind. But I tell you, I left something in the doorway as a trap – I'm not saying what it was – and it was moved when I came back. I know someone been in here."

Now it was Ann's turn to come to the rescue.

Through her various non-profit jobs, Ann had worked with several city supervisors, whom she apprised of Gordon's circumstances. One of them, Bevan Dufty, suggested that Mayor Newsom might be approached about declaring a Gordon Bell Appreciation Day. Ann wasted no time in calling the mayor's office and informing first his minions, then him, how Gordon had risked his own life to save Lance and had lost his job because of the injuries he had sustained in the fire and his mission of mercy for an old, blind woman. Leaving little to chance, Ann organized Jul and us tenants in a letter-writing campaign to city officials and the mayor. Jul's letter to the mayor went beyond anything I would have expected: "With disregard to the obvious personal danger, Mr. Bell entered the completely smoke filled rooms to reach the moaning (occupant) and then drag him to safety in total darkness. In this amazing and heroic rescue, Mr. Bell had the forethought to take the hall fire extinguisher to the fire. Mr. Bell has sustained pulmonary injuries and a dangerous twenty-five pound weight loss, required medical treatment at his own expense and lost work time without pay or other compensation … I recommend him for the highest meritorious recognition available from the City of San Francisco…"

By the time Ann was done lobbying on Gordon's behalf, city officials planned to give him three different commendations – one from the board of supervisors, one from the mayor and one from the fire department. Armed with these tributes, Ann launched the second part of her plan. She arranged a meeting with Gordon's supervisor at the cab company. Of course, I offered to go with her, as did Jul and Mary. Every cabbie in the company seemed to know why we were there; several called out good wishes to our friend Gordon as we climbed rickety steps to the supervisor's office. There, we met the kind of person who had risen to a position of authority in a business that didn't allow for much advancement, especially for women. We took turns singing Gordon's praises, describing the risks he had taken, his good deeds, arguing that he should have been rewarded for helping Mae rather than fired, detailing the impact the loss of his job could have on him, his wife and daughter.

If I ever needed an advocate, I would hire Ann. She simply offered the supervisor a strategy for rehiring Gordon without losing face or putting the company at risk. "Hire him back on contingency," she suggested. "Give him a few weeks to get back on track. You can still let him go if things don't improve, but I know they will." Then she said, as if it were an afterthought, "By the way, Gordon is going to be honored by the city of San Francisco for his courageous deed. He'll receive three different citations for risking his life, saving the life of a neighbor and saving the building. There are going to be several articles written about his acts of bravery. You wouldn't want your cab company identified as the employer that fired him after his heroic deed. Surely, you wouldn't want the whole city to know that."

Next came Jul: "I've been in the rental business for forty years and I've had few tenants who would take the risks that Gordon took. He was thinking of others, just like he did when he took the cab to get Mae, an elderly blind woman in our building who is suffering over the recent death of her friend Noel. Did we mention Noel? Like a father to Gordon. I'm sure Noel's death contributed to Gordon's state of mind. I understand it was his taking a cab to check on Mae that got him fired. I also understand that's not out of the ordinary, that employees with seniority do so regularly. Isn't that what happened here?"

"I can't speak to personnel matters," the woman said, dismissing us.

Ann had us write thank-you letters to the supervisor, reiterating our points and asking to arrange for us to speak to the cab company's board of directors. I was stunned when I read Jul's letter, which ended with these words: "I and many others could go on and on about how much we trust and even rely on Mr. Bell on a daily basis, but as we both know in our respective lines of work, talk isn't worth much. Contracts can be, however. I am willing to formally indemnify (the cab company) for one year to the maximum amount of $5,000 for any uninsurable loss due to any wrongdoing of Gordon Bell."

Days later, Gordon's supervisor told us the board had declined to meet with us. The decision was the same. But as it turned out, being fired was exactly what Gordon needed. His health improved and shortly before I returned to Vermont for my summer break, he was hired at a competing cab company, one that was happy to have him. I was sure, however, that the various commendations along with the support he had received from Jul and Mary, Ann and me had also contributed to Gordon's improving health.

PART THREE
(2005-2006)

From bitter searching of the heart,
Quickened with passion and with pain
We rise to play a greater part.
This is the faith from which we start:
Men shall know commonwealth again
From bitter searching of the heart.

F. R. Scott, "Villanelle for Our Time"

I returned to San Francisco in time to see the eight trees on our block chain-sawed down in seventeen minutes. I know how long it took because the Polish immigrant from the apartment building next door timed their destruction on a stopwatch. We stood together as block after block was denuded of vegetation. The destruction of Octavia Street and the construction of Octavia Boulevard had officially begun.

The men in hard hats had arrived at 7 a.m. with their chainsaws, loud enough to draw me out of my apartment and our Polish neighbor, too. He was famous on the block. He had been an Olympic diver. He rode his bicycle all over town and walked about in training clothes, flexing muscles. Yet, he used a handicap placard when he parked his car and, according to Jul, collected disability payments. He had lived in the rather dilapidated building next door for more than a decade, since emigrating there from Poland with his wife and mother-in-law. The couple had three children, all beautiful and impeccably behaved.

Over the years, Jul and the Pole had many disagreements stemming from the proximity of the family's apartment to Jul's building. Their rented rooms were on the ground floor and their windows, which were quite large and opened just above sidewalk level, looked onto a small walkway that ran between our two buildings. The garbage cans, meters, and utility boxes were located there, presenting a dozen opportunities for annoyance every day. The Pole used every opportunity Jul gave him to complain to various city agencies, bringing inspectors to our building and slowing down projects, large and small, unnecessarily. Meanwhile, these same city officials seemed blind to the deteriorated condition of the building next door, a veritable rat-trap, at least if one considered pigeons flying rats. They roosted in empty apartments; their shat stained the sidewalk.

Now, as my neighbor worked the mechanisms on his stopwatch and flexed his muscles, he clicked off a list of insults he predicted we would soon experience, speaking in a thick Eastern European accent: "The lights, they go next. You will see. Then the street itself. They will come and tear it up, making much dust, much noise. Then our sidewalk. You ready for that, girlie?"

Until that moment, I hadn't given full consideration to what it would be like to live in a construction zone. Indeed, I hadn't really believed the project would ever begin. "But it's for a greater good," I said to the neighbor. "We'll have a beautiful boulevard out front when it's done."

He looked at me like I was crazy then said, "You are crazy woman. When they are done, we will have traffic and noise and exhaust. And you wait and see what will happen to our buildings." He pointed to the for-sale sign I hadn't noticed on the front of his building. "The rich will buy, they'll try to move us' out. They will not move me easily, I tell you that."

Later that day, Ann and Alexandra and I were standing on the sidewalk surveying the damage when Gordon rode up on his bicycle, his curly red hair tied in a bushy ponytail and a jaunty black beret angled across his brow, making him look like a hippie Frenchman. Workmen were already erecting metal fences as barriers along the sidewalk, showing that my neighbor knew what he was talking about. Within a few days, we would be an island. Not only was our street now closed to traffic but the men were fencing off the cross streets as well, making each a dead end, from Market to Hayes. Other than work vehicles, there would be no traffic along the four long blocks of Octavia for the duration of the construction. And the city predicted it would last the better part of a year.

"Gordon's errand service at your command," he said, bowing from his perch atop the bicycle. "Errands large and small for the duration. No mucking stalls or pens but otherwise while the street is under construction, call on your Gordon to navigate through the upcoming muddle. I was here for the removal of the freeway ramps; I know it will take longer than planned and be a pain in the ass beyond anyone's imagination. A bicycle is the perfect means of transportation under circumstances like this."

"Thank God for Uncle G," Ann said. And I seconded that emotion.

And then, as if on cue, Lance returned.

In the months since the fire, Jul had alluded to efforts he was making to get Lance's parents to understand the seriousness of Lance's condition and ship him home. Apparently, those efforts, like the nonsmoking ban, had failed.

"Oh, you're back," I said lamely when I saw him. What else could you say at a moment like this?

"I am," he said. His eyes went liquid.

It was pouring again as I made my way down Waller toward Octavia, wondering what havoc the road crew had left in their wake that day when I spied Stretch squatting on a pile of clothing in his old alcove. I hadn't seen him in ages but he looked the same. He grinned as I approached.

"Stretch, you're back," I said.

"Oh, I been here off and on the past week. Lost my room. Lost all my stuff. I was fucked over," he said. Language I'd rarely heard from him before.

"What happened?"

"I got in some trouble. Went to jail. Got out and my room had been rented to someone else. All my stuff was gone."

I didn't ask for details. I didn't ask about the boyfriend.

"I think I've got an old sleeping bag if you want it," I said.

"Nope, I'm good. I got some stuff from the church. Jack saved it all from some other guys who were sleeping here while I was gone. I like to travel light."

It sounded so funny hearing that expression coming from a homeless man.

"Well, what can I do for you?" I asked. "Can't I do anything?"

"Make it stop raining."

"You thinking about Care Not Cash?"

"Nope. Nope. Like I told you before, I'm better off by myself. Besides, with the street closed off like this, it'll be quiet here. Quieter than that flophouse I was in. Quieter than jail."

"Well, I'm happy to see you. I'll go get Daniel so you can say hello."

One of the best things Jul did was introduce me to his friend Rebecca. Jul had told Rebecca that I wanted to meet some interesting people, people from whom I might gain a better understanding of San Francisco. He was concerned that I saw the negative too often, that the constancy of begging and bodies on the sidewalk overshadowed the city's pleasantries. He wanted me to get to know people who had lived in the city for some time, creative people who were continuing to make it a vibrant place. Rebecca was interesting in and of herself. She used to design jewelry that she had manufactured in Brazil, where she had nurtured and partnered with local artists; now she worked promoting architectural designers, artists and their work. She was connected to the art scene in the city not just because of her own work but also because she had lived in San Francisco during the city's artistic renaissance, the years when San Francisco rivaled New York in art, clothing design and music. She had also lived through its dark days, the days when gay men died daily, and she had cared for and loved several of them. Like so many others in her wide circle, Rebecca had to live with the memory of what was. Still, there was no shortage of "interesting people" to meet. Thanks to her, I met architects, designers and artists, partied with the literati and spent time in half a dozen fabulous homes, each with its own calling card – the city's best view; multi-million dollar artwork; rough-hewn furniture juxtaposed with African masks and metal sculptures. Rebecca knew the best place to get Burmese food or buy homemade taco shells. She had an eclectic music collection, which made our forays to Sonoma to visit her artist friends or a new winery all the more decadently interesting. On top of all that, she was a voracious reader and movie viewer so our times spent together were filled with engaging conversation and entertainment.

She phoned one day to say that a fellow named Leif was expecting my call. Rebecca said just enough to tempt me: You need to see his art and his apartment, she said. You need to see the clothing he's made and the costumes. He's a San Francisco institution. You should know him.

Leif lived above a store in a rent-controlled apartment. You rang a bell mounted on the doorframe and waited for him to come downstairs and open the reinforced metal door and then the heavy wooden door that together protected him from the craziness of the street. If my neighborhood was dicey, his just a few blocks away was treacherous. There were surveillance cameras mounted on nearby corners, not to catch red light scofflaws but rather to monitor the drug traffic and crime in the neighborhood. Two people had been shot dead nearby in the weeks before my visit.

After the gate and front door, you climbed a long, dark flight of stairs along which Leif had arranged driftwood sculptures, fantastically shaped pieces, some left in their natural state, others gilded or otherwise enhanced to suggest a shape or emotion. In one, a gargoyle hid in the gnarled and weathered wood; in another, the suggestion of a sail, the wood washed gray and hoary from salt spray. Leif led me through the flotsam to the top of the stairs.

"Our brother and sister," he said, pointing to two pieces of driftwood posed on either side of the landing, "Ask and Embla."

"Huh?"

"Our ancestors. You don't know the story? Norse mythology says we humans were formed from two pieces of driftwood. They're the Norse version of Adam and Eve. Don't you love the names, Ask and Embla? Ask is the male although it always seemed to me it should be the other way around. Of course, I'm interested in this as my namesake, Leif – it's Lifprasir in Norse mythology – was the last male to survive the Ragnarök ...."

"The Ragnarök?"

"A series of natural disasters out of which the world we know came to be."

And so I told Leif the Gnostic joke about Adam and Eve. Then, crossing the landing, I left the 21st century behind and stepped into the 19th-century sanctuary that Leif had created above a scummy storefront, a royal refuge, an artist's retreat. He'd painted the walls of his flat a delicious gray that looked ancient and warm at the same time, which is something you can't say too often about gray. He had sewn the fitted white slipcovers on the divan and chairs throughout his apartment as well as the elegant velvet curtains, a soft fawn color with gold tiebacks, that adorned his windows. Leif had created padded portieres from silk salvaged from an ancient mansion. They not only kept out the draft but also the street noise. He'd opened them partway so that, as I stepped into his parlor, light streamed into the room in scrumptious beams of warmth. He had painted a mural on a far wall that from across the room looked like an arched window with a view of San Francisco Bay, perfectly rendered with the sun filtering down through soft clouds onto the golden hills beyond. And he had painted ceiling inserts that he'd constructed to look like skylights, one daytime with realistic clouds against a blue sky; the other nighttime, with a sprinkling of stars and clouds lit from a distant moon. He had crafted the lamps and Victorian sconces throughout the apartment, stitched the pillows and throws, painted the oil paintings on his walls. He had sewn the vest he wore, designed the ring on his finger. It was no exaggeration to say that Leif was living in his art, wearing his art, reclining on his art.

His latest projects, terra cotta sculptures of friends, populated the rooms like half-born gods and goddesses. One evoked a young Greek god. It was a bust of Leif's latest boy lover. Another was of a friend of Leif's named Christopher, a lawyer and gardener; that he'd named "Joie de Vivre." Another, the headless torso of a chiseled male, was constructed from Fixwall, papier mâché and butcher paper, but it looked carved from marble and the figure itself, so perfectly formed, called out to be touched. Leif and the man had been lovers for decades.

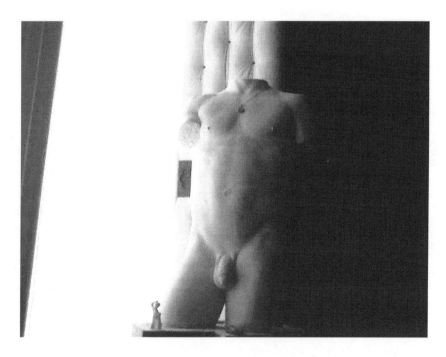

Leif's Statue in Front of His Portieres.

"He still looks that good," Leif said of the man he'd modeled the sculpture after, as I oohed over the perfect roundness of the buttocks, the marbled chest, and the well-formed penis. "The magic of seeing his perfect body here in my apartment has kept his body beautiful," Leif said. "I first recognized that possibility years ago when I saw a photo of Mae West in her apartment. She was shown in a room surrounded by photographs and a nude statue of herself, all made in the prime of her life. She was in her eighties at the time, but still looked great. She was standing next to the statue, posing like her own image, and she told the interviewer something like, 'Seeing myself in my perfection has kept me beautiful.' I think it's been so for Clifton. Maybe that's why he keeps coming back, because I captured him in his prime."

"I know Mae West," I said, laughing. "She lives in my building."

And there was that story to tell.

"Mae West – *the* Mae West, the fabulous Diamond Lil – also outfitted her apartment in white silk and satin furniture. Were you thinking of that when you made these?" I asked, pointing to his white furnishings. I could not imagine living with such virginally upholstered furniture. But no, Leif said he chose the fabric because it made his friends act civilly.

My favorite sculpture in Leif's atelier – I'd already begun to think of his apartment that way; it was the perfect allusion since the French word for an artist's studio originated with the Old French word *astelle*, meaning "splinter of wood" – was a stunning bust of a patrician woman with upswept curls and perfectly budded nipples adorning her modest breasts. The hair, piled high like that of a Roman goddess, matched the nipples in color, a color reminiscent of burnt orange, of rust, an orange-red so delectably vibrant that you adored her immediately.

"Everyone has that response to her even though she's not finished," he said. Then, as if he were a god creating a living form from clay, he described how he envisioned her ears more perfectly shaped, the combs he planned to mold and arrange in her hair, and a collar of leaves, modeled after the taro plant that the Romans had imported from Egypt.

Leif's Roman Goddess with Tarot Leaves Arranged Around Her Bodice

Other Works in Leif's Atelier

After the gawking and praising, we traded stories. He told me the sad love story of the Greek god-boy who had just broken his heart and he told me his secret. "No one believes me but I am channeling Oscar Wilde. I've always had an affinity for him. There are many parallels in our lives," he said, thumbing through a book he had nearby that told the sad tale of a man brought down by prejudice. Leif's hands were beautiful; a ring whose gem he'd purchased from a street vendor, then set himself, decorated one finger; a ring that had belonged to his father another. As he began to tell me details of Oscar's and his own life, making connections I sometimes followed, often didn't, it occurred to me that between Jul and Wisdom Man, Rebecca and now Leif, the people I'd surrounded myself with were stories in and of themselves, agents at work in their own dramas, as we all are, but they were working overtime, and the scenes and actions in each of their stories mimed shifts in society that both defined them individually while also reflecting the social order of life in San Francisco. For Leif, like Oscar Wilde, art was always at the center of the drama.

This was how the Oscar Wilde connection had been confirmed for him. Leif had been quite ill one day, suffering from the flu or a broken heart. He had been working on his various projects in a kind of delirium and for a minute experienced a sense of the whole, how the clothing he had sewn and the apartment sanctuary he had created, the driftwood, the paintings and sculptures together comprised what the art world might call an oeuvre, a total statement or environment in the manner of artists like Charles Rennie Mackintosh or Aubrey Beardsley, an approach to life and living that was no longer practical or honored, one in which art and artifact were entwined so that the artist strove to create not just beautiful items to hang on walls or exhibit in public or, heavens, to sell, but rather to create a world separate from everyday life or, at least, an asylum from that world. Leif was concentrating on this insight, undoubtedly feverish, when he swooned and fell to the floor. A painting tumbled from the wall. It was an old painting, something he'd done as a teenager, and when it fell upon him the glass shattered and several pieces stabbed him like stigmata, cutting his forehead and slashing deeply into his flank.

"When I came to, I wrapped my side in a towel to stem the bleeding, went to bed and slept for two days," Leif said. "When I awoke, I knew I was channeling Oscar Wilde."

I was not sure what to say after hearing a story like that from a stranger but I didn't try to make sense of it. It was so melodramatic I could see Sean Penn acting it out. But I could also see genius all around me in Leif's sculptures and driftwood, his beautiful paintings and furnishings. There was certainly some powerful juju going on there. Yet Oscar Wilde's last years had been so pitiful that I thought one should never invite such imagery into one's own life.

Of all the people I'd met so far in San Francisco, Leif was the most interesting. I knew from the minute I met him that we would be friends. Daniel liked him too. He curled up on Leif's lap and went to sleep while we talked of Oscar Wilde and Aubrey Beardsley and the artist's life.

"Did you ever hear the famous line about the two of them?" Leif asked as I was leaving. "It went something like this: 'Aubrey Beardsley was so precious of speech and languid in his poses, so extravagantly foppish, that Oscar Wilde claimed him for his very own.' I don't have it quite right but it's how I feel about my Greek god-boy. I want to claim him for my own."

"Channel it," I said. "Ask Oscar what you ought to do."

When the metal door closed behind me, the first thing I heard were the boom boxes. This was not a quintessential San Francisco neighborhood, even thought it was Haight Street. A pitifully skinny woman, her face cadaverous, screamed obscenities as a car full of men drove by, the passengers hanging out and laughing at her. It made her scream all the louder. The street was littered and dirty. I carried Daniel for a block or two, until we got closer to the now-closed campus of UC Berkeley-San Francisco, scheduled to be leveled in the next year or three, who knows, for an apartment complex. When I'd arrived at Leif's, the day had been warm and sunny; now, fog rushed down Haight Street as if some force were chasing it. Back at Leif's, the sky in one room was still blue with just a scattering of high clouds while in another, moonlight lit a room inhabited by a Greek god-boy and a Roman goddess.

And when I got home I called Rebecca right away.

"I knew you'd love him," she said.

Long moments of silence as Silent Guy and I watched the world go by, then this from him: "I bought me some bongo drums."

"You're rather flush."

"Oh, they only cost $5. I got them at the secondhand store. They're broken in already. You ever hear that drum circle in Golden Gate Park?"

I had. On weekend afternoons and sometimes during the week, the drummers gathered on Hippie Hill – always one or two Rastafarians, some old hippies, a couple of straight men, a red-haired girl in flowing silk, three or four people from a place where the culture revolved around the drum, a neophyte on the outskirts timidly swaying, and the young hippie wannabes in loose clothing and ratted hair smoking dope and dancing. I loved it best when the twirler was there; she was a young beauty who effortlessly coiled a Hula Hoop around her sinewy frame, doing the knee knocker, the wrap the mummy, the arm gyro, the neck break and the stork, a champion Hula Hooper capable of changing tempo and moves in time to the music as if she were hot-wired to the drummers' collective pulse.

The Hula Hoop girl was a regular at the Drum Circle or, as here, at the San Francisco Love Fest, held in the Civic Center each fall.

Sometimes the drummers were one voice, deep and rhythmic, celebrating the heartbeat, rocking in placental bliss. Other times, you heard their individual poundings, mocking, rocking, rapping, tapping, blending, bending, sounding, resounding. And then the voices might join in. "Play it, sistah," the Rasta man would say. "I hear your story."

Silent Guy interrupted my reverie. "I'm thinking of buying one of those little folding chairs too. I can't sit on the ground too long. My knees won't take it."

"I hear your story," I said. "There's a bench the drummers collect around but it's always taken. But you probably knew that. Have you been?"

"Nah, I seen it on TV."

"You could take the bus there. I do. We could go together."

"Maybe I will some day when I get better at the drums."

More silence. Then this: "I'm getting a little inheritance. My mother's house finally sold. I could take lessons, maybe."

Work crews came by day. They moved their fences around. They drove big trucks. They dug the pavement up from one end of the boulevard to the other. They deposited huge mounds of dirt and then moved the mounds around. They hauled in loads of gravel. They moved the loads around. They would work in front of my building, then move to the other end of the street four blocks away, work there for an hour or two, then disappear. Why didn't they finish one block at a time, I wondered, save us some misery?

Mike Powers, the project manager for Ghilotti Bros., the company building the boulevard, said the delays were caused by frequent discoveries of odd and unexpected obstructions, undocumented fuel lines, old basement walls, abandoned conduits and the like.

A city worker named Mitch was our lifeline. He had an official title, Octavia Boulevard Ombudsman or Public Liaison or some such horseshit, but Ann and I considered him our private prince. We took turns calling him at City Hall. We called when the workmen moved the barriers closer to the building, further diminishing our egress. The fences were equipped with metal footings that poked out into what was left of the sidewalk. You couldn't see them in the dark, making them particularly treacherous. We called Mitch when the crosswalk was a foot-deep puddle or when people dumped their trash at the end of the side streets so that we had to navigate around broken televisions and pawed-through garbage bags to get home. Mitch, ever patient Mitch, actually listened. He actually tried to do something about each and every one of the problems we brought to him. But there was only so much he could do for people living through a transformation. The air was full of noise and dust. The trucks made clouds of it when they dropped their loads of dirt or gravel. It blew into our apartments. Glenn couldn't sleep. Ann couldn't maneuver the stroller through the mess. Mae was essentially a prisoner. Gordon ran our errands, wheeling through the obstacle course skillfully. Nighttime was even more difficult, of course, when, without street or car lights, we had to maneuver through it all in the pitch dark.

Of course, the very worst was when the trucks and the men disappeared, when days went by without any work or progress, when the homeless took up residence on the sidewalk during the day rather than waiting for the work crews to leave. Then, besides the obstacle course of footings and puddles and signs and mud, there would be the bodies and the shopping carts to navigate around.

And so we called Mitch.

Sound asleep. A door slammed, jolting me awake.

From the hallway, Robin's lovely Rita, the peter maid he'd described as a sex therapist, yelled out, "You just want to stick your dick in someone's mouth."

And from somewhere upstairs, another voice: "Me, too."

Stretch was not alone in considering the lack of traffic in our neighborhood an invitation to bed down. More homeless people had taken up residence on the side streets. There were needles on the sidewalk; this was something new. Human shit, too. With the rainy season upon us and no streetlights, night descended like a shroud as you turned your back on Market Street and climbed Octavia. I didn't like feeling afraid. Of course, once I got home there would be another challenge: walking Daniel, a white dog in a dirty land.

Another week passed, no Wisdom Man. Silent Guy said he was working at the library. Then one Saturday morning there he was on the corner, sitting with Guy, drinking black coffee and officiating over the scene as before.

"Where have you been?" I asked, hoping the answer was not jail or the mental ward.

"Tending the orchard," he said.

"Tending the orchard?"

"My school. My students. I'm nurturing my future. I'm tilling the fields of monetary possibility so that later I can harvest the fruits of my labor."

This was the first time that Wisdom Man had spoken of his material needs, if ever so metaphorically. I had imagined a back story for Wisdom Man as the son of an old moneyed family from a preppy town back east, the smartest kid in class, odd but protected because of what old money used to buy, money that he now lived off. How else did he get to spend his days prognosticating and portending?

"The fields of monetary possibility?" I asked. "Do you mean you got a job or that you're fund-raising?"

"I have a job. I've been cultivating my student base," he said. Wisdom Man often spoke in allegories. I decided to go blunt before he left for the Zen center.

"Do your students pay for their lessons?"

"Learning cannot be sold or purchased," he said peevishly. "I am not in the business of making money off of knowledge."

"Just asking. Weren't you the one who spoke just now of monetary possibility, of harvesting the fruit of your labor?"

"Well of course you wouldn't understand my meaning," he said, reinforcing my discomfort. "You *do* make your living selling knowledge."

Of course I understood his irritability. No one else questioned Wisdom Man about his "school." Guy didn't interrogate him about its workings. And what difference did it make whether it were real or imaginary? Either way, it was entertaining. And now I had hurt his feelings and he had hurt mine in return.

Still I said, "Well, that's a rather crass way of putting it, even if you are right."

Silent Guy cleared his throat. He made a fuss over Daniel. He scraped the legs of his chair.

"Whoops. Late," Wisdom Man said, then scooted across the street to the Zen Center. As he stepped onto the far curb, he turned and smiled, apologetically.

"May the farce be with you," he said.

Lance was drinking again. Gordon was pissed. Patrick was pissed. Patrick was looking for a way out; neither he nor his wife could handle living next to Lance much longer. Gordon simply wanted Lance out. What made matters worse was that Lance had never apologized or thanked Gordon; he just returned from the hospital and drifted back to his old ways, apparently unaware or unconcerned about the damage he'd done. And Ann certainly didn't want to spend another night on the sidewalk in her plaid bathrobe. I took my building mates' concerns to Jul, accepting my role as intermediary. My expectations were not high.

"Lance is certifiably mentally ill. Evicting him would be seen as an act of discrimination against a handicapped person. Oh, pardon me for misspeaking." Jul's voice dripped with sarcasm. "A person with a handicap," he corrected. "I'd probably face a hefty fine not to mention a lawsuit if I even suggested he might be better off with supervision. Haven't we been through all this before?"

"I know. But he's drinking again. Would you call his parents again?"

"Apparently they don't want him back either," Jul said.

Later, Patrick confided he had put a deposit on a condo, tiny but with a great view. On a clear day, you could see the bay.

"That ought to be great for your wife. At least she'll have a view for comfort if she doesn't get out much," I said, trying my best to be diplomatic.

"Oh, no. She hates heights. But I love them. The view is for me."

Mae and I were waiting for her Jewesses. They parked on Waller or Haight now and walked to the building to fetch her. She was particularly chatty that morning, having been stuck inside for days.

"You wouldn't believe what this street was like before," she said. "This ain't nothing. This will end. We had prostitutes right over there. Right there." She pointed across the devastation. "Ha, they call upstreet Hayes Valley. We used to call it Hell Valley. Where's that Daniel? Let me feel him. What color you say his hair was? White? Pure white like an old man? Hmmppph. That freeway, that was the divider. On the other side, it was safe. Over here, you put your life in God's hands every time you stepped through the door. I should have a little doggie like this."

"How would you walk him, Mae?"

"I'd get you to do it," she said laughing. "You would, wouldn't you?"

Mae's Jewesses arrived, three lovelies in their fullness, a splash of color against the rain-drenched barrenness of Octavia Boulevard. Mae took their arms and walked between them as they wove their conga line through the muck. If Mae had a dog, I was sure she'd find someone to take him on as a project.

Jul was not quite sure she was as blind as she appeared. Indeed, one of his workers swore he'd seen her bend down and pick something up from the floor. Now that was not proof of anything. Blind people see with their other senses, as Mae had described. But sometimes it was just too uncanny to see her maneuver around her apartment or the perfection she brought to her outfits. I asked Gordon if he thought Mae was totally blind.

"What's that Vermont expression you taught me, hard telling not knowing?" he said.

The torrent returned. Mud oozed down the hill, flowed over the sidewalk, puddled up in dark shallows. The workmen disappeared. Then one evening Ann was at my door crying. Alexandra clung to her. The two were stippled with mud. Ann had tripped over one of those frigging metal footings; she and Alexandra and the stroller had tumbled into the mud.

"There are three single women in this building," I yelled into Mitch's voice mail. "There's a blind lady, me and my very white dog, Ann and her baby. Four single females, counting the baby," I told him – or his answering machine – what had happened to Ann. I knew it was stupid, my complaining. We should just shut up and let them get the work done. It was not Mitch's fault that the rain continued to fall, that the drains didn't drain, that the construction crew didn't return, that the punks and vandals and crazies and curious moved the fences during the night and wandered through the wasteland, vandalizing city trucks, stealing copper wire, leaving obstacles for us to trip over in the dark.

In the morning, Ann could hardly move. She was badly bruised. And a day later, after I'd told Jul the story, he climbed onto the fire escape and attached floodlights to the front of the building to illuminate the sidewalk below. Without even being asked. And why hadn't the city thought of such accommodations?

Robin had joined the missing. I'd heard music and voices from his apartment off and on, and had run into Acacia in the hallway several times. But when I asked where her father was, her answers were indecipherable. She seemed to have moved from slim to skeletal and the way she avoided further questioning filled me with concern not just for her, but also for Robin.

When I asked Jul about Robin, Jul asked if I'd like to rent his apartment, pointing out that it would be cheaper than mine. "Do you know something? Is he moving?" I asked. "Is he okay?"

"One can only let someone go without paying rent for so long," he said.

"Oh, how long?" I asked.

Stretch was annoyed with the newcomers on his block yet did nothing to protect his turf. In the months since the construction had begun, other homeless men often beat him to his alcove. If that were so, Stretch just slept in one of the shallower openings along the church's exterior, ones that offered less protection and privacy. When I asked why he didn't defend his right to his sleeping niche, he said the new one was actually a better location, further away from the construction dust. I didn't buy it. I thought there was a street etiquette that had been violated by the usurpers, but apparently it was one Stretch either wasn't comfortable defending or the usurper was someone he knew not to challenge. Stretch was not a fighter. It was I who wanted to kick the newcomers out.

"Oh don't go doing that," he warned. "Street people are crazy. Don't go messing with them on my behalf. Something happen to you and I'll …"

I cut him off. "No, I wouldn't be rude. I don't know exactly what I'd say but it's not right. You've been sleeping there for years …"

"The rules of the street are first come, first dibs. They ain't doing me no wrong. But I gotta' work. I can't be laying down in the afternoon like they do."

"How about another room in an SRO?"

"No, it's too much trouble with my cart. This'll work out. You'll see. Street's done, they'll be gone and I'll have my sidewalk back."

One day in mid-November, after months of construction hassles, I heard a loud boom from the street and just a few moments later, Ann called to ask if my gas stove and electricity were working. Mae was at the door with a similar question. No one had bothered to tell us that the workers had hit a gas main and had to shut off the gas and electricity to all the structures along Octavia to prevent an explosion. Or at least that's what I think the rude fellow on the bulldozer working near a big hole not far from the building barked by way of explanation.

Jul was away on a motorcycle trip; Gordon was at work. And so it fell to me to deal with the problem. I was on the phone to Mitch right away. A few hours later, he called to say PG&E would have the gas and electricity restored soon. Three hours later, however, he called to say a utility employee would have to come into the building to physically turn on the electricity and enter each and every apartment to relight gas heaters and stoves. An hour later, Mitch called to say the building owner had to be there to let the PG&E guy into each apartment. After a half-dozen phone calls, I tracked Jul down and he designated me his proxy and made arrangements to get the keys to me. That was how I learned this axiom: Never go into the apartments of your fellow tenants unannounced unless you are prepared to see some things you wish you hadn't.

First, there was Robin's hovel, knee-deep in clothes, magazines, ashtrays and the general detritus that came with too many people sharing one small space. If Robin had moved out, he'd left his life behind. Acacia had made her own crib in a small cubby off the kitchen, probably intended for storage. Mattress on the floor, printed material papering the walls, a small bouquet of flowers on a tiny stand in the corner. The PG&E guy had to clear debris from atop the stove to light the pilot. Tell these people it's dangerous to leave flammable items, like matches and paper towels, on the stovetop, he said, removing the bong as well.

Ann's apartment was fine and Mae's was nothing new to me, although the PG&E guy looked askance at the candles burning in pots of water. Brendan apparently owned no dressers or clothes hangers. Indeed, his apartment was almost void of furniture. His bedroom consisted of a mattress and two piles of clothing. Hopefully, he knew the clean pile from the dirty.

About the time that we were deciding we didn't need to go in Noel's vacant apartment, Gordon arrived to help with the keys and the lighting of gas heaters and stoves, but as we made our way to the third floor, Lance appeared on the staircase, looming over us like a flaccid balloon.

"What's the fuss? Why's the power?" he stammered.

Now we had an entourage: me with the keys, the PG&E guy, Gordon and Lance, weaving on tiptoes, always in the way. I could smell the liquor on him. He was barefoot; his foot was bleeding and he trailed bloody footprints up and down the hall.

"Leave," I said. "Wait in your apartment."

By the time we made it to Patrick's apartment, I was glad to bequeath the task to Gordon, but there was still Lance's to deal with. I thought it best to hang around. We stepped inside his apartment, me wondering what Gordon must be thinking, then seeing more bloody footprints, a broken Jack Daniels bottle. The smell of alcohol permeated the air. The PG&E guy made it clear he was not going to get down on the floor amidst the glass and blood and Jack Daniels.

"This man needs help. This is an unsafe situation," he said, surveying the mess, the pill bottles that spilled their contents across the counter, food drying in to-go cartons on the counter, the smell of decay in the air. I was astounded by how much havoc Lance had created in the short time he'd been back from the hospital. All the while, as the PG&E man lectured us as if we had any control over the situation, Lance staggered about the small kitchen, bleeding, knocking things over, but silent, his big face moonlike and oddly blank.

Eventually we all became accustomed to the routine interruptions of our electricity and gas service but one day something quite outside the norm occurred. During the night, someone threw a lit gas can down a manhole near the end of the street. The manhole provided access to the circuitry for telephone and cable TV serving a broad area throughout the neighborhood. The blast had short-circuited our phone and Internet service and that of hundreds of others. For almost a week, workers restrung wires to the circuit boxes. They'd think they had it fixed and would pack up their equipment and leave and the phone in my apartment would ring and it would be a call for the Polish family next door. Ann was without phone and Internet for three weeks. And so, we called Mitch.

The blast had also undone some of the progress the workers had made on the new boulevard, causing them to dig up some of the road, repair water pipes, then lay down gravel and macadam again. In the midst of all this, Chuck arrived for his visit from Vermont. He brought a good perspective. It was fifty-five degrees and sunny in San Francisco the day he arrived; when he had left Vermont it was twelve below zero without the wind chill and snowing sidewise. And, as he pointed out, the construction looked to be halfway completed.

Metallica opened for the Rolling Stones there in that beautiful stadium overlooking the bay, giving new meaning to the term Wall of Sound. Metallica had first tasted success in San Francisco and the audience, including Chuck and me, was appreciative. Yet, from the moment that Keith Richards delivered the familiar opening chords to "Start Me Up" and Mick Jagger flashed onto the stage in his skin-tight black jeans, red T-shirt and gold lamé jacket, it was clear that the Rolling Stones were still the world's greatest rock 'n' roll band. They may have been old and wrinkled but those British bad boys could play.

The night was clear and crisp. And cooler still when Jagger played harmonica and acoustic guitar on "Sweet Virginia" or Keith Richards got on his knees and played the guitar with his teeth during his solo ballad "Slipping Away." Of course, neither "Sweet Virginia" nor "Slipping Away" was what the crowd and Chuck and I had come to hear. We had come for down and dirty, swaggering, stomping, rock 'n' Rolling Stones. We wanted "Satisfaction," "Let It Bleed," "Sympathy for the Devil," "Paint It Black." They played them all.

After the firework finale, we walked with the concert crowd along the Embarcadero from SBC Park to the Ferry Building, then piled onto the F train at Market Street for the trolley ride home. Every so often, someone would sing, "Whoo, hoo" from the song "Sympathy for the Devil" and dozens of other Muni riders would answer from somewhere in one of the cars, "What's my name?" Call and response: "Whoo, hoo. What's my name?"

The day before I left for winter break, I finally ran into Robin. I'd heard Jul was trying to negotiate his departure from the building rather than reach the same result through the legal system. Robin looked older and thinner as he struggled with the key at his door. His hands shook.

"I've been staying out of town with friends," he said by way of explanation but he, too, went vague when pressed for details. He seemed distracted. I told him I was leaving for Vermont the next day.

"Don't know if I'll be here when you come back. I'm thinking of moving north to be with my daughter and grandkids. I just don't know …"

"Well, how will I find you when I get back?"

"Maybe you won't. Maybe this is your last chance." The old lecherous spark lit his eyes, marvelously blue in his ravaged face. Oddly, when I told Ann about the conversation that evening, I was surprised by my emotions. Robin and his circle of oddballs were certainly more than an annoyance but for reasons I could not articulate I realized I would miss him if he did move away.

The next day, as I hauled my heavy suitcases through the mud and around the corner to Waller, past the Baptist Church, to wait for the shuttle that would transport me to the airport, I came across a sleazy fellow hiding in the shadow of a sturdy bush that had survived the demolition. I wish I hadn't looked. I wish the last thing I'd witnessed before leaving San Francisco for my six-week winter break was anything other than the man's pants rolled up to his calf and his dirty fingers holding the needle that he had stuck into the abscess on his leg.

My bi-coastal life had settled into a manageable pattern. Not only had I learned the practicalities of what to cart across the country and what to leave behind, but my comings and goings were no longer a trauma for me or those I loved and depended upon on either coast. Of course, I was always missing something – my granddaughter's play at school on one coast or an evening dinner party at Leif's on the other. While there would be more plays to watch and I would surely get roped into attending them and with any luck more dinner parties in Leif's atelier, there were the events and passings that could not be replicated, the sadness that reached across the miles when only a few days after I'd left San Francisco, Ann called with the news that Mae had died. It is so hard to get news like that on the telephone, again.

When I thought about it, I realized that I hadn't said goodbye, hadn't thought to remember her with a gift upon my departure, that she had warned me not to take her for granted, and I had. When was the last time I'd seen her, the day we had waited together for her young lovelies to fetch her, the day of the explosion out on the street? Life had been so disrupted by the street construction that I'd not paid much attention to Mae's comings or goings. Beyond that, the semester had been ridiculously busy with demands at school where I was simultaneously heading up our department's promotion committee and serving on the university senate and on the union's executive board. Again this year, like a stuck record, the governor, His Excellence the Terminator, was cutting the state university budget and the university was rife with grumblings of a possible strike. Academia is full of small and large dramas, comedies and tragedies that I have not burdened this book with, but the semester had brought more than a heavy dose of both, although no deaths until Mae's.

This is what I learned long-distance, another chapter in which Gordon played the crucial role and from which I was separated by time and space but not emotion. Apparently, a few days had gone by with no one seeing or hearing from Mae.

Eventually Gordon became worried when she didn't answer his knock and climbed down the fire escape to look into her apartment, then forced a window open and climbed in. Mae looked asleep, tucked nicely in her bed but her body was cold as stone. He told me she had a peaceful smile upon her face, small consolation for my failure to have said goodbye to her.

I was heartbroken, and glad she had not suffered. I put my U-2 disk in the Walkman and listened to those words, over and over:

> Take this soul
> Stranded in some skin and bones
> Take this soul
> And make it sing

The Program from Mae West's "Homegoing Service"

And so I returned to San Francisco from my winter break in time to see Mae's relatives empty her apartment but too late for her funeral, which had been held on New Year's Eve. Jul and Mary were the only people connected with our building to attend the service, held in her black Hebrew church, the only white people. They provided a detailed report, including a description of the orange African robe that Mother Mae Rose West was buried in. In the few years I'd known Mae, I'd never seen her in a dashiki or kaftan, never mind the color orange. I was not sure she would have approved of meeting her Yahweh dressed as an African princess. I have the program from her service, thanks to Mary who saved me a copy. I look at it often and think of how she slipped away, angels finding their way to her, perhaps following the light of her candles, there in an apartment transfixed within months into a place I did not think she haunted.

I had hoped that more would have been accomplished on the boulevard while I was in Vermont but thanks to December and January's torrents, the street looked worse than when I'd left. No one hated the mess more than Glenn.

"Really," Glenn said the first morning I ran into him as we surveyed the gully of sludge, a mix of mud and street litter that had been deposited on what remained of our sidewalk. His voice was so loaded with annoyance that Zipper, a dog who was always on a mission that involved either getting food or getting rid of food, pivoted his head to look at Glenn in a sorrowful way and refused to leave the building. Daniel was of a like mind. We stood there and watched the sky open up. Rain pelted down. The sludge turned to something that resembled diarrhea.

"I'm going back to bed," I said to Glenn.

"Good idea."

"Your buddy Noam Chomsky's on his way out now, Yvonne. His whole theory's gone right out the window," Wisdom Man said as soon as I sat down with my coffee. It was a Saturday morning, the only time we saw Wisdom Man now. Most mornings, if I ventured through the muck and mud to the coffee shop, I'd just find Silent Guy, sitting silently, smoking. I had no clue where Tom or Ted or Jay had gone, probably staying close to home given the miserable weather.

"When did Chomsky become *my* buddy?" I asked.

"MIT and Vermont are both in New England, that's one. You're both university professors, two. And you're both teaching something to do with language. Three strikes," he said.

"Trust me, Vermont and MIT may both be in New England but that's one of the only things they have in common," I said. "And I don't have a clue what Chomsky's linguistics is about. But why is Chomsky out? Aren't more and more Americans opposing the idea of war that he's long argued against?"

"It's not his political positions but his language theories that have been proven wrong, especially the most essential of his hypotheses, that humans are the only organism able to comprehend recursive grammar."

"Bush doesn't comprehend recursive grammar. Does that mean he's not human?" I asked.

"That's not my point," Wisdom Man quipped. When he had a point he wanted to make, he did not welcome interruptions or tangents, especially when we were talking about the ability to follow tangents. "Some psychology researcher from UC San Diego – his name is Timothy Gentner – has discovered that songbirds, starlings actually, are capable of learning simple grammar."

"I believe it. Starlings are so smart that they lay their eggs in other birds' nests, the bird equivalent to surrogate motherhood. And the cardinals at my Vermont home have a whole language. They grumble, 'shit, shit, shit' in the morning when they wake up and trill 'prego, prego, prego'– thank you in Italian – in the evening. They have a litany of songs they call out to one another, 'Watch out,' 'Hey, you, wanna be my sweetie?' 'Kids, it's time to come home.'"

"Do you think Daniel knows that – what did you call it, recurrent grammar?" Silent Guy asked.

"Recursive," Wisdom Man said, "The repetition of a rule or procedure with successive results."

"Speak English," I said. "It means inserting an explanatory clause or rearranging known words in a sentence. Daniel definitely understands it. For example, first he learned, 'Danny boy, go get your leash,' then other versions of the same sentence, like 'Danny boy, let's get your leash and go for a walk.' I think he can speak it, too, combining various yaps and barks to communicate to Guy that he wants some salami," whereupon Daniel gave a little yap and hopped about on his back paws, demanding more salami.

With that, Wisdom Man got to his feet.

"Are you leaving us already?" I asked. "Don't go. We're lonely for you. We miss you. Do you have to run away? And why don't you come by more often?"

"Austerity. I'm on an austerity campaign," Wisdom Man said.

I said not a word.

Apparently, Robin had moved out of the building while I was away, but Acacia stayed behind in his apartment, a sweet, lost beauty who continued to adopt strays so that the parade of people in and out of the building persisted. She collected a small zoo of abandoned creatures, a gecko, kittens and a school of koi fish she'd rescued from an abandoned pond. She kept the fish in a kid's swimming pool installed in the front room. The smell of dead fish permeated the foyer. It was apparently easier to dump the fetid water out the front door or, better yet, out the apartment's front window than haul it to the kitchen sink, but she rarely made it without spilling half along the way. Once or twice, one of us would discover a dead goldfish on the sidewalk. I was glad to have her next door, nonetheless, rather than listen to the banging and sanding that filled the air as one after another apartment emptied from deaths and evictions, or contend with the people applying to rent them. Besides, with her there, there was the outside chance of seeing Robin or at least learning of his whereabouts.

Jul would invariably bring prospective tenants by for my approval and I'd give what became a practiced spiel about how we were an informal family in the building and how we looked out for one another. I liked that he sought my endorsement. The building's composition was changing. Younger people were moving in, people who expected that once the boulevard was constructed, the neighborhood would be quite charming and desirable. My vote for Patrick's renovated apartment went to Emmett and Deanna, the latest prospective tenants. They owned a store in Hayes Valley that specialized in designer 1950s furniture. Emmett had grown up in the neighborhood. As a child, he'd known Jerry Garcia and other musicians from the Sixties and Seventies who'd once populated the area, learning guitar from them. Deanna was a Midwestern girl who had come to San Francisco for the weekend and stayed. She'd been a diva in the day, modeling hairstyles for top salons while she collected her own entourage of performers, artists and musicians. Now they were among the applicants vying for Patrick's old apartment. When I stepped into the flat after Jul's renovation, the apartment so stunningly appointed, the view from its floor-to-ceiling windows so commanding. I considered moving upstairs myself, but the additional $200 a month and four double flights of stairs deterred me.

Jul introduced me to Emmett and Deanna quite grandly, overstating my credentials, and asked me to answer any questions they might have, with the unspoken expectation that I would gauge their reliability as tenants and provide a report on them. Deanna and Emmett were willing to move in during the street construction because they wanted a place where they could settle for at least the next decade, a place close to their business. If they were to move to the fourth floor, sans elevator, and give up their rent-controlled apartment in the Mission, however, they wanted responsible neighbors and a caring landlord. All this made them preferable to the wannabe hip-hop stars and computer nerds who also came by for their interviews.

What could I tell them about Jul? He had been good to me, I said. He cared for the building. I mentioned that they, like me, might find themselves debating Jul over most anything from race relations in America to the Beatles, while wishing he would just fix the goddamn toilet. They had already picked up on his oddness, his need to impress, his desire to be surrounded by people he could brag about knowing to others with whom he had surrounded himself so he could brag about knowing them. Jul was the first to concede he liked to drop names, that he was impressed by titles.

I did not tell them about our recent argument, one that had left a chill between us. Jul had offered to deliver a television and some other heavy items that had been left in Mae's apartment to a woman from Mae's temple named Sala. She lived in the Hunters Point neighborhood of San Francisco, the neighborhood my dead student Adam had first feared, and then learned to love. I asked to go along, hoping to learn more about Mae and her temple.

After we delivered the TV, Sala, Jul and I stood outside her house, chatting near a pile of donated food she would be distributing around the neighborhood later that day. Sala was running for city supervisor to represent her neighborhood. At the time, the city of San Francisco and the federal government were developing plans to address the pollution problems that had long plagued Hunters Point, the neighborhood populated largely by African Americans, prior to a huge redevelopment project planned for the region.

Sala feared she and her neighbors would be further exposed to environmental toxins stirred up by the decontamination and construction only to be priced out of the neighborhood, much as they had been during redevelopment projects in the Fillmore and Western Addition. The Navy had estimated the cleanup would cost at least $266 million. Sala thought the Navy should also compensate residents for their exposures from years of living with the pollution. And, if there were good-paying jobs to be had, she wanted some of them to go to neighborhood residents.

Sala knew her campaign for supervisor was a long shot but that didn't discourage her; she was using it to promote her causes, to ask questions, to represent her community. I tried to ask about the African American Hebrew Center, but Sala just referred me back to Mae's pastor. The conversation had segued back to her campaign when Jul leaned forward and abruptly interrupted our discussion. His voice was conspiratorial as he bent his tall, thin, white frame forward toward Sala. "Would you let me give you a bit of advice?" he whispered. She leaned forward in response. A pause, that Adam's apple of his bobbing for a minute before he said, "Leave race out of your campaign. You must agree that the race issue is dead, that we've all moved beyond that, that race and gender are no longer issues in San Francisco. Take my advice. Don't drag race into your politicking."

We were standing on a broken sidewalk in a crime-ravaged neighborhood with a woman who had lived there all her life, someone who worked with kids who might have been in gangs, a person who delivered food to the elderly and knew first-hand how much race and gender still mattered in America. I saw how regal she was then, how tall, nearly as tall as Jul. She simply fixed her nutmeg eyes upon him and asked if he wanted to accompany her on her rounds delivering the donated food piled on her sidewalk. I was glad when Jul declined but then I had to get in the car and decide to speak not a word to him ever again or else tell him how idiotic his advice had sounded. He might have called our words during the ride home a debate or discussion, but anyone listening to our raised voices would have thought differently. It wasn't pleasant.

The thing is, he believed what he said. Jul had accomplished much through hard work and determination. I had as well. Yet, I thought, neither one of us was entirely self-made. He had grown up in Malibu, for criminy's sake. And, while my father was a throw-away child, raised in a Boston orphanage and by people who essentially took him in for the labor he could provide, and my mother had been a poor immigrant who'd been so torturously taunted in her first American school that she dropped out, they had benefited from their whiteness, from being born at a time when people of their race were making their way up America's social ladder. I had benefited from their ability to move beyond the circumstances of their births. I was well educated, well fed, given the tools I needed to make a success of myself. I remembered something Lyndon Johnson had said while promoting his anti-discrimination programs, something to the effect that you cannot take a person who has been hobbled by chains for their whole life and suddenly liberate them and expect them to be able to compete with all the others. There was a divide that still held people of color back while also creating among some a suspicion of people like me who wanted to cross over it. Mae's spiritual sisters – I couldn't remember her mentioning male members of her temple – were not going to provide me with much information about her or their "cultural center." I sensed they had an inherent distrust of me, a self-protection, even though Mae and I had become friends. Jul might interpret their reluctance to share their stories with me differently, just as he thought that Sala was wrong in running as a candidate for her people rather than for all the people. The thing was, we could have these arguments and remain friends. He didn't hold my outspoken East Coast bluntness against me and I didn't expect him to agree with my view of the universe, which was I was sure as flawed as anyone else's.

I didn't tell Deanna and Emmett any of that, of course. I'd already decided I wanted them in our building.

I often spent the afternoon in Leif's refuge above the grime of the Lower Haight, listening to his sad or scandalous or sweet love stories and watching him create his various miracles out of the most basic materials: clay, driftwood, cloth and thread. One day he worked on his terra cotta sculptures, the next on a painting or his latest sewing project, a fake-fur coat with gold satin lining and bone buttons. He'd cut the material against its natural fall so the fur was punked out and the bone buttons echoed the colors in the fur, which reminded me of a wild animal's pelt, a perfect adornment for someone channeling Oscar Wilde.

Leif was a handsome man with a chiseled face and intense blue eyes. He wore his hair short like a Roman cap and shaved his sideburns to resemble a sideways V. He assembled his clothing with care, much of it homemade. Since I am a person who dedicates very little attention to my dress, he often fussed over my clothing, picking off stray hairs or sewing on a loose button.

In many ways, his lifestyle was rather precious, something from a bygone era. When he wasn't working on his own art, he studied art and history, numerology and the rotation of the planets. He read the dictionary and rented DVDs about royal families, going back to Cleopatra. He had an astounding memory and blended facts and conjecture, traditional beliefs and esoteric divinations in the most entertaining ways to come up with his own theories about the end days and the future of the human. Like Acacia, he, too, took in strays, pretty boys whose childhoods or education had left them bruised, even bewildered by the business of growing up, of caring for oneself, of staying healthy. They came in assorted colors. There was the young Mexican, probably illegal, who caught the measles shortly after coming under Leif's care. Of course, I was the one to diagnose the disease and to offer remedies. Another young man, a boy really, also illegal, had just been diagnosed HIV-positive; he thought his life was over. It was Leif who taught him how to negotiate the health system. When the boy ended up in jail – the story too convoluted to follow – it was Leif who visited and helped the fellow get into drug-treatment. All the while, Leif created his half-born gods and goddesses, often modeled after these gorgeous creatures he met at the clubs, the gym and the beach.

Leif was perpetually annoyed with his neighbors, the loud-mouthed vagrants who inhabited the public housing units down the street, many of whom were black. He sometimes made remarks that I'd consider racist and I'd get into a disagreement with him, urging that he not judge all by the actions of a few and reminding him of the prejudice that gay men like him have had to fight. He wasn't having any of it; he particularly disdained a scrawny woman who spent most afternoons across the street from his apartment, shouting and singing as her boom box blared out rap and hip-hop at decibels that must have violated some city ordinance. Leif and the woman had argued several times with the result that the woman's male friends had taken to sticking their penises in his mail slot and pissing in his entryway.

"Why don't you rig up the mail slot with an electric wire, like they use in an electric fence? I don't think it will do any real harm but that will put an end to the pissing," I suggested, teasing, then added what I really wanted to say. "On the other hand, maybe you should ignore it, not up the ante. You are outnumbered here on this street, you know. You could get hurt."

Leif had no intention of ignoring the problem. It wasn't right that his ability to work was being thwarted by people who hung out all day, shooting drugs or each other. He had a point, of course. Much of the behavior on that street was just plain obnoxious. Yet it pained me that his exposure to those marginalized by poverty, substandard housing and drugs had so poisoned his thinking, especially as a person channeling Oscar Wilde should have understood the damage marginalization could do.

Black flight can alter a city's character in ways that are incrementally damaging, seen for example in Leif's growing impatience with the violence and noise, the apparent waste of human life that he often witnessed on the streets beneath his comfort zone. Like the dreams of the counterculture, San Francisco once held great promise for African Americans but now the city was experiencing the fastest out-migration of blacks of any major city in the United States. Some city officials pointed out that many of those left behind were the '80s babies, born during the crack boom and nourished on the drug's culture of violence; they had basically raised themselves and now had few role models of how to make it out of the cycles of drug use, crime, gang warfare and poverty. I was the one arguing for pity, for compassion, but just a few blocks downhill, I didn't have to live with noise and crime every day, as Leif did. And, as with the homeless problem, I didn't see a solution.

When I voiced some of this, however, he educated me about my neighborhood, making it clear that these were not the neighborhood's darkest days, that indeed when he had moved there two decades ago, rescuing his flat from cockroaches and rats while negotiating a territory in which he was one of only a few white, gay men, muggings were a regular occurrence. He had a friend who'd turned a mugger's knife back on the mugger, then was sent to jail for manslaughter.

"I was a lamb to the slaughter when I first moved here, with no foreboding about what it might be like. I found out right away I was not welcomed, I was not respected," he said. "It was hell on earth for the first ten years. Now no young person disrespects me. You have to show people you won't take disrespect."

I had to accept that my morning entertainment was pretty much gone. Tom must have left the city, which was fine with me; I'd never liked his poor-me routine. But I did miss Ted's political quips and Jay's art by distraction. I suspected I'd see Jay again somewhere around the neighborhood; the streets were his supermarket, his art supply store. But, Ted? I was fairly sure we wouldn't see him again, that his health or living condition had changed, maybe for the worse. And I had to admit that morning coffee was not the same without a dose of Gnostic repartee.

Silent Guy, however, could be relied upon for a line or two.

"Have you been coming here during the rain?" I asked.

"Oh yeah. This awning's good cover," he said.

A long pause, then he said, "I guess we're going to war with Iran." In all our mornings together, Guy had never initiated a conversation involving politics or current events.

"I think it's just posturing," I said. "But it's like the bully in the schoolyard. Sooner or later, things escalate and someone gets hurt."

"That's why I stopped going to school."

I waited.

"There were some real bad bullies there."

I waited.

"Course, if I had some smokes or something to drink, they liked me fine."

I waited some more.

"But then they'd get mean again. Ain't no one meaner than a mean drunk."

Eventually, I told him I had been following Wisdom Man's debates with other visitors to Gnostic websites on the Internet.

"He got into some rather heady arguments with the other bloggers," I said. "I couldn't understand much of what they were arguing about. It was all so entirely over my head. And I'm a college professor."

How elitist that sounded. I tried to recover. "I mean, it's not that these sites are so intellectually challenging, they're just so ..." I was searching for the right word, one that would include Silent Guy. "Obscure" was what I came up with.

"Unfathomable," Guy said and smiled in a most forgiving way.

"Have you read his postings?"

"Oh yes. I look him up on the Internet, too."

I loved that. "Well, where do you think he is? Do you think he's moved? Could he be in jail or the hospital?" I asked. "They have Internet access in jail. I don't think he's off on one of his walkabouts in this weather."

"No, he's not in jail," Guy said with conviction. "I think he's hanging low because he ran out of money. I'll look for him at the library later."

Just then, almost as in the old days, Jay came sauntering down the street, carrying a piece of metal, a frond of leaves, a pencil and a ragged piece of paper.

"Another found poem?"

"No, no poem. It's from a kid's textbook on Washington Irving. Can you believe they're still teaching Washington Irving?" He smoothed the wrinkles on the page, an excerpt from Irving's *Sketch Book of Geoffrey Crayon, Gent.*

"I grew up in Washington Irving's home town, good old Sunnyside," Jay continued. "Sleepy Hollow was near our house. Some might call it a coincidence, but people are always placing useful or symbolic things in my path, pinwheels with prophetic words on them, for example, and other items of delight."

He blew his nose, went inside for a cup of coffee and joined us at the table. Without Wisdom Man there to monopolize the conversation, Jay talked without interruption, spilling out random bits of his life that kept coming back to his hometown, his family and, oddly, to protest songs. Listening to him was like following a record played at the wrong RPM. He was jeeped up on something.

"Have another coffee, Jay," I said and he chuckled as he told us he'd been practicing anti-war songs with the other regulars at the hash bar in the building on Market Street near where I lived.

"How do you get into this hash bar?" I asked. "I've been wondering that. Is it a legal hash bar? I mean legal here in San Francisco. Do you have to be invited or can you just go?"

"Semi-legal. You have to have a government-issued health card as a medical marijuana user or as a registered caregiver for someone with the diseases approved for medical marijuana," he said quite officiously.

"I've thought of doing that, registering," I said, "but I don't want the government having my name on their list."

"Oh, I know all about the government's lists," Jay said, grinning. "It's one of my areas of expertise. I also know about deceptive names for a deceptive government. I could give you one." He smiled sweetly. "Lots of people have invented names in the medical marijuana world. No one wants to be on the government's lists."

The conversation wound back to the war. "It all makes me so nostalgic for the SNCC singers and Pete Seeger," Jay said. "We're living in the time of hypnosis, actually the latest time of hypnosis."

His fixation with the protest music of the 1960s, he explained, was the result of another gift left for him on the streets of San Francisco a few weeks previously. He'd been walking one day shortly before his mother's seventieth birthday when he passed a box literally packed with vinyl records from that era, not just Pete Seeger but also Phil Ochs, Buffy St. Marie, Zager and Evans, Barry McGuire, each album a gem from a past era. Jay figured the albums were the universe's reminder to call his mother, who had dragged him to dozens of protests as a kid.

After he called her, a surprise as he didn't always remember to call on special days, Jay decided to really listen to the music, to study it for clues on surviving difficult times. "It was a revelation," Jay said. "I grew up on those songs. I want that hope back. It's what I'm doing with my life now so I don't feel like I'm wasting my time. I'm getting ready for the movement. I'm letting those songs fill me up with faith in the human spirit. A change will come when enough people are fed up. Are you fed up yet?"

"I've been fed up for a long time," I said.

"Well, join our group, both of you. I'm sure you already know the words."

"Will that get me into the hash bar without registering?" I asked. "Actually, you might regret inviting me. When I sing, people shout 'Sing solo' as in so low no one can hear. But I do know all the words. Guy, do you know the words?"

Then I remembered that Guy had been straight and sober for two years; he shouldn't be going into any hash bar. He didn't say no to Jay's offer, which probably wasn't an offer at all, just a way to make conversation. Guy said nothing; he just smiled and smoked his hand-rolled cigarettes. I probably wouldn't be going to the hash bar either but I needed that hope Jay was offering.

Meanwhile, of course, Jay had been fiddling with the detritus from his morning scavenging, arranging it one way, then another. The piece of metal was flat on the bottom but its sides formed a circular funnel on one end. Jay laid it down on the table and stuck the frond of leaves into the funnel hole, like a fountain pen in an ink well. Then he inserted the pencil into a groove in the front of the piece of metal, so it stuck out, making a pointer. He wrapped the story about Washington Irving around the pencil, tightly like a sleeve. Just then, the wind picked up, caught in the leaves and spun the whole contraption around like a pointer for a game.

"Well, I guess that means I'm on the path of righteousness," Jay said when it stopped, pointing at him. "As you can see, I've found my moral compass."

Thanks to Rebecca and Leif, I made friends with a cadre of other interesting people. There was Christopher, the lawyer and landscape artist whom Leif had celebrated with the sculpture he'd named Joie de Vivre. It took one evening to identify Christopher as a hedonist, a delightful hedonist who sucked the marrow of books and movies and educational TV, the UPS deliveryman, the oysters at the Anchor restaurant where they served the best seafood in San Francisco, all the while earning the designation Leif had bestowed. And Cevan, a landscape and mixed media artist whose gardens combined exotic plants with ancient Asian artifacts that he collected on forays into Myanmar, Thailand and Cambodia, bringing back also spices and recipes he culled from cooking classes he took while traveling. And Edith, an attorney who specialized in employment law and favored the underdog. She knew Paris, Shanghai, Los Angeles. She and her sister were the last of their line, Russian Jews whose parents' entire families had been killed by the Nazis. As a result, she adopted the adult children orphaned when their mother would not get sober or a client injured beyond healing. And Celestine, an African prince raised by French monks; his body when he danced was a delusion, no body is that lithe, that sensuous, that shy, but his was. And he could write. Celestine was a person whose story should be published.

Each of these new friends had a long history in San Francisco and shared their stories generously – not just their personal sagas, but also their versions of San Francisco over the last few decades, complete with observations of its challenges and rewards, rewards that Jul was hoping would broaden my appreciation of the city. And they did.

Edith took me to the ballet where invariably the one number I didn't appreciate would be the one the ballet aficionados adored. How I loved the outfits not just of the dancers but also the audience; for example, the middle-aged, Botoxed woman in leopard-skin jeans and baseball shirt sitting next to a woman in a floor-length purple gown designed by Ream Acra. How I loved sitting in the War Memorial Opera House, so stunning, surrounded by people who knew ballet – I didn't – and watching the magic of bodies, of youth, of choreography, then meandering to one of the small ethnic restaurants that Edith knew of to sample baba ghanoush at one, green curry at another, before walking home together in the cool night air.

Or the splendid, farcical traipse to the Palace of Fine Arts for a Lalique, Tiffany and Fabergé show with Leif and Christopher. We ogled the beauty that was both stunning and obscene, the goo-gahness of the jewels, diamond upon diamond in tiaras that Christopher and Leif appraised, rated, lusted after. This bling came in dog collars and eggs encrusted in precious gems, in sterling coffee services, necklaces, glassware, the capitalist vernacular of another age, the one called the Golden Age. You cannot think of the homeless and simultaneously examine the lavish ornamental eggs that Fabergé produced for Tsar Alexander III. And if I were to complain about the vulgarity of any of it, either Leif or Christopher would chastise me for my failure to appreciate the inherent beauty of the gems and the cleverness that the artist had brought to their use.

We sometimes escaped to Cevan's gardens where we sipped martinis infused with the citrus fruit I'd bought at the farmer's market years ago and not known what to do with; it's called Buddha's hand and it perfumed the vodka deliciously. We ate the Thai or Burmese food Cevan had learned to cook while collecting literally hundreds of Buddhas and Shivas that populated his hidden paradise outside the city. When we traveled there, we would climb from the car and step beyond the crenellated metal gates that separated his small property from his neighbors and immediately experience a magical geometry. The property was small but so cleverly designed that one could get lost within its curving gardens and small plantings of tall bamboo. Large-leaf Ligularia in ancient urns flanked two koi pools, each with floating lotus flowers, and troughs from China were filled with flowering ginger, all so exotic. One evening, Daniel nosed amongst the giant slabs of granite, stepped atop a lotus leaf and sank immediately into the koi pond, his long hair heavy with water, so heavy it would have been a very unhappy evening had I not been there to fish him out, then sit by the fire Cevan built in a giant brass kettle, sipping my martini with a rescued puppy in my lap.

And Rebecca? We often drove north to Sonoma where she took me to horse farms, artists' retreats and upscale wineries where everything from the wine to the furnishings was organic. Or we traipsed together through the Mission, gathering the makings for a feast, then worked together in her kitchen, fashioning empanadas, gordita, agua fresca and coconut flan to serve to our cadre of friends.

This was also my life in San Francisco, rich and privileged.

Ann was exceedingly clever at many things, one of which was making cutesy scrapbooks for brides, new parents and puppy owners. She had an arsenal of paper products in her apartment and supplied military personnel oversea, shut-ins in San Francisco and a constantly changing array of people celebrating precious moments of their lives with the proper materials. Often, when she had clients in her apartment, I would take Alexandra on an adventure. On one occasion, Alexandra was exceedingly happy when I announced we were going to Starbuck's for Madeleine cookies and a latte. It was dusk as we maneuvered down Octavia, balancing on one foot then the other through what was left of our sidewalk then skipping down Market Street, singing "Did you ever see a lassie go this way and that way" as we went this way and that. A blue tarp had been stretched along the fence surrounding the former Sue Mills uniform company on Market Street. The building was going to be torn down for a new apartment complex. Alexandra and I stopped to peek through a hole in the tarp, me squatting to her level to assess the progress. Then we skipped some more, Daniel prancing along on his little legs, keeping up with us as we went this way and that way. As ever, I looked for Ruth in the Duboce Alley; I looked for Hudson Bay Blanket Man at the Redemption Center. I looked for Stretch. My life felt so full, I wanted to share my surfeit with those whose lives seemed like ships upon the water, adrift, at nature's mercy.

Alexandra and I sat outside in a little grove of tables and chairs between Starbucks and Safeway. Alexandra was four years old then and full of questions as she dunked her cookie in milk and I drank my latte.

"Where's your daddy?" she asked.

"My daddy? What do you mean?"

"Chuck. Your daddy. Where's he at?"

"He's not my daddy," I laughed. "He's my husband. He's in Vermont."

"Where's Vermont?"

"Far away, all the way across the country."

"What does Daniel call him? If you're his Mommy, is Chuck his daddy?"

"Well, we're his human mommy and daddy. We're his owners. He has a real mommy and daddy, a girl and boy dog, but he doesn't live with them anymore."

"How come?"

"Well that's what happens when you get a dog, it leaves its mommy and daddy. Well, a lot of dogs don't ever get to know their daddies. They just know their mommies at first."

"Like me, I don't have a daddy."

"But you have a mommy."

A homeless man was scarfing a muffin at the table next to ours. I'd silently watched him salvage the muffin, a carton of chocolate milk and a Hershey's bar from the depths of the oversized parka he wore, its pockets perfect for purloining. He caught us staring and asked for a quarter. All I had were dollar bills so I told him no, I didn't have a quarter. Alexandra broke off little pieces of her cookie for Daniel and told me not to talk to strangers.

"He's dirty," she whispered.

When she needed more milk, I gave the change to the homeless man.

"Why'd you do that?" she asked.

"'Cuz he's not lucky like us to have a mommy and lots of friends and Daniel to play with."

"How come?"

"Now that, my dear, I don't know."

Every week or two Cevan, Leif, Rebecca, Edith, Christopher and I would organize a dinner party at one of our homes. At each outing, to this group were added others in their wider circle – Michael, an art gallery owner and collector with his own repertoire of extravagant gestures; Julia, epicurean chef and environmental scientist who brought her own lusty conquests to the table; Mayan and Annie, a lesbian couple who had lived in Israel and turned the simplest of culinary fare into art objects, and others of course, men and women with handsome faces and bodies and agreeable taste and talent.

One night Leif served us salmon roe on delicate wafers and sashimi in gorgeous carnival glass dishes shaped like conch shells, followed by the most perfectly poached salmon presented on a bed of risotto with creamed spinach on the side. Rebecca brought dessert, adorable mini-cupcakes and chocolate bonbons from the red café. There were martinis before dinner and pinot grigio with our meal and, of course, Leif's specialties were amply tasted.

On another evening, we feasted in Christopher's garden beneath his third-story apartment in the Castro. Roses and wisteria bloomed as we stuffed ourselves with homemade sausage rolls, bacon-wrapped figs, green beans with raspberries, a delicious salad with pistachio nuts, and cheesecake for dessert. Christopher and Leif were famous smashball players. They played at the gay beach in the Presidio, a former military base now part of the Golden Gate National Recreation Area. They played naked, of course. There they tormented or were tormented by the National Park employees who deigned to interrupt the casual shore-side trysts of the men who frequented the beach. They tormented or were tormented by the tour guides who brought their customers along to show them where the queers bathed in the nude. The beach had long been favored by gay men, long before it had become part of the national park system and thus its frequenters had a natural hostility toward the "watchers," as Leif called the people in uniform who stood above the beach surveying them. He could be confrontational. Most of the time, however, San Francisco and its traditions reigned and the men played their games and flirted and fucked without surveillance.

Because they played and frolicked with such enthusiasm and energy, Leif and Christopher could eat the kind of food that Christopher created, full-fat, decadent, delicious offerings; they kept their bodies trim and tanned in places I would never see. I would host my first dinner when Chuck arrived. I wanted these yummy boys to meet my best boyfriend. I'd show decadence a thing or two.

By the time Chuck and I had walked amongst the 1,525 pairs of black military boots, each pair representing a dead American soldier, and another hundred more everyday shoes of all sizes from kid to adult, representing the thousands of Iraqi dead, we were done in. The boots stretched across San Francisco's Civic Center Plaza. We were among the hundreds of people who had gathered there to see the exhibit, a symbolic protest against the war. As they do at the Vietnam War Memorial, people left notes, photos and flowers by various pairs of boots so that the exhibit engendered another exhibit, created by the viewers. The boots of the American dead were organized by states; we stopped longest at those representing the twelve Vermont dead, more per capita at that point than any other state.

So often I'd been in the plaza at an anti-war demonstration or some typical San Francisco celebration, the LoveFest or the LGBT Pride Parade. Even at an anti-war demonstration, something would make you smile – posters showing the entire no-carb quartet: "No Cheney, No Ashcroft, No Rice; and definitely No Bush," for example. But at the "Eyes Wide Open: The Human Cost of War" boot exhibit, organized by the American Friends, no one was smiling.

Richard Farina once wrote that the best thing a person could do after seeing something especially disturbing or after suffering a truly devastating experience was to curl up with the one you cherished, to damn the darkness with your lovemaking. And we tried.

We spent the rest of Chuck's time in San Francisco doing things that gave us comfort. We hiked along the Pescadero estuary and ate artichoke soup at Duarte's. We climbed the hills of San Francisco, exploring neighborhoods away from the homeless. The rains were biblical; the city's bookstores and museums and public library provided ample remedies. Schedules being schedules, we couldn't all get together for my big dinner until Chuck's last night in town: Organic rack of lamb with rosemary and garlic and braised root vegetables, coleslaw with pears and blue cheese dressing, popovers with homemade pepper jelly and a pear pie for dessert.

The night of the feast we were engaged in another biblical story, feeding the masses with a miraculous, never-ending bounty. We listened to Chris Botti play his magical trumpet and talked about our favorite books and movies. We told the funny stories about ourselves in the easy way that came of a full belly and good companionship.

Chuck was grilled, of course, about our bi-coastal life, my San Francisco friends curious to hear what he thought of my living so far away. Chuck said the right thing, endearing him to me and simultaneously to my new friends: "I learned a long time ago not to try to tell Yvonne what to do. We couldn't do this if we were thirty, but we have been together too long to let 3,000 miles get in our way. Besides, I like my time alone too. And thanks to her I get to come to San Francisco for a month twice a year and meet great people like you."

Leif took the last piece of pie home with him. The night was that good.

I avoided telling Ann that I was planning to take my sabbatical from the university in the fall semester, which would mean I'd stay in Vermont for seven months, rather than just the summer. I planned to schlep my new book on Vermont's literary history, finally published, around to bookstores and literary gatherings. And I'd begun writing a new book, the one I planned to call *Octavia Boulevard*. I was looking forward to culling through the notes and emails I'd written over the last few years to see if there actually was a book there.

"That's not fair," she said when I finally broke the news, and when I told Alexandra, she used the exact same words. But I was excited to spend the autumn in Vermont, to watch summer wane and experience autumn come on with its full-color palette spreading up the mountainsides then down through the valleys. I tried to assuage Ann with the news that she would be among the stars of my next book.

"Do I get a say in who plays me in the movie?" she asked, fast-forwarding to a future as unlikely as world peace. But later when the subject of my departure came up again, she said, "Still not fair. What gives you the right to write about Octavia Boulevard when you get to avoid the mess for the next seven months?"

True. I had wandered down Hayes Street and seen the next stage in the roadwork. From Hayes to Lily, the sidewalks had been jackhammered away for the construction of new, narrower sidewalks. Asphalt was coming, too, and tar – all those obnoxious smells. With luck, the street would be done when I returned.

PART FOUR
2006 - 2007

The moral of the story
The moral of this song
Is simply that one should never be
Where one does not belong
So when you see your neighbor carryin' somethin',
Help him with his load,
And don't go mistaking Paradise
For that home across the road
        Bob Dylan, "The Ballad of Frankie Lee and Judas Priest"

The summer unfolded with the usual routines of children and grandchildren, the budding of gardens, writing assignments and book readings. Emails and phone calls kept me current on dramas inside and outside of the building. That was how I learned that through Jul's efforts Lance had returned east to his parents' care. The details remained vague, but apparently the scene with the PG&E man had figured prominently. I knew that Mary and Jul had truly cared for the man; to the end, they remained sympathetic to his condition. I was glad their efforts had paid off.

About the same time, Glenn wrote to say that he wasn't waiting for the construction to end; he'd be moving to Florida before I returned. Jul had managed to get Acacia out of Robin's old apartment, although where she had gone, no one seemed to know. Jul also sent news that a couple of lawyers had bought the building next door and were clearing it out. I wondered about the Pole and his family. What would become of them? All these changes were upsetting in an odd way. The building and neighborhood would be quite different when I returned.

But, later that summer, an email arrived that sent me *and* Chuck back to San Francisco sooner than I had planned. During the previous school year, I'd met Debi, the owner of two chubby Maltese dogs named Shaylynn and Zoe. Debi had wanted Daniel to mate with her dogs, but he was rather young and not very proficient in the mating business. Lo and behold, she called in early summer to say both dogs were pregnant and, per our agreement, we could have the pick of the litter – a wonderful birthday present for Chuck. As it turned out, it was a blessing that we traveled to San Francisco in August, using the occasion to check on the apartment between sub-leasers. I'd found over the years that law students made great tenants, too busy to party or make a mess, but unfortunately the couple I'd rented to that summer had left our apartment fairly trashed. I had a new tenant arriving in a week and Chuck and I used the opportunity to clean the apartment before his arrival.

The puppy arrived wearing a blue ribbon in his hair, a white puffball as adorable as my own sweet Danny Boy had been when I first rescued him from a penthouse apartment. In between cleaning the apartment and visiting our West Coast friends, we played with the puppy. Chuck named him Augustus, but it quickly morphed to Gus, Gussie and other nicknames. "Come here you little wind-up toy. Come here, you little Turkish taffy," we'd take turns saying and Gus would twirl around, showing he had inherited Daniel's ability to do the twirly-girlie.

Here's Gus in my arms with Daniel in front of the Greenwich steps. We posed at their base where someone had painted this mural in a little trough where only "teacup poodles" were allowed to take a drink. Daniel and Gus were close enough.

At the Laguna Sidewalk Café, Silent Guy reported that Wisdom Man had to give up his apartment and now rented a small room in the mauve building.

"It's a come-down but he still stops by on Saturday morning," Silent Guy said, "He doesn't drink coffee any more either, just water. You'll see, but get here early. He leaves for the Zen center around 8:30. "

"Hallelujah, the dogs multiplied," Wisdom Man shouted as we rounded the corner. "A miracle, from the Latin *miraculum*, 'object of wonder.' I didn't think Daniel had it in him."

It was true. Wisdom Man was drinking water from a clear glass. He was very thin. His blond hair, always trimmed in what I thought of as his choirboy haircut, now brushed his collar, but his clothing was neat and clean as ever. He sipped his water and said little after the exuberant welcome.

"You gave up coffee?" I asked, breaking the awkward silence.

"Had to. Couldn't afford it," he said candidly.

"But you still live across the street? That's good."

"No, I don't live there any more. Haven't in months. I live in a shelter now," he said, and then added matter-of-factly, "It's not so bad."

"You're shitting me," I said without thinking. Wisdom Man in a homeless shelter? That was inconceivable. "Where's your stuff, your Austrian hunting jacket, your books? How do you meet with your students?"

"My material possessions are in storage," he said. "I find almost everything I need in the library. My students and I still communicate on our network. We're not dependent on me being in any one place. You understand that by now, I would hope."

A nice dig. He spoke with dispassion as if he were telling us he'd moved a piece of furniture from one side of the room to the other. "Really, it's fine," he said, finally turning to me. "I'm having a temporary cash crunch. I've planted the orchard but the fruit hasn't ripened yet." That goddamn orchard again.

We all sat speechless as each of us registered the news that Wisdom Man's problems were greater than being able to afford a cup of coffee. Why had he told Guy he was renting a room in the mauve building and then told the truth upon our arrival? But as was routine, rather than explain what had happened, how he'd become homeless or how he was managing, Wisdom Man launched into one of his seminars.

"We were on the network the other day and one of our members said the ivory tower approach to knowledge places too much emphasis on theory rather than providing students with a solidly pragmatic preparation for life. I thought of you, Yvonne; I think you'd agree."

It was then that I understood what he had been saying all those years. His network was simply the intersecting conversations he had both inside his head and all over the city, in a shelter packed to capacity with men and women who had no home of their own or there outside a café where Elise was giving and taking attitude. I wanted to offer him something. I wanted to say, "You could use a solid and pragmatic preparation for life," but I didn't. Was that why he had been disappearing off and on over the past year? Why he'd become so testy? Had he been on the road to homelessness all those years and I'd not seen it?

"I wonder why he told you one story, then told us another, this one ostensibly the truthful one," I thought out loud after Wisdom Man left for the Zen center.

"Beats me," Guy said.

"Because he knows you're writing a story and he's part of it," Chuck said.

Silent Guy rolled a cigarette. He scraped his chair across the cement. He cleared his throat. Finally, he pulled a small notebook from his pocket.

"I've been writing too," he said. "I guess they're poems, what I've been writing,"

Here is the one I showed to Chuck, the one Silent Guy game me for a present. I asked him to make me a copy so he could have the original in his worn notebook:

Sitting on a corner
Cars go by
People too
Time moves in coffee cups, in cigarette ashes.

Mature date palms, their long fronds bundled and tied with cordage like huge green ponytails, had been installed at the intersection of Octavia and Market, marking the entrance to the new boulevard, a welcome home to San Francisco, January 2007. The palm trees, costing thousands when purchased full-grown, were left tied up until they had established their roots. Otherwise, a strong wind might blow them over. I considered it another example of over-indulgence: thousand-dollar palm trees while people slept on nearby streets.

Beyond the grove of date palms, two hundred and sixty-one trees, Lombardy poplars, evergreen elms, flowering cherries and pears, lined the boulevard. At twelve locations all along Octavia, the city had actually installed the kaleidoscopes it had promised on its website all those years ago. The artist Wang Po Shu had designed the scopes, entitled "Ghinlon/Transcope." Each was comprised of different combinations of mirror lenses, providing ever-changing views of our small universe. There were two at each corner, one at adult eye level and one lower, for children and persons in wheelchairs. And, to make the experience more diverting, poems had been inscribed on each scopes' column. One near my building read:

> Good morning traffic
> I have come to witness the congestion of my mind
> Stumbling in this jumbled spectrum of a rainbow
> Resonating all through my molecular being
> I am only my holographic self
> Mirrored into existence

John King, writing in the *San Francisco Chronicle*, described the boulevard thus: "Drivers heading north or west descend from the freeway at Market Street and are greeted by the most attractive entrance into the city after the Golden Gate Bridge: a boulevard with poplar trees in the middle and Chinese elms on each side of the four-lane thoroughfare between faux historic lampposts. Most freeway exits drop you into a mess. With this one, you feel you've arrived."

My decision to explore the street was immediately rewarded as I heard, "Hey, stranger," the corollary to Robin's "Hey, stuck-up," and turned to see Jack coming from the Baptist Church parking lot. After we shared the pleasure of the boulevard's completion, I asked about Stretch. "Same old, same old," he said. "No predicting that boy."

Days later, I was walking with Daniel and there he was, assembling himself on the sidewalk. As usual, Stretch had a story to share, a story of victimization that I wasn't sure whether to believe. He said he'd been living in a single residence hotel again but that someone had broken into his room, stolen his ID, his social security card and cashed his SSDI check. He said the thief bought a ton of meth with his money. Social Security was trying to get his money back but, meanwhile, he was broke and back on the street. Could I spare two dollars? Always two dollars. I didn't regret giving him a few bucks, but I was uncomfortable with the story. It seemed rather convenient that he'd been ripped off just as I returned to the neighborhood. Still, I gave him five.

Noel's apartment had been rented and Jul was busy working on Glenn's as well. When I stood on the threshold to peer into Robin's old place, I could see smears of black, red and purple paint on the walls, the floor warped from the koi pond. "I'm not sure what to do with it," Jul said, explaining why he hadn't renovated it. He offered it to me again, making me wonder why he was anxious to move me.

I feared Ann had grown weary of my arrivals and departures but my first night back she took me to the new Thai Restaurant on Guerrero – our old favorite had been turned into yet another wine bar – and we slipped seamlessly into our friendship. Alexandra was growing up; she could ride a bike and read simple words. She shouted them out as we walked down Market Street to home: Stop. Pizza. Tattoo. Gold Teeth.

Within weeks of the boulevard's completion, journalists, Realtors and property owners were referring to the neighborhood as the new Soho and using words like hip and diverse to describe it. The closer you got to Hayes Street, the center of Hayes Valley, the more ridiculous were the prognostications about the neighborhood's future. Eclectic art galleries and designer stores emerged overnight. It was certainly more pleasant to walk along the boulevard, even with the increased traffic, than it had been before the construction. Homeowners and apartment dwellers cleaned, painted and repaired their buildings while city employees tended the new park created where Octavia T'ed into Hayes Street.

The homeless moved in to the park overnight, sleeping on its new benches while we ate croissants at LaBoulange, the tony new cafe across the way. There was an installation of homeless people on Lily, near the Blue Bottle Café where they made the coffee cup by cup in a renovated garage. A grizzle-haired fellow slept in a bedroll of rags there, while the young and upcoming drank their cappuccinos.

Stencil on the Corner of Oak and Octavia

I began to think of message stenciled on the corner of Oak and Octavia, "Crying is Okay Here," and the street itself as a symbol of the inherent conundrum living in San Francisco presented. The more the city gussied itself up, the greater would be the need for people who would prepare and serve our food, repair our roads, clean our offices, haul away our trash. But where were those people going to live? Where would the artists and dancers and musicians and others who lived from hand to mouth reside? And my students, where would they find shelter? Or the families, already disappearing from the city, families with children, where would they reside? Statistics from the mayor's office from 2006 showed that one in every 268 residents was homeless; that figure included only those people the city found actually living on the streets, not those without permanent homes who were living in shelters, cars, transitional housing, treatment and stabilization centers, jails and hospitals. When these were included, estimates were that one in every 117 people living in San Francisco had no home. Wisdom Man was among them now.

During the intervening months, Leif and the "skanky bitch" had continued their battle. I heard the latest chapter the day I climbed Leif's narrow, driftwood-lined staircase to enter the sanctuary of his apartment, so happy to find it still there, to find him still there. I worried about his health. In the months I'd been in Vermont, more people I knew and loved had died. The deaths seemed to fall upon me, one after another, inevitable, I knew. With the help of Willie and Chuck, I had come to accept the reality of death, to accept that because I was rich in family and friends, rich beyond measure, I would experience many such losses in my life, until I too no longer lived.

I wasn't pleased when he told me the latest version of his battle with his neighbors. After listening to the yelling and the constant throb of the woman's boom box and cleaning up the piss on his doorstep, of closing the portieres on his window to block the incessant cursing and shouting from the woman and her jeeped-up friends, he had stormed downstairs to confront her, only to find the boom box blaring on the sidewalk and no one around. Without hesitation, Leif picked it up, held it over his head and dropped it, smashing it onto the sidewalk. The next time the woman saw him, she screeched to her girfriends, "That's him! That's the homo who broke my boom box. There he is," whereupon two of them took off after Leif with the skanky woman leading the way.

As he ran ahead of the rabble, the woman hit him over the head with a board. Fortunately, Walgreen's had a fulltime security guard on duty. Leif's assaulters backed off when he ducked inside. His assailants were dense enough to wait outside until the cops arrived to take Leif's complaint.

"You can't arrest me unless you arrest that homo," the skanky bitch screamed. "That boom box cost $250 and he smashed it to smithereens." Leif admitted to breaking the woman's "ghetto blaster," but said he had found it abandoned on the sidewalk, set at top volume.

The responding cop was ready to walk away, but Leif insisted that the woman should be arrested for assault and when the officer searched her, he found a small amount of crack cocaine. Off to jail she went.

"Are you crazy?" I asked. He was gleeful with the account. He'd shown them. "Of course, I'm crazy," Leif said. "I live in San Francisco. But I'm not vengeful. After she'd been in jail for two months, I got a call to come to a hearing on the assault charges. I thought, two months, that's long enough and I declined pressing charges. There's been a very quiet détente between her and me since they let her out of jail. She knows I could have kept her in there. I've weighed this out and I've decided I'm going to defend the quiet enjoyment of my home."

Then he told me about his other acts of guerilla welfare. His targets were two other neighborhood women. He called one the crack-selling grandma; she sold her wares from a wheelchair she often parked under his windows. He called the other one the screamer. "She'll be out there in the middle of the night, screeching nonstop for hours," he said. Leif would climb to the roof of his building and throw water balloons at the women. "Sometimes I hurl plates. I buy them cheap at sidewalk sales. The plates really shut them up." He chuckled with the image of himself hurling plates from the roof of his building.

"You are really asking for it," I said.

"No, you don't understand. This is how I know you're not actually a city person. The crack-selling grandma and the screamer? They are always so nice to me when they see me on the street," he said. "The screamer always smiles and says, 'Aren't you a ray of sunshine,' when she sees me. And the crack grandma, she tells everyone I'm okay, to just leave me alone."

"You think they know you're the one throwing the water balloons and plates?"

"Of course they do. But they're crazy. You can't wimp out around people like that. You have to show them you're just as crazy as they are or they don't take you seriously. Oh," and here the look of delight in his eyes suggested he really was nuts, "I scream right back at them. I toss those water balloons and plates. I yell, 'Shut up, you old coot. Shut your fucking mouth.' And they see me on the street and they smile and say, 'You're a ray of sunshine in my world.'"

Absolutely nothing can be counted on. Without warning, Elise quit her job at the Laguna Sidewalk Café, leaving the coffee making to several unfriendly Arabs. It about broke my heart. No warning, just a barked, "Coffee? How you want it?" She had taken a "real job" as personal assistant to an upscale real estate agent. Alas, there went the free refills for regulars. There went the New York sarcasm with the latte. There went the Wall of Shame.

The lawyers who purchased the building next door bought out all the tenants they'd inherited except for the Polish family, at least that was the story on the street. Speculation was, they were holding out for a big settlement. The lawyers were planning to convert the building into what is called a tenancy-in-common building, in and of itself a complicated process. TICs were the latest arrangement devised to help people own residential property in San Francisco. In a TIC building, each apartment or flat was sold individually. The arrangement served two purposes: it allowed a property owner to make more money from his property than he would selling the building outright; and it provided renters a way to purchase property, usually at much less than they would have to pay for a condominium or house. TICs were particularly successful for conversions of three or four-apartment complexes. Long-term renters who knew one another and got along could pool their resources and become property owners, sharing expenses and upkeep.

Advocates for renters and some city officials, however, viewed the TIC process as a tactical move aimed at circumventing the city's efforts to stem the loss of rental properties by limiting the number of rental properties converted into condominiums, at that time set at no more than two hundred a year. The need to preserve rentals was especially important in San Francisco where two-thirds of the residents were renters. And while those TICs had indeed helped many people buy a home in San Francisco, tenant advocates argued that the loss of these rental units inevitably led to even higher rents and would ultimately turn the city into a place of upper middleclass and wealthy homeowners and rather poor renters, the latter holding on to rent-control apartments or delegated to subsidized and often substandard housing. The figures said it all: As a result of TICs and other creative forms of financing, San Francisco lost more than 18,000 rental units between 2000 and 2006. At the same time, of the roughly 14,000 new units built in the city, nearly 12,600 were condominiums, many selling above $600,000.

California had passed a law called the Ellis Act in 1986 to address this complex problem. It established rules under which a building owner could remove tenants from a building, in part to prevent them from doing so simply to charge the next renter more money. The act also established rules under which a landlord would be required to compensate a tenant forced to move through no fault of his own. Owners who removed tenants for major changes such as TICing a building or converting it, say, into retail space, were required to compensate renters between $4500 and $7500 each, depending on the tenant's age and ability. The elderly and people with handicaps got the extra $3,000, a situation that could easily be abused. With my letter from Willie, even I qualified for the extra money.

However, it was not uncommon for property owners to pay a tenant more than the prescribed $4,500 to $7,500 to avoid the long and costly process of court action that often ensued when, for example, tenants refused to move. The legal process might take months or even years, costing far more than $7,500. Indeed, a healthy cadre of attorneys had made gobs of money representing tenants fighting property owners and Ellis Act evictions.

As with many of these TICs, the new owners of the building next door planned to fix and sell one apartment at a time. It was hard to imagine how the building could be saved given its deteriorated state and the amount of time it would take to restore it. But Jul said money could do most anything. He was intrigued with the process and pleased, as improvements to the adjacent building would only increase the value of his. And, with the street work completed, he began restoring the exterior of our building, as well.

It was the afternoon that I first visited Christopher in his garden apartment in the Castro that I realized how much I missed a garden. People who do not grow things may not understand how gardening maintains mental health. Simple tasks, planting, weeding, watching things grow, these restorative acts take little mental energy while allowing the brain to work out dilemmas, to practice conversations, to take part in the diurnal cycles of life and death. Writer Harriet Doerr once told me, "I do my best writing with the sun and plants."

Christopher understood that. He had invited Leif, Edith and me over for lunch in his garden. It was late February and already his roses were delirious in color and scent; he had riotous bushes of orange-yellow calceolaria, salvias blooming purple-blue, scarlet and chartreuse, poppies in bud. Christopher worked as an attorney only when absolutely desperate for money; his avocation was landscape gardening and he had a small clientele who paid him enough to support his own lust for growing things, along with his other hedonistic pleasures, which roughly coincided with mine: food, drink, theater, music, politics and books. When I first met him at Leif's, I knew we would be friends as we immediately launched into a deconstruction of Roth's *The Human Stain*. Back then he was in a relationship, which had recently ended. He was having the luncheon in part to pull himself out of his doldrums, to get beyond the misery of not having someone equally delicious to share his garden with. Besides the roses and the calceolaria, his plot was chock full with cymbidium orchids, dozens of sedum varieties, clematis, agapanthus and other species into which he'd tucked a couple of chairs and a coffee table. We drank wine and ate tea sandwiches and arugula salad before attacking the most decadent desserts I'd ever not made myself, a medley of delicacies loaded with chocolate and cream and butter and calories that Edith had purchased at a French bakery. As I sat surrounded by the spicy and sweet scents coming from all sides, I wished my Octavia building included a spot of soil for planting.

"I need a garden," I whined to Christopher as we sipped espresso and munched crème de pirouline, reminding myself of how I'd whined to Ann about needing a dog. Leif was having a side conversation with Edith, describing his theories on global warming, the Egyptians and Oscar Wilde.

"You should have a garden," Christopher agreed, eerily reinforcing the memory. Daniel tunneled through the undergrowth, sending waves of pungency and perfume our way as we sipped our espressos and held the crispy, rolled piroulines with their bittersweet chocolate tips like cigarettes.

"These piroulines are remedy for a broken heart," I said to Christopher, who had slipped back into his gloom. He moped. He repeated the story of Jim's inconsideration. He ate a pirouline.

"It's better to end it now rather than after you've invested years and years into the relationship," Edith said, always the realist.

"He wasn't worth the anguish," Leif offered dismissively. He'd never liked Jim. "He wasn't worthy of this much effort. Do you think he's thinking about you right now?" His words were cruel but his point rang true. Christopher didn't want to hear it. Why wouldn't Jim even tell him what went wrong?

"If a person won't talk about problems early in the relationship, there's no future there," I said, adding my two cents worth.

Simon and Garfunkel's song, "So long, Frank Lloyd Wright," played languidly somewhere in the neighborhood:

> So long, Frank Lloyd Wright,
> I can't believe your song is gone so soon.
> I barely learned the tune.
> So soon. So soon.

It seemed a particularly unfortunate intrusion into our garden reverie, certainly not a remedy for a broken heart.

> All of the nights we'd harmonize 'till dawn,
> I never laughed so long
> So long. So long.

"Hey," I said, "let's do the heart-repair calculation." I was winging it. "Okay," I said, "count the number of weeks you knew Jim before the relationship turned romantic. Divide that by two. Got that? Then count the number of weeks you were romantically involved. Add the two together. Then, count the number of days per week you saw Jim during the romance and divide that by two. Then multiply the two sums together; that's how long it will take."

By then, we were all laughing, the calculation so convoluted no one could keep track.

"Oh, I won't survive," Christopher said, and opened a fresh bottle of wine.

$

A team of laborers attacked the structure next door, uncovering the original tin wainscoting and fireplaces inside, painting each flat in sunny colors. Decorators outfitted each in uber-Pottery Barn hominess, while restoration painters dressed the building's exterior in complimentary shades of tan, burnt umber, ochre and plum, complete with gilded moldings and cornices. Rebecca called it a painted pig; we knew what lay under all that paint.

Advertised as a "trophy building on tree-lined Octavia Boulevard," its two- and three-bedroom units went on the market for between $650,000 and $889,000. When I had snooped around the building last year, entering through the unlocked front door and sticking my nose in a vacated flat, I'd noted the stained ceilings and broken plaster, the husks of dead flies, mouse and pigeon droppings everywhere. During the building's open house for prospective TIC owners, what I saw seemed impossible, the kitchen, for example, now outfitted with granite countertops, Jenn-Air dishwasher and Viking stove. I wanted to hate what had been done out of some sort of solidarity with the people who had lived there and the family holding out downstairs.

The whole idea of a TIC seemed ridiculous to me, paying $889,000 for five or even six rooms in a 100-year-old building owned in common with a bunch of other people. In a TIC, individual buyers or "tenants" purchase shares of a building under a single deed; they don't technically own their own flat or apartment. Yet, up and down Octavia and throughout the neighborhood, those with the means were getting theirs while those without were moving elsewhere, many involuntarily. On Waller, not far from Stretch's alcove, the top floor in a Tudor that had been converted into three condominiums was selling for about $1 million even though the large lot between it and the LGBT would be a construction site for the next few years. Two streets over, a handicapped guy in a wheelchair and his aide, along with their Maltese dog, Star, were fighting an Ellis Act eviction. He'd lived in the apartment seventeen years. The owner wanted to convert the building into four TIC units. The new Soho.

The Baptist Church hosted weekly meetings for city officials to give their PowerPoint presentations, detailing future construction projects, plans for the use of empty lots and ideas for art installations in the Hayes Green. The residents, however, had other issues on their minds – the nightly car break-ins, the occasional muggings and shootings. As those of us living in the neighborhood had discovered, you could put up all the artsy kaleidoscopes in the universe, but if you didn't address the disparity between the haves and the have-nots, which was manifesting itself in living color there in our neighborhood, you would reap the results.

When I ran into Stretch after weeks of not seeing him, he said a new resident on Waller, perhaps the owner of the million-dollar condo, had repeatedly complained about him sleeping on the sidewalk across the way. After he'd been hassled awake by the police five nights in a row, Stretch had found a new place to live and it wasn't in an SRO. For whatever reason – there was a new one every day – he was back on the street to stay, but his new abode was closer to downtown, in an area far sketchier than our neighborhood.

"He'll be back," Jack said as he painted over the graffiti that had been scrawled across the church overnight, "He always comes back."

"I don't think so, Jack," I said. "Not this time."

The bullhorn blasted and we fell to the ground, 30,000 strong, young, old, a rainbow coalition dropping like stones onto the street in a symbolic die-in to protest again, again, the war, to protest the thousands, hundreds of thousands maybe, of Iraqis killed since the Bush/Cheney war began in 2003. Christopher was actually grinning from where he lay on Market Street, right in front of Octavia Boulevard. The die-in had blocked traffic on either side of Market and the blaring of car horns and shouts of the addled drivers only added to the bullhorn's blast while the crowd lay silent where each person had fallen.

"It's a die-in; you're not supposed to be grinning," I stage-whispered.

"Can't help it; it's my first die-in," Christopher said and grinned some more.

Later at Dolores Park, we listened to Dennis Banks, the American Indian Movement leader, congratulate the many young people in the crowd, but I saw mostly white and gray heads, the Raging Grannies, the Gray Panthers, old Socialists, Code Pink mothers, labor activist geezers. Then I spied my student Lauren in a crowd of students from SF State.

"Hey, you radical, you," I shouted, and she grinned almost as broadly as Christopher who had forgotten about his broken heart at least for the moment.

$

That fusty gray was gone and our building now wore celery green with raspberry trim and a generous dollop of gilding on the drip moldings. Jul then turned his attention to the interior, pulling up the old carpeting upon which the street construction had left indelible evidence, and installing oak floors in the halls. He refurbished the old wooden stairway, itself now quite beautiful. He had contracted a bonded painter for the exterior work but chose to hire someone else for the interior painting, which was rather basic. The man's name was Reuben, a Salvadorian. Reuben showed up early every morning with his crew of handsome fellows who filled the halls with Latin music and quickly covered the grime of ages with a fine shade of green picked out by Rebecca, whom the whole world should consult on such matters.

One afternoon returning from work, I walked in to the building to find Reuben lying on the floor while Mary and the paint crew rushed about with rags and buckets of water, cleaning spilled paint that had splashed all over the new floor as well as the recently sanded stairs. Jul directed them from splatter to splatter then rushed to Reuben's side, urging him to lie still before returning to marshal the forces in the clean-up. Mary explained that Reuben had been painting on the second floor landing when he fell backwards off a ladder and down the stairs. "Just lie there a few more minutes. Don't move," Jul told Reuben every few minutes while pointing out the scattered splats of paint.

Eventually Reuben got to his feet and eventually Jul drove him to the hospital, where they found him to be bruised but not seriously injured. Hours later, however, Reuben was at Jul's door. His family was outraged. They told Rueben that Jul should have called an ambulance right away, rather than worry about the spilled paint. They thought Reuben should sue.

Jul was practically apoplectic. "I offered to take Reuben into my home where Mary and I could care for him until he got better. I said we would wait on him hand and foot. He could have the upstairs room where we have the flat-screen TV. He wouldn't have any of it. What more can I do?" Jul asked, scratching the hair on his arms nervously, pacing. "And now he's going to sue me."

"What you should have done was attend to him first and worried about the splattered paint later," I said. "Did he actually say he was going to sue or that his family thought he *should* sue? He was probably hoping you'd give him some money to keep from suing, you know, like the dentist from Mendocino."

"Giving him money would be admitting culpability. This isn't the same as that rotten deck you fell through. This was Reuben's fault. He didn't set the ladder up right. We knew he wasn't hurt. But his family will make him sue. I can just feel it."

I was convinced there would be no suit, and said so again. A suit would only bring scrutiny upon Reuben, his business and his employees, who may not all have been legal. No matter my assurances or anyone else's, Jul was unable to deal with the situation unemotionally, which is why I designated the day Reuben fell from the ladder as the moment when my venture on Octavia Boulevard was destined to end.

The 11 o'clock Mass was beginning as I walked by the Mission Dolores to Dolores Park for the Sisters of Perpetual Indulgence's annual Easter egg hunt. I had been contemplating going to their annual Easter party when Leif showed me the material he'd used to sew a costume for one of the sisters. It was a rabbit costume with ostrich feathers inside giant fuzzy pink ears. Leif had created the bunny outfit from layers of pink tulle and distressed satin, generously sequined and trimmed with fur, pink of course. We were at a dinner party at Christopher's on Good Friday when Leif brought out the samples and described how he had designed the ears to stand three feet high.

The Sisters of Perpetual Indulgence are not a recognized religious order, of course, but rather an association of social activists who dress as nuns while proclaiming the joy inherent in everlasting tolerance. If the Pope can grant perpetual indulgences, a kind of get-out-of-jail-free card for sinners who repent, the Sisters of Perpetual Indulgence reasoned that they should grant eternal joy to those who practice self-gratification and perform corporal works of mercy. The group is one of the last bastions of street theater in which drag queens, transgendered people, transvestites and anyone else who enjoyed dressing up wandered the streets of San Francisco in inventive attires, the years of the Cockettes and the Angels of Light, far more outrageous than the current gay scene.

The Sisters trace their beginning to an Easter Sunday in 1979 when three gay men donned full, traditional nuns' habits and strolled through the city and down to the nude beach, fluttering false eyelashes all the way. Perhaps they were responding to what was then called the Gay Clone movement, in which hyper-masculinity – tight jeans and shirts to show off pectorals and penises à la the construction worker in The Village People – had become so fashionable that the queens and fem-dragsters were feeling outnumbered. Or, as likely, these men dressed like nuns to simply protest the Catholic Church's position on homosexuality.

Soon the three "nuns" in drag grew to a half dozen, then a dozen. They next showed up in 1980 at a Three Mile Island protest. Then they began running bingo games, holiday galas and street races around San Francisco to raise money for non-profit groups that promoted tolerance and HIV prevention. One of their first fundraisers was a baseball game for gay refugees from Cuba. By 2007, the Sisters of Perpetual Indulgence numbered roughly seventy members of all genders and orientations with "orders" around the world. They've taken names like Sister Anal Receptive, Sister Ann R Key, Sister Anni Coque L'doo and Sister Constant Craving of the Holey Desire. Of course, the Catholic Church disavows them.

Two Members of the Sisters of Perpetual Indulgence

One Sister Models Her Outfit While Another Knits

The Sisters modeled their habits after the wimple or headdress worn in the fourteenth century by Flemish ladies-in-waiting and cloistered nuns, complete with oddly shaped bulges above the ears, which the Sisters of Perpetual Indulgence called ear brassieres, as in hear no evil.

My plan for the day had been to simply check out their Easter egg hunt then head to the Mission Dolores for the noon Mass in Spanish, but while watching the Sisters cavort with the neighborhood children, I heard there would be a lusty band of strumpets entertaining in the afternoon, along with a hunky Jesus competition. That sounded like something I should not miss.

By 11 a.m., the park was full of men in togas, chaps, sequined gowns, and a mixed bag of homemade Easter bonnets. One bonnet featured a ski slope with marshmallow peeps shushing down the hill; another was a six-layer cake complete with birthday candles. There were women decked out like Roller Derby babes, women in prison stripes, in sailor-girl get-ups, in push-up bras and little else. The weird thing was that the children looked like normal, all-American kids, especially the girls, many of whom wore frilly Easter dresses, white stockings trimmed with lace, and black patent leather shoes. I watched one mother and her curly-haired beauty, maybe four, interact with one of the Sisters. The girl wore layers of stiff crinoline and pink barrettes in her hair. She snuggled against her mother who was holding her up so she could get a good look at the nun's face and headdress, a black voile veil with elaborate ear brassieres. The nun wore a low-cut peasant blouse that showed ample chest hairs, a black cummerbund, an elaborate cross hanging mid-chest and a long, flowing purple skirt, almost as frilly as the little girl's.

"What's that?" the little girl whispered, pointing shyly to a thorn that looked as if it were about to burst from the nun's forehead. "Oh, it's just a little thorn," the Sister said in a most saccharine voice. "It's just a little decoration, sweetheart." Sister ever so gently touched the rather large thorn glued to her forehead. She fluttered her eyelashes deliciously. The girl curled closer into her mother's bosom.

Nearby, another Sister was running the bowling contest in which the kids had to knock over three-foot-tall, blow-up bunnies with a big beach ball. You would be hard-pressed to miss the giant rabbits, which was precisely the point. This nun's habit immediately threw me back to girls' Catholic school and Sister Mary Thumbtack, the name I called the nuns in grammar school because I couldn't tell them apart. The bowling sister even wore the classic white wimple. It was creased and folded elaborately and pressed against the sides of her cheeks so tightly that she could say "Funny bunny" funny without anyone having to pinch her cheeks together; they were compressed like an MP3 file and her high-pitched voice dripped with sugar as she helped with the ball rolling.

A few feet away, another nun, trim red mustache and beard resting upon a bib literally slathered in holy medals, was running the spoon and egg contest. The kids just took the nuns in stride, along with bearded men in red lamé dresses and stiletto heels and two beautiful women emerging from Easter baskets, one all in pink, the other in blue, from the tips of their feet to their Dolly Parton hair. I hung around until it was time to go to Mass, wondering what that would be like after viewing such sacrilege.

Mass was held in the beautiful basilica next to the original Mission Dolores, the oldest surviving structure in the city of San Francisco and the sixth religious settlement established by the Spaniards in America as part of their chain of missions. I grew up during the silent Mass era when the only voices you heard were those of the priest and the choir, none of this "Peace be with you" hand shaking and hugging that goes on at Mass today.

There are three kinds of Catholics: regular Mass celebrants; wedding and funeral Mass-goers, and Christmas and Easter Catholics. I am an Easter Mass girl. That is because the crucified Jesus is traditionally swathed in cloth during Lent; in the church where I worshipped as a child, the covering was left on until after Easter to signify that He has risen. I was always so relieved not to have to look at Jesus with his wounds, the nails through his palms and feet, the wound in his side, the crown of thorns upon his head, that the only Mass I went to voluntarily was on Easter Sunday. My parents thought I was being dramatic with my terror of the crucifix, but think about seeing that as a child, the rail thin body stripped almost naked, the wooden cross, the blood. Who wouldn't be traumatized? But there in the Mission Dolores on Easter Sunday, Jesus was risen and all the crucifixes in the church were draped in virginal muslin, and the lilies, hundreds of them, glowed magnificently white on the altar.

Precisely at noon, the choir arrived with much fanfare, from the heavyset teen wearing a giant Giants baseball shirt, rapper pants and a bling-bling crucifix about the size of a CD disc to a woman in head-to-toe black so old the other choir members practically carried her. The musical director, a tall, proud man in a brown corduroy jacket and pants, yellow tie, ponytail and mustache presided with gusto, arms waving enthusiastically in time to the salsa beat the organist played. This was my kind of Mass. The Spanish was close enough to Latin to deliver me back to the Mass of my youth, yet there was a joviality, a participatory element to the service that buoyed my soul.

When the priest strode the aisles, dipping a brush into holy water and flinging the water at the parishioners in blessing, I tried to position myself so I would get splashed, but he seemed to know I was a heretic. He wasn't wasting any of that holy water on me. Still, after Mass, when I saw the pastor standing outside and went to tell him how much I'd enjoyed the Mass, he interrupted my blathering and placed his big hand upon my head, forcing my head down as he recited an exorcism over me, or at least that's what I imagined.

That didn't stop me from joining the blasphemers back at the park where the Bad Kitties, a luscious trio of women singers, were belting out a little ditty about the res-ERECTION and a fellow with washboard abs like you see on the cover of Men's Health magazine was crowned the Hunky Jesus.

Toward the end of the day, when was getting ready to go home, Leif finally showed up on his bicycle, wearing *his* bad kitty costume.

Leif in his Bad Kitty Costume

The rumor on the street was that the Polish neighbor had turned down $80,000 to move without bringing the family's situation to the attention of city officials. Obviously, I needn't have worried about them; the Pole had learned the American way. Yet, almost every week you heard about someone squeezed out of his or her apartment to make way for a condo or TIC conversion. No wonder. The average advertised monthly rent for a two-bedroom apartment in San Francisco in 2006 was $2,300. People who could afford one of those new no-interest mortgages were signing up. Meanwhile the number of homeless people in the city and those applying for public housing was reaching historic proportions.

As I went to community meetings and talked to homeless people, experts and advocates, I kept expecting to find potential solutions to the problem. I held out hope that in an inventive place like San Francisco, someone would figure out a way to serve the needs of a diverse population. But it became more and more evident every day as the availability of low-rent housing declined precipitously and redevelopment and gentrification shifted into high gear while funding for community health centers plummeted that there would be no solutions there, that Care Not Cash would translate into A Little Care for Some, No Cash for All.

As for me, I wondered how long I would be able to afford to live there.

Robert was a gay hairdresser with no hair. Not on his head or eyebrows or anywhere else that I could see. I imagined he removed all the hair from his body, but I hadn't gone so far as to ask if that were so. There was among certain gay men a desire to be perfect, to have muscles that swelled and rippled without the distraction of hair, to exhibit skin that was unblemished as an infant's, an older version of a twink, which is gay slang for a young or young-looking man with little or no body hair. When Robert and Christopher danced, their sweet abandon was reflected on their faces. Christopher was still recovering from Jim, trolling the gay dance clubs for a replacement. On this particular evening, after we had spent a small fortune at the new French restaurant in the Castro, where they served decadent food and refolded your napkin whenever you got up from the table, we wandered over to The Club, the second-floor dance bar above Twin Peaks. The old queers hang out at Twin Peaks, the young studs at The Club. It used to be a lesbian bar but now handsome, tight-bodied Latinos twirled and kissed and gyrated on the dance floor to music that was half salsa/half trance. Heterosexual couples danced among them, a constant mixing and remixing of young bodies, almost all svelte and muscular. I'd been longing for this: to go dancing with the gay boys, to be the voyeur to their fantasies, without the details, of course, while the music, the beautiful bodies, the alcohol and other enticements washed away my obsession about the homeless, the war, and the economy, at least for the moment.

We were dancing together, the guys and me, each in our own reverie, when all eyes turned away from the dance floor. A tall, slim woman had climbed atop a pool table and the crowd turned as one to watch her. She wore black leather boots, torn fishnet stockings over a g-string, a tiny skirt that flared about while she danced, her upper torso naked other than a lacy black bra. The mandala tattooed on her back was one of the few adornments on her body. She had a tiny jewel in her navel and very short hair. Her torso was that of a snake, undulating above the circling crowd of women and men who proffered dollar bills, exchanging words and desires in movement but little touch other than to insert the bills in some crevice of her body or tuck them into her waistband as she smiled in a most beguilingly anonymous way and gave each paying admirer a personalized slink or swirl, falling to her back to spread her legs lasciviously, or standing tall on the heeled leather boots to lean over and jiggle her breasts and butt, making eye contact for the merest of seconds, then turning instantly remote and almost removed from her own gyrations.

When the dollars jammed into the band of her skirt or bra became too plentiful, she shoved fistfuls of cash down her knee-high boots. One bull dyke wanted her; you could see it in the shy yet stolid way in which she took up residence at the end of the pool table, the way she offered her folded bills; another woman's adoration as she came close enough to count the pores on the little patch of skin peeking through a tear in the dancer's stockings was too embarrassing to watch. And the Latino guys, two studs in black, they, too, were enticed, their bodies locked together, back to front as they mimicked the dancer, their bodies spooned together until they separated to tender their own dollars to the dancer's spinning torso. And the music pulsated, on and on, and the couples of all sorts on the dance floor exuded sexuality, and Christopher and Robert danced. As did I.

Jul was driving over Portola Avenue when he saw Mayor Newsom holding a press conference on the street corner. He whipped the car around, parked and ran two blocks to where the mayor was making an announcement about potholes.

"Mayor, Mayor," he said, gaining Newsom's attention just as the cameras were being turned off. "Oh, you've been doing such a good job, lowering our deficit from $100 million to $80 million, but you must admit $80 million is still a huge chunk of change. Let's see, you've got roughly 28,000 employees in this city and a budget of what, $5 billion, roughly half of that on salaries. That's where I can help. I have an idea on how to cut your budget substantially. Those of us who have city employees as friends or those of us who do business in the city …" and here he went off on one of his tangents, outlining his long career as a property owner … "we know that the average city employee only works half a day. That's substantiated by the fact that whenever we call City Hall, we never get anyone on the phone. And if we go down there, there's no one to talk to."

By now, Newsom had gone on automatic pilot. He'd heard it all before and employed his well-rehearsed responses to citizen advisors like Jul, balancing between outraged defense of city employees and deep-felt concern for Jul as a citizen who felt neglected by his city employees.

"No, no. I'm not looking for personal redress," Jul told Newsom. "I'm trying to help you fix your budget problem by determining which city employees are actually working and which are not." Jul's Adam's apple bobbed vigorously and his eyes had a gleam of self-congratulation. The cameramen were driving away. The mayor's assistant gestured it was time to move away from this particular citizen.

Jul tried the soft sell: "It's not your fault, I understand. You inherited a lot of dead weight, lifetime appointees anointed by your predecessor. My idea will make them either do their jobs or give up their jobs. Hear me out." The mayor looked as if he might be listening.

"Okay, you equip every city worker with a video camera mounted on his head. You want to see their hands and bodies moving, shuffling papers, fixing our roads. Call it the Jul Worker Cam if you like. You installed cameras on street corners to catch criminals and red-light runners. Use them to crack down on employment scofflaws. Why should citizens be subjected to surveillance when workers paid with citizens' hard-earned tax dollars go unobserved?"

Newsom was backing away, moving toward a waiting car. Still Jul persisted: "On the other important issue facing the city, my general suggestion is that we stop encouraging homeless people to move here. Discourage them. Change the city's reputation. Rehab, work or jail. There's freedom in that."

And the mayor got in his car and drove away with Jul still offering advice. Jul tried to get me to help spread the word about his Worker Cam to journalists, economists, lobbyists and City Hall watchers.

"Jul," I said, "you are your own best advocate. You don't need me to promote your idea. Just bring it to the next supervisors' meeting. I'm sure the employees union will embrace the idea."

I had allowed myself the delusion that I was the catalyst, creating a family with pies and Thanksgiving leftovers, that my presence in the building had made us kith and kin. But while pie is as powerful an enticement as most any item on this planet and food often brought us together, it was Ann and Alexandra who had united us. A family's history is not necessarily told in big moments but rather in the smaller milestones of life: a child learns to walk, to talk, to ride her bicycle. A child learns to write her name and draw pictures that show relationships through her eyes. In my year of discontent, the year in which I had my car accident and experienced death after death, Ann was my friend in need just as she was for Gordon and Liya during their difficulties after the fire. There were others in the building, Emmett and Deanna especially, with whom we socialized and held communal meals. We did what family members do for one another: we gave rides, loaned money, ran favors, commiserated, advised, and whenever schedules allowed, we ate together. Our favorite meal was when Liya cooked Ethiopian. First, she placed a large round of Ethiopian flat bread called injera on each of our plates. The bread was mushroom color and spongy. She had explained that in Ethiopia the injera would be your plate and your fork. You cover the injera with samples from the various dishes, then tear off small pieces of the bread and use them to scoop up bits of food. Alexandra particularly liked that it was okay for us to eat with our fingers.

The first thing that goes on the Injera is the chicken, which Liya cooked with whole eggs. "We never serve chicken without the egg," she said, her beautiful face shining with pleasure and shyness the first time she described the daylong process of making the meal.

"I do that thing with the butter … what's that word for neter kiba? … Clari-something? It's making the butter pure of the milk, and then I cook red onions, so many onions they fill the pot up to here." She held her hand about seven inches off the table. "After the onions have cooked down for three or four hours, I add garlic and ginger, cardamom and paprika, and lots of spices from Ethiopia that I keep in my refrigerator, korerima, berbere, wot kimen and mitmita, but I only use a little of the hot ones when I cook for you."

By this point, Ann and I were laughing with our mouths full because we were trying to remember the words Liya was using for the ingredients, but when Liya said words like injera, korerima and berbere, it was as if the words had no vowels. The j's and r's rolled off her tongue like sweet sambusa and we knew we wouldn't be able to spell the words without looking them up and that neither of us would be able to replicate the meal. Why should we? We had Liya, beautiful Liya.

"Then I clean the chicken. No … what do you call that stuff on the outside?" she continued. "Right, no skin, and I pick off all the fat. We don't have any fat in our doro wat," which was the name for the chicken dish that we were savoring. The chicken fell from the bones and had been steeped all day in the gravy made from the onions and butter and spices, so it was densely yet subtly spicy.

We were all shoveling food into our mouths and asking questions about the preparation of the meal and life in Ethiopia where Liya's father, now 108, and mother, in her late-80s, still lived. Meanwhile, Alexandra was long done with eating and had sprawled out on the couch, whining, "No one's talking to me."

Poor girl. All these adults who have for years taken turns pampering her were in her house all at the same time and no one was paying a whit of attention to her.

The front page of the *Chronicle* read, "SF moves to stem African American Exodus." The writer, Leslie Fulbright, quoted Joseph Blue, a black resident of the city, who said, "San Francisco no longer has a viable black community. The middle class is gone, and what we have left is underprivileged, uneducated, poor black folks." Statistics in the article confirmed my observations; African Americans had fallen from 13.4 percent of the city's population in 1970 to 6.5 percent in 2005 – from roughly 96,000 residents to 47,000, the largest drop of its kind in any American city. (Most recent statistics are about the same.)

The city had conducted its annual homeless count in January during which volunteers wander the streets literally counting the homeless population, not just people living on the streets but also those living in shelters, hospitals, jails and treatment centers. They reported 6,377 homeless people in 2007 compared to 6,248 individuals in 2005. Newsom said the figures were misleading, that there had actually been a decrease in homelessness because the most recent tabulation had used twice as many volunteers than in previous counts, five hundred in all, and they had conducted a much more thorough search, peering under highway underpasses, going into enclaves in all 189 city parks, looking in cars and examining jail populations. More than 530 people were living in their cars. The volunteers were not required to write down the race and gender of the people they counted, but where they did, they reported that almost 31 percent were black, 28 percent were white, and 4 percent were Latino.

March: Chuck escaped Vermont at its most bipolar season again, when one day it might be 65 and sunny in the morning, 20 degrees and snowing by mid-day, the snow wet and heavy on the telephone and electric wires so that power outages were as routine as the deluges that would follow, melting mounds of snow overnight, saturating the ground and turning every dirt road in the state into a quagmire that ate cars alive. March was a good month to be out of Vermont.

This year's peace march on the anniversary of the Iraq war felt like a dirge. There was the usual array of clever signs and T-shirts but the demonstrators chanted in the most desultory manner; even the Socialists, the most fervent at this sort of thing, appeared to be going through the movements. Nothing seemed to make a difference with this president, this Congress. The Democrats were as bad as the Republicans, hopelessly pursuing this hopeless, endless war.

On the way home, who should we run into but Jay, whom I hadn't seen in months. He was sitting at the counter of a coffee shop in the Civic Center and quickly provided another opportunity to learn how wrong assumptions can be. All those years at the café, I thought Jay lived in the building near my street that he referred to so often, the building that housed the tattoo parlor, the heroin shooting gallery and hash bar, the kind of place where people one step up from homelessness or the newly immigrated lived. As we learned that day, Jay had lived in a rent-controlled apartment just west of the Civic Center for several decades, a one-bedroom apartment that cost him only $209 a month. He was a prime example of Jul's argument that rent control had led landlords to convert their buildings into condominiums or sell them for tenants in common partnerships or simply give up on the landlord business, that the well-meaning concept of rent control actually contributed to the high cost of living for more recent renters in the city.

Jay was having nothing to do with that concept. "No," he said, "those of us who live in rent-controlled apartments are being rewarded for the stability we bring to neighborhoods," he said. "Cities like this one are full of transients, people who don't set down roots and in any number of ways use the city's resources without giving much back. Meanwhile, people like me who have lived in the same neighborhood for decades, know the neighborhood; we support our local businesses; we clean up our streets; we look out for one another."

"I was paying $249 a month for several years after my landlady raised the rent when my girlfriend moved in. When my girlfriend moved out and I asked for a rent reduction, I discovered that it had been illegal for her to have raised my rent in the first place. You can't charge more for two people," Jay said. "So she had to pay it all back, with interest. You gotta love this city."

Jul's latest obsession was with America's image, how badly it had deteriorated, especially with our European friends. Jul considered himself a citizen of the world. He had lived in Germany, traveled extensively throughout Europe and Asia, South and Central America, and planned to continue to do so. He didn't want to go overseas and have to defend himself as an American. He certainly didn't want to have to defend the Iraq War. He wanted the Brits to love us, to be our friends again, and the French, too.

"We're lonely for the Europeans," he said plaintively as if speaking for a larger group of people. Frankly, I didn't think George Bush was lonely for the Europeans; he had his own puppet, Tony Blair, and seemed to prefer pedaling his $5,000 Cannondale mountain bike, the one the manufacturer had given him, rather than strolling the Champs-Élysées.

Jul had a plan he wanted to present to the beleaguered mayor of San Francisco, his prettiness Gavin Newsom who, oh gosh, oh golly, had just gotten himself in a bit of trouble for having an affair with the wife of his top political aide and had subsequently joined the line of those confessing to a little problem with alcohol, a problem that might have clouded his judgment. Hizzoner wanted to run for governor, for president. He needed to repair his image if he were to be a candidate for higher office who both supported gay marriage and was sleazy enough to have an affair with the wife of one of his best friends, a woman who by the way was employed as Newsom's appointment secretary. This idea was better than the Worker Cam; it could bring new revenues to the city while restoring Newsom's image as a forward-thinking leader. Essentially, Jul proposed that Newsom create a safe zone for Europeans, a place where they wouldn't see freedom fries on menus or hear justifications of Abu Ghraib tactics.

"Gavin should turn on the charm, which is his main calling card anyhow, and get together with all the other West Coast mayors, from Santa Cruz to Washington state – just the coastal mayors, mind you, and no one from south of Santa Cruz – and make a big regional push to get the Europeans to come over here where the Euro will buy them so much more, given the exchange rate. And, while they're here, those Europeans will see how civilized we are," Jul explained. "We'll make a map of safe zones for Europeans, a small thin green zone that'll say, 'We agree with you, you Germans and Frenchies. We want you to come and teach us some civility. We'll market ourselves as the precious few areas in the country where we've always known the president was an idiot maneuvered by two nuts named Cheney and Rove. Once they see that we're not all warmongers, when we go to their countries, we can identify ourselves as from the safe, green zone, and they'll just love us."

One day when Daniel and I were walking down Market Street near that building Jay liked to frequent, the one with the hash bar in it, Daniel spied Jay coming our way with another fellow, each carrying an open cardboard box. "More treasures from the street?" I asked as the two men juggled the box into the trunk of a car, the stranger arranging his body awkwardly to keep me from seeing what was inside, which, of course, piqued my interest even more.

"No, just some health-giving babies. She's cool. She's a friend of mine," Jay said to his companion as I poked my nosy little head into one of the boxes and started laughing as the poignant smell of marijuana seedlings wafted my way.

"Smells good," I said.

"Oh, they don't have that great smell yet. Give 'em time," Jay said, turning again to his companion, obviously a paranoid botany geek who didn't appreciate a strange woman poking her nose in his trunk, which was full of pot plants.

"Now, any time you want some more of these beauties, you come see me," Jay said as the geeky fellow tried to make a clean getaway. Jay was not letting him off that easily. "She's a journalist, writing a book. I'm already in it and here we are, giving her another chapter," he said, eyes twinkling with amusement.

With that, the fellow scooted into the car and, much too quickly for someone trying to avoid notice, peeled out of the parking lot and onto Guerrero.

"Did you finish the story you were working on the other day?" Jay asked.

"I did."

"What was it about?"

"You."

"That's great," Jay said unconvincingly, then scratched his scalp vigorously. "Precisely, w*hat* about me?"

"About you finding your moral compass." We had a good laugh about that.

"Oh, that's good. I was afraid you'd written about the hash bar."

"Of course I wrote about the hash bar. That's part of the story."

"Oh, what the hell. I don't care. They've got to know people bend the rules there a little. You know, two news stories have been written about me already."

"Really. What about?"

"Well, one of the headlines read, 'Boy Slips; Storm Rips.'"

Jay explained that when he was a boy, one of his friends – "I use the term loosely" -- pushed him into a river during a freak flood, a river that normally wasn't more than a stream, no big deal except he got swept under water and into a sewer pipe. It carried him under a busy street and out the other side.

"I raised my hand and felt the ridges in the storm drain like an accordion against my fingertips as the water pushed me along. Bing, bing, bing. Felt weird. Obviously, I survived," he said. "It must have been a slow news day, though, because they wrote a story about my ride through the sewer pipe."

If I had written the headline on his story, it would have said, "Boy Slips; Storm Grips; Boy Trips," forecasting Jay's adventures into the future.

He got a kick out of that.

"A year later, they did a follow-up story on me. That must have been a *really* slow news day. Still alive and well despite sewer water up my nose."

"Or, that someone knew your moral compass would take you through the spin cycle a few more times," I said.

"Or that I'm full of shit," Jay said and headed off to the hash bar.

Five days after I heard the Pole had accepted an offer to move, the final amount not revealed, I received a letter from Jul and Mary, informing me as they had all the other tenants in our building that an inspector would be coming to measure our building as the first step in Jul's plan to make our Octavia Boulevard apartment house into a tenants-in-common building. Roughly, for us, that meant cough up a ton of dough or move. I had been half expecting this announcement for months as he defended the acts of the lawyers next door. I had even given some thought to buying in to this or some other TIC building; bankers were certainly making it easy enough to get a mortgage for a TIC, ignoring a buyer's ability to pay with what they euphemistically were calling "creative financing." But the reality was that I couldn't afford to do so, even if I qualified for one of those no-money down loans that the Realtors were promoting.

"What was that Jul said when we moved in, that we had to meet certain criteria that the longtime residents approved of, that we had to fit into the mix? Hadn't he paraded me into your apartment for my obligatory interview?" Deanna asked when we talked about Jul's plan. "He told us he wasn't planning to sell for at least ten years. They bring prospective buyers into my apartment and I'll put up signs to scare them off. I'll write, 'If you buy this place, you will be displacing two adults and three cats from their homes.' Or, 'Prepare yourself for a long legal battle.'"

Ann wasn't worried. "They've got laws in this city to protect the tenant, remember?" she said. "How easy do you think it'll be to evict me? I've got a 4-year-old. I'm a single mother working three jobs to pay the rent. I've built a community here. He'll have to pay me $20,000 or more to move me out."

Although Jul's profit would be many times higher if he sold each apartment outright, rather than sell the building as it was, I wondered if it would be worth the grief and the time it would take, maybe two years, to go through the process of removing all of us, then renovating and selling each apartment. The apartments in the building next door had sold quickly enough, several for three-quarters of a million, which, of course, had given Jul the idea in the first place. But the market was starting to cool down, making me think that perhaps Jul was feeling some pressure to get his while he could. While others in the building thought he was operating from a place of greed, I was slightly more sympathetic. I understood that a combination of factors were at play; these included his fear of an economic recession, the constant aggravation of tenants calling with needs, and his aversion to lawsuits. In truth, I traced his desire to sell the building to the day that Reuben had fallen from the ladder even though, as I had predicted, there had been no lawsuit.

Still, I was as upset as everyone else in the building with the prospect of having to look for another apartment, especially as rents had gone up considerably in the years I'd lived on Octavia Boulevard, not to mention the hassle of moving. On top value of that, we had come to depend on one another in this building. What was the recompense for that loss?

On a practical level, I thought Jul's plan to TIC the building was just too ambitious. How would he sell twelve units in a 1906 building individually? He kept telling me it was being done all the time but it seemed harebrained to me. And then there was the emotional toll. And so, I tried to reason with him.

"Jul," I said, "You are asking for a world of hurt."

He didn't appreciate that comment.

"What? Everyone wants me to work myself to death? Is that what the tenants want? They want me to work myself into the grave? They want me to have a nervous breakdown? I'm over the landlord business. I'm done with it."

"No, Jul, they don't want you to have a nervous breakdown. It's that they don't want to have a nervous breakdown. They don't want to move. This is our home," I said. "Why don't you just sell the building to someone else if you're over being a landlord, as you put it?"

"And that person will just turn this place into a TIC. That's the way all the properties are going now. Why should I let someone else reap the benefit of all my hard work? It will be worth a lot more to me if I sell it unit by unit."

"I know that but I'm just worrying about you, about the stress you'll be under," I said, keeping my voice as calm as possible. "Will it be worth all that, really? Think of the grief you've experienced every time you've been involved in a lawsuit. This will be a gazillion times worse. You saw how Ann worked to get Gordon back his job, to get him recognition for saving Lance. Imagine that energy directed at you to save her and Alexandra's home …"

Mary said not a word, but she was listening intently.

"Everyone warned me not to tell the tenants what I was considering," Jul said. "Everyone said to keep my plans to myself, to just set the process in motion and let the tenants know when everything was ready to go. But no, I try to be the nice guy. I'm up front with everyone and give notice. I'm creating an opportunity for everyone in the building to be a property owner. And this is what I get?"

"What did you think, that everyone would be thrilled, that Gordon would say, 'Oh thank you, Jul, for making me leave a home I've lived in for 30 years, the place my daughter was born and grew up in?' I'm just trying to point out that it's going to be a horrible business for you to go through. You're going to turn a lot of people in the building whom you've befriended into enemies. It won't be pretty."

"Don't try to tell me how to run my business," he said, his voice flat with restraint. "I've been in the property business for years. I know what I'm doing. Of course, I can take it." Jul's face was ashen white, his jaw clenched.

"Jul, don't be angry with *me*. I'm just trying to talk to you about it."

"Well, you don't know anything about it. I know what I'm doing. This is the appreciation I get," his voice gone cold. "Fixing up the building, painting it, putting down hardwood floors in the lobby, new carpeting. All that work I did for everyone – and this is what I get."

"Well, apparently, Jul, you didn't do the work for us, did you? You did it for yourself." And the memory of T.C. Boyle's Vogelsang came to mind.

Days later, Jul tried once again to convince me to be his first sale, offering to lower the cost of my apartment. He'd talk to his agent and see what he could come up with. I only needed 10 percent, he said, to which I replied, "Jul, even if you sold to me for $400,000, which I don't think you'd be advised to do, I would have to come up with $40,000, plus closing and other costs. No thank you. I do not want to own even one-twelfth of a 100-year-old building in earthquake-prone San Francisco. Do you know my home in Vermont cost $43,000?"

"How many years ago was that?" he asked. "A bigger earthquake is coming, an economic one. And I for one want to get my money before it all collapses."

"Oh, I see. You think the economy's going to go bust and property values will plummet. So, you want us to help protect your investment by buying while property values are high. How altruistic of you."

End of that conversation.

And so it began for us: The city's agents came through each apartment. They measured our space. Jul filled out the proper forms. He hired the top TIC agent in the area. Still I persisted. One day, I sat in Jul's car and cried and cried while I tried to get him to see the havoc he was about to cause. It was only later that I came to understand that the more I argued against the idea, the more I said his TIC scheme wouldn't work, the more determined Jul was to make it happen. My arguments actually worked against me. Jul would show me. Indeed, the more I argued and the angrier Ann and Deanna and the others were toward Jul, the more he wanted to get out of the landlord business. We were a self-fulfilling prophecy.

Meanwhile, I had to pity Mary. She understood what the future held if they went forward with the TIC. I couldn't stand the fighting, the sense that we were being pulled apart by money. I couldn't stand the idea of Ann having to leave the secure nest she'd made. I couldn't stand the idea of Gordon having to leave a place he'd lived in for his entire adult life, a place he'd cared for as if it were his own. I was the flexible one. I was the one who had another home, who came and went and did not consider the apartment on Octavia Boulevard, much as I loved it, the place where I would spend my old age.

And so I came up with a plan.

My logic went something like this: Robin's apartment was empty but needed a lot of work before it could be sold. Mine was in very good shape. If I moved out, Jul could do a quick refresher on my apartment and put it up for sale. If it sold, he could use that money to fix up Robin's apartment. Rather than TIC the whole building at once, he could sell apartments one at a time, beginning first with mine, then rehabilitating Robin's. I thought the process would quickly show Jul how difficult a full conversion might be. The solution appeared when I learned there was a vacancy in the other building that Jul owned. It was a small complex of five apartments located in Noe Valley, a neighborhood I'd walked through many times with Chuck. Noe Valley is uphill from the Castro and has many of those staircase walks that we'd been exploring over the past year or so. The neighborhood is full of old homes and gardens and shops. When I first discovered it, I was attracted to living there but thought it was outside my reach economically. I was a bit unsure that I would be comfortable living in a neighborhood often referred to as Stroller Valley because so many dot-com couples had moved there to have their babies. Every day the nannies and young parents strolled 24th Street with their perfect babies ensconced in high-priced strollers, posh as a Cadillac.

But after I spent a couple of afternoons walking the neighborhood streets and talking to its residents, I came to see that Noe Valley was really a village within the city; it had a main street lined with stores, several coffee shops and bakeries, a park, a branch library, a small church that hosted folk musicians and leftist talks, in other words a neighborhood in a way that Octavia would never be.

"It will be good for you to move, healthier," Jul said, immediately accepting my proposal. "You won't be in such a state over the homeless. I'm telling you, you'll like Noe Valley."

I had second thoughts when I saw the apartment for rent. It was ridiculously tiny, about a third of my Octavia digs with a kitchen the size of a portable toilet. I cried as I walked through it, simultaneously aware that I'd already made the decision to move and disgusted with myself over my emotions. It wasn't a pretty scene: Jul ignoring me while I walked around the apartment, tears rolling down my stupid puss. Poor Mary. I felt for her. She understood how upset I was and was doing her best to help me see the benefits of the Noe Valley apartment while also responding to Jul's impatience with my requests for enhancements to make the place more livable. It was our most difficult time together.

Looking back, I don't know as I can explain why the whole process was so emotional for me. I was afraid that moving would be seen as a kind of disloyalty by Ann and my other neighbors, as if I were aiding Jul in his desire to TIC the building by offering up my apartment as the first space for just such a conversion. Yet I felt fairly confident that my moving would result in no one else having to move. I thought the idea of converting my apartment would show Jul how difficult the whole conversion would be.

I had to admit, also, that even though it was ridiculously small, the Noe Valley apartment was quite cute. It had a fabulous deck overlooking a huge back yard. It was the deck and the yard that convinced me as I remembered the day I sat in

Christopher's garden and realized how much I'd punished myself by not picking an apartment with growing space.

Later, after I left Jul and Mary and took a stroll around the surrounding blocks, reminding myself of my tour of the Octavia neighborhood years previously, I counted four coffee shops, two bookstores, three florist shops and a dozen or more restaurants. Not only were the sidewalks clean, there were no bodies sleeping on them. Much as I hated to admit it, I had lost my tolerance for the constancy of the homeless. Best of all, my rent on the new place would be slightly less than what I paid for the Octavia apartment.

Of course, I would make Jul pay me the requisite $7500 to move, reminding him that I had been diagnosed by Willie as a person with a disability, making me qualify for the $4,500 all tenants removed for TICs received and the additional $3000 for a person with a handicap. I knew exactly what I'd spend the money on, a new kitchen in my Vermont home.

Ann and Deanna and Emmett, Gordon and Liya all went through a ration of emotions when I presented them with my idea. Deanna wanted me to stay and fight alongside her and Ann; she knew I'd be a formidable opponent. Ann thought moving was unnecessary. She dismissed the TIC plan as another of Jul's ridiculous schemes, like web cameras for city workers. Surprisingly, Gordon supported my move. He had worked on the Noe Valley apartment and could see its charm. "Don't worry," he said. "We'll always be friends."

Silent Guy and I were sitting at the café, staring morosely at the mauve house across the street, worrying about Wisdom Man, when a stranger strolled by, walked past once, turned around, sat down.

"You Yvonne?" he asked tentatively. "I'm Tom's son." I could see the resemblance.

"He asked me to tell you he moved back to Vermont," he said. "And something else. I don't know what it means exactly but he said to tell you there was no woman in Paris. I imagine he made up some story to make himself seem more interesting, more … I don't know … I've lived with it all my life. He's a bullshit artist."

"We figured that," I said, "but he had me convinced anyhow."

"I know what you mean," he said. "My mother can't say no to him though. I told her not to take him back but I was just as glad to get rid of him."

I didn't say, us, too.

Through all this, the 2007 mayoral election provided comic relief. One day as I exited the Castro Muni station, I saw one of my students photographing the action near the corner of Market Street. My eyes focused on what he was focusing on: a 60-something, bearded man, essentially naked, holding a sign that read "George Davis for SF Mayor 2007."

George Davis Campaigning on Castro Street; you can see my student photographer in the window behind Davis.

My student's instincts were correct: a man running for office on the Right-to-Be-Naked ticket was news even if it were unlikely that he could publish the photograph in most publications, given the candidate's full-frontal nudity. We were standing there watching the reaction of out-of-town visitors – "That man is NAKED!" – when two cops showed up.

"You're naked," the male officer told candidate Davis.

"No, I'm not. I'm wearing a hat and shoes," Davis responded.

"Well, aren't you going to put some pants on?" the cop asked.

"No, I'm not. This is my campaign statement," Davis said.

"Well, how long are you going to be out here like that?" the female cop asked.

"I don't know. Most of the day, I reckon."

The cops stepped away to assess the situation and talk on their cell phones. Ten minutes or so later, another officer arrived, a supervisor.

"You're naked," he said to Davis.

"No, I'm not. I'm wearing a hat and shoes," Davis responded.

"How long do you expect to be out here like that?" the cop asked. "Can't you put some clothes on?"

"No. This is my campaign statement." Davis, who's 61, continued to hand out flyers promoting his major platform, which was that Golden Gate Park should become a clothing-optional recreational area. I didn't even want to picture the drum circle with a bunch of naked people beating away.

Early on, the list of challengers for mayor had dwindled down to a mere thirteen candidates, most of them falling into the "only in San Francisco" category, given that it was generally accepted that Newsom was a shoe-in, despite the affair and the little problem with alcohol, not to mention that his aide had quit and the woman had gone into rehab.

Besides Davis, there was Grasshopper Alec Kaplan, a 27-year-old vegan taxicab driver who lived in a purple cab, had been jailed for assaulting a passenger and otherwise had endeared himself to the local constabulary.

Candidate Chicken John Rinaldi listed his employment as "showman." His supporters included the Cacophony Society, an anarchist group that had initiated Burning Man. Rinaldi's campaign slogan was "Chicken, the other white mayor," and he campaigned on the "idea of San Francisco."

But wait. There's more. Michael Powers, the 42-year-old owner of the Power Exchange sex club, ran on the platform that his ability to run a nightclub that welcomed gays, lesbians and heterosexuals, as well as assorted devotees to domination and bondage qualified him best to serve the needs of San Franciscans.

Lonnie Holmes, a juvenile detention probation officer, ran as the U.S. Marijuana Party candidate. And one of San Francisco State University's graduates, Josh Wolf, ran on the Socialist platform. Wolf's claim to fame was serving a record 226 days in federal prison after refusing to turn over footage of an immigration protest in the city's Mission District.

Other candidates campaigned to protect Hunters Point, for affordable housing and to slash the city budget. In the end, though, Newsom won with 74 percent of the votes. Chicken John, who came in sixth with 2,508 votes, hosted a Loser's Ball the night of the election. Davis garnered 644 votes. Democrat Quintin Mecke, an advocate for the homeless who expressed rational concerns about the rising crime rate in San Francisco, came in second with 9,036 votes compared to Newsom's 105,596. It wouldn't be long before Newsom announced his intention to run for governor of California. (He later downgraded his ambitions to lieutenant governor.)

I had no way to get in touch with a whole group of people I wanted to alert to my move. I couldn't telephone or email Stretch or Silent Guy or Wisdom Man or Jay. I had tried communicating with Wisdom Man on various Gnostic websites but he had not responded. I decided to track as many of my neighborhood pals down as I could and make appointments, if they were willing, for actual interviews. I knew now that I would write a book that would chronicle my years on Octavia Boulevard. I knew it would be about the natural conflict between progressive politics and capitalism, that it would tell the story of how a small neighborhood had been transformed, improved in so many ways, but how that transformation might never help those who deserved, or at least needed, those benefits the most.

I began my search with Stretch. Day after day, I traipsed the few blocks to the homeless camp in the Ivy alley, looking for him. No one I talked to admitted to knowing a man named Stretch or anyone answering his description. And then one day I saw him working at the plant supply store on Market Street that catered to marijuana growers, just a block away from the Baptist Church. Stretch was unloading pallets of planting mix, his bare chest a thin bellow of bones above jeans held up with a rope. I told him I was moving and that I wanted a real sit-down talk with him before I left the neighborhood. We agreed to meet later in the week and I'd take him to J's Pots of Soul for breakfast.

Stretch's basketball sweatshirt was filthy and his pants and shoes were tattered, but the smile that spread across his face as he saw that I was actually keeping our breakfast date was that of a young boy about to have a treat he'd been anticipating for days. Stretch had a series of mannerisms and tics that began with a twist of the head and a quick squint before he could look or talk directly to you. The gestures were on full display that day, he was that nervous. But I didn't even have to ask for his story. He began to volunteer it from the moment we set off for J's, as if he knew this was the deal, his story for a big grub feast. Some of it, like the stories we all tell of success or demise, some of it seemed fantastic, unbelievable, but Stretch had never struck me as a liar. Sure, he had his tales of woe that he employed when he needed money but there were no hard feelings there. And, as the story unraveled from him, he admitted to many mistakes along the way, never in shame but rather in a matter-of-fact voice, just letting the story spill out as if he had no choice in his own life, cranking his head around and scratching here and there between the words. I wanted to slow him down so that I could concentrate on the story once we got to J's, where the Number One – bacon, sausage, potato wedges, eggs, three pancakes with bananas, real maple syrup – might begin to fill him up.

As we waited to order, Stretch sweetly began his tale anew; he liked the idea of being in a book. "I ain't ashamed of being homeless," he said. "I work for a living, don't I?" And then he began the story again from the beginning: He was born in Toledo and had a younger sister but she was dead. He couldn't talk about her. When he was a young teen, he said, his father won the Lotto in a neighboring state and, overnight, became a millionaire. The family moved from Toledo to the rural town of Holland. There, they built a big house with a pool. The rug in Stretch's huge bedroom bore the Pittsburgh Steelers' symbol, his favorite team, and a poster of Isaiah Thomas filled the wall over his bed, a bed finally long enough for his long frame. Stretch loved the suburbs. He rode his bike and played basketball every day until well after dark, practicing, practicing. He dreamed of being an NBA star. A girlfriend gave him his nickname, Stretch. "You're a lady so I can't tell you why," he said, as he ordered the Number One and poured three sugars into his coffee.

"That's my real name, Dennis Paul Jones," he said, taking out his ID. "Dennis, that's Daniel in Spanish. That's why I like Daniel so much. I figure you named him after me."

Where he'd gotten the idea that Dennis was a Spanish name or that it was related to the name Daniel was beyond me. I just loved the way he'd put it all together, that I'd named Daniel after him. Besides, Dennis Paul Jones was most likely not his real name; it sounded made-up to me. Denny and Danny were close enough, though.

"Stretch, did anyone ever call you Denny?" I asked.

"How'd you know? My mother. When I call her – and that ain't often; *he* might answer – she still calls me Denny."

I'd learned my lesson. I just listened.

Stretch was the star of his high school basketball team. At 6 feet, 11 inches, he got lots of notice and a scholarship to the University of Toledo – at least that's what he said -- then notice from Ohio State University. He figured he was on his way to a big college school and then the NBA. He could taste it. When he wasn't on the court, he practiced, practiced. Sometimes when the weather was cold or he was tired, he'd get a coughing spell or have trouble catching his breath, but he ignored it and stayed focused on the hoop. At night, he dreamed of wearing the Buckeye uniform. Then, halfway through a game in his second season at Toledo, with scouts watching from the stands and the score tied, Stretch was running down the court, about to make a lay-up when suddenly he was short of breath. Not tonight, he told himself, and kept playing, running even though his chest burned, scoring basket after basket. Near the end of the game, he went up for a rebound; that was all he remembered of the next month. He'd had an asthma attack and had literally stopped breathing, there on the gymnasium floor. When he returned to the team near the end of the season, the coach benched him and later told him he could keep his scholarship but his playing days were over. The school couldn't risk having him play. His asthma might kill him.

"I was going to play for the NBA. Basketball was my life," Stretch said, adding another sugar to the coffee. "I told them they couldn't bench me, that I had to play. But no one would take a chance on me. They just cut me loose."

Could he have tried harder? Should someone have advised him, gotten him health care, helped him stay in basketball? Did they? Or was this just the story he'd invented to explain why he lived on the streets, why he used to be a drug addict and had been in jail? And, if he did indeed suffer from such bad asthma, how had he survived so long sleeping out of doors?

I just let him talk.

"No one would take a chance on me," Stretch said again, but his voice held no rancor. There was more to the story – the discovery of his sexuality, a fall-out with his father, perhaps the beginning of addiction. "I'm not gay," he said, answering a question I hadn't asked despite the boyfriend who kept a cowboy outfit for him. "I'm bi. But my father called me a faggot and disowned me. He threw me out. My mother knew. Said she knew since I was 9 or 10."

Stretch said he didn't see much sense in staying in college if he couldn't play basketball and the allure of San Francisco was so attractive that he headed west, hitchhiking and catching rides on freight trains, following that road so many others had taken there. One morning along the way to the Golden State, not knowing exactly where he was, he jumped off a train and started a campfire to warm up. When he awoke, Stretch was surrounded by flames. He had made it to California just in time to go to jail for starting a wildfire in a national forest. There have been other jail sentences, including the more recent one.

"Five jail terms maybe. Or three. I don't count overnight, nothing less than a month. The longest was when I was using methamphetamine and crack, addicted bad, living across the street from J's Pots of Soul, right over there," he said, pointing across the boulevard as he shoveled forkfuls of food into his mouth.

Stretch said he was healthy now, off the crack and the meth. We were sitting in J's surrounded by other customers and he was pulling up his sleeves to show me how beautiful they were, his veins, and to show me that he had no needle marks. I caught the gaze of the regulars at a nearby table and stared them down.

And the story continued.

Back then, he had a bad addiction, he said. One day, he was looking to make a score when he saw a black wallet on the ground, again not far from J's. "There was no ID in it, just $800 cash. I pocketed the money and threw the wallet back into the gutter, walked over to Mission and Washburn to buy a load of crack."

"To sell?" I asked.

"Shit, no. To use," he said, cranking his head again, first to the left, then to the right, starting to pick at his teeth. I'd never spent so much time close to him and hadn't noticed how engrained the various tics were, a kind of repertoire of nervous movements that had become so routine that he had to stop himself from going through them in the restaurant. The time frame of his story didn't make sense with other stories he'd told me but I didn't interrupt. What did it matter?

"So then I see this black couple. I knew they had some good shit, so I go over to where they was standing under the overpass and they say, 'Hey, Whittle, what you looking for?'"

"What's that they called you?" I asked. "Whittle?"

"White boy. That's what they call us. So, I ask them, 'You a hoodie?'"

"Hoodie? What's that?"

"A cop. That's what they call them. A pig. That's funny, me knowing stuff the professor don't know. I asked him three times. 'You a hoodie?' And he said, no. Three times, he said no, he weren't no cop. So I pull my money out and make my score and then I feel something on my chest, and it's a .45. He's got a .45 on my fucking chest. 'Scuse me. On my frigging chest. And I say, 'Hey, what you doing? You trying to steal from me?'

"And, you don't know this about me," Stretch said, interrupting his story, "but I know karate, kung fu. I grabbed the nose of that gun and we wrestled with it for a while and I get it away from him. And I put it to his head and I say, 'So, you're gonna steal from me, mother fucker, you give me all your money.'"

I might have been staring because he stopped his narrative again and said, "You didn't know I know kung fu? I got a green sash and a black belt. I pointed that gun down at my side and I shot two bullets into the sidewalk. The woman, his partner, she jumped a mile. And then I see she's on a walkie-talkie, screaming, 'Back up. Back up. He's got my partner's gun.'

"And next thing I know I'm surrounded by cops and I'm yelling, 'Put your guns down or I'll blow his brains out.' And then to the cop, 'You told me you weren't no cop. Let me see your badge.' And he showed it to me. And I'm putting the gun down real nice because now I know it's a set-up. That was when one of the cops hit me over the head, right here …" He pointed to a place on his forehead where there was a slight notch. The guy at the neighboring table was staring again; probably everyone was following the drama.

"And I got charged with attempted murder. You believe that, attempted murder? But the judge threw that charge out. It took a year to fight it but he said I was right, the cop should have identified himself. I got a year for attempting to buy. I got off probation April 1."

Stretch was an eating machine. While he told his tale, strips of crunchy bacon disappeared into his mouth. The pancakes vanished in Guinness World Record time. I had ordered the pork chops, grits and eggs and I offered him my second chop. I was stuffed. He took the chop, inhaled it.

"I got a ticket last night," he said apropos of nothing and pulled a much-folded paper from a back pocket. He'd been over by Zuni – the Zagat-rated restaurant where a hamburger costs $15; $2 more if you want a slice of tomato on it – waiting in the alley to sell the scrap metal he'd collected during the day. He explained that a truck driver met scavengers like him there a couple of nights a week and bought whatever scrap metal they'd gathered, no questions asked.

Apparently, the valet parkers didn't like him hanging out in the alley and he got into it with them. "I have a temper, you know," he said, which surprised me, given that he had never revealed his temper when other street surfers stole his alcove at the Baptist Church. I realized then that he had probably avoided those confrontations because he had been on probation.

After a few choice words with the valet drivers, Stretch walked further down the alley to await his buyer, but a few minutes later, he said, three cop cars pulled up and a horde of hoodies piled out. Stretch said they shoved him against the wall and asked for his ID.

"I told them, 'I'm off probation, you can't fuck with me anymore,' but they did anyhow. I told them I was just waiting to sell the scrap I'd picked up and then I'd be on my way. But they showed me the No Trespassing sign on the wall and they hassled me some more and then it came in over their car radio that I was off probation. So they stopped hassling me but they gave me a ticket for trespassing anyhow. And as soon as they left, my guy showed up. But by then it was too late to get my cart somewhere safe and get a room, which is what I'd been planning to do. Instead, I had to sleep on the street last night. That's why I look the way I do. I was pissed because I wanted to look good for our date," he said, acknowledging his filthy clothes for the first time.

On the words, "our date," one nearby patron's head shot up and he gave me the strangest look, head to toe, as if he were trying to put us together some how. Stretch had picked up the pork chop and was busy nibbling the remnants of meat off the bone. He saw me watching him and dropped the bone, wiped his hands on his napkin, resumed his story.

"My checks got screwed up while I was in jail and on probation. I think I finally got it straightened out. I might have $2,000 coming to me from SSI, all my back checks at once. I'm going to put a bunch of it toward a room and then I'm going to get all dressed up and take my friends to Zuni's," he said, this last change in the direction of the conversation coming so completely out of the blue that it took me a minute to grasp his meaning.

"You want to eat at Zuni's," I asked, "even after they called the cops on you?"

"You can come too," he said. "I told them last night. I said, 'You keep your eye out. I'm coming back and you won't know it's me.' You remember I told you I got me a whole western outfit at my ex-lover's place. I'm going to fix myself up good and go over to Zuni and order the most expensive meal on the menu. I'll show them I'm not just some bum."

"Stretch," I said. "You want my toast?"

When I showed up at J's with Silent Guy, Lorna brought us hush puppies right off, on the house. Unlike Stretch, Silent Guy wore his best clothes for our meeting – not his jean jacket and jeans, but a Hawaiian shirt and straw hat. Unlike Stretch, Silent Guy's story came out in fits and starts, but once he got going, it was like he'd been waiting years to tell it to me all at once, confidentially, the way he did that morning, taking deep sucks of coffee into his mouth then cleaning the liquid from his mustache before leaning forward over his coffee. His story was not much prettier than Stretch's. Indeed, as he disclosed a more detailed version of the story Ted had told me years ago now, I thought my heart would break.

"I stopped going to school by sophomore year but they let me hang out in the schoolyard. I guess that's when I got my habit of just sitting and watching, back there in that schoolyard. There was a door – what d'ya call those things they have that go down to basements? Yeah, a metal bulkhead. They had one on the back of the school and it was in the sun and I'd go there after school started. Just sit and watch the clouds and smoke. Rules was a lot different then. During recess some of my friends would hang out with me and sometimes in the afternoon I'd run errands for my mom or hang out in her store. I told you about her store, right? Notions and some such. I always liked that word, notions.

"That's when I started drinking. My mother got disgusted with me. She smoked cigarettes, too, but she didn't like to see me smoking and drinking and hanging around all the time so, well, we had this shed-like building behind the house." Here, he paused shyly, ate his toast, dipping it in the egg yolk. "She told me to go live in the shed if I was gonna be a bum, so she didn't have to look at me hanging around, and I did. But I burned it down and for some time I didn't have no place to live."

He stopped then, looked up. "You writing this stuff down? How you gonna remember it all if you don't write it down? You gonna' put me in your book, right?"

I was so embarrassed then, so downright chastised by his sweet trust in me, the offering of his story. "Guy," I said. "I'm listening to every word."

"Well, it might help someone else, not be stupid like me."

He stopped again, played with his food. "I'm sorry," I said.

No, It's okay. I guess I just kind of lived on our front steps for a while. Slept there. Drank a lot. I started talking to myself and I guess I got a little crazy. That's what they said. Said I had a disease. I don't know what you call it, disassociation or something, and that's when I got on the SSI. And so, then Mom felt bad and she let me move back home.

"She weren't working no more, store had gone under, and we just there together. Those were happy times, watching TV together. We liked old movies. I wasn't eating much then, her neither I guess. I'd just walk to the store every day and get a pack or two of smokes or rolling tobacco and a couple bottles of beer and a sandwich or something for Mom, then sit on that porch and watch the world go by. I had medicine, too, but I didn't take it much. I'd forget."

Christ, whole paragraphs, pages of dialogue poured from him. His story. I felt awful, but I let him continue.

Just as Ted had said, his sister came to visit one day and saw the house a disaster, the mother a disaster, the brother a disaster. Things moved pretty fast after that. One day his mother was put in a nursing home and Guy entered rehab. He's never had another drink. His mother died a year later. And, after treatment, Silent Guy moved into the group home where he now lived. And five or six years later, just a few months previously, his mother's house had finally cleared probate and sold and he'd received a small inheritance.

"Don't worry. They say I can live where I am forever," he said, answering my unspoken question. "They divvy my money out so much a month. Not supposed to spend it on tobacco but I do. Don't have nothing else," he said, drawing in his upper lip to suck the coffee from his mustache.

Wisdom Man was far less cooperative when I found him in the library and invited him across the street for lunch at the Mexican place he favored. For each question I asked, there came a look of suspicion followed by an answer that was not an answer. It went like this:

"So, where did you go to college?"

"Oh, one of those institutions of higher learning where the higher you go the less you learn."

"East Coast?"

"East of here."

"And the job you got when you came out here," I asked, taking another tack, "it was in Silicon Valley?"

"Synthetic Valley, yes. Silicon too. The eighth most common element in the universe. By mass I mean."

"Where'd you work?"

"I labored in the protective shells of the microscopic diatoms."

"You've lost me."

"That's the point," he said.

"I've written this book, you know. You're in it."

"So you say, but is it really me or a construct of me?"

"Well, I write about your Wisdom School and your thesis on the gender of the seed ..."

"Neither one of which, I trust, you fully understand."

"That's the point," I said.

We ate our burritos. There was none of the warmth that I thought had been between us there on the corner of Page and Laguna.

"Are you upset with me for writing about you?"

"You haven't written about me," he said. "You have created a non-existent reality, a fusion of cyberspace and New Age gnosis."

"So you're upset that I've written this book with our morning dialogues in it?"

"Upset? Of course not. I'm honored, thrilled. But don't for a minute delude yourself into thinking that it is actually me you've captured in your paragraphs. It's just a paradigm of me."

"Well, you're one of the most interesting paradigms I've encountered in this life," I said.

"That has always been the point," he said, and smiled. Finally.

Shit, I would miss those mornings together, I thought again as we finished our meal.

"I wanted your story," I said, "but you won't give it to me."

"Of course not," Wisdom Man said. "What did you say you called me in the book? Wisdom Man? I'm too wise to give my story away. The greatest wisdom is of course *docta ignorantia*, that is recognizing the wisdom of knowing none of us knows a thing."

"Our coffee shop has closed," I said. "They've turned it into a fancy samovar."

"According to the Gnostic viewpoint, resurrection is the transition to a new beginning."

"And you?"

"I'm always transitioning. That's the human condition. Don't worry about me."

"I can't help it."

"A sphere is a circumference whose center is everywhere. I need no worry on my behalf. "

And with that, he returned to the library stacks.

My efforts to find Robin finally paid off. He was living in the North Bay, a man quieted by new and unimaginable loss, one only those of us who have lost a child can begin to understand. No one knows the depth of another's misery. A year after Robin had moved from our building, his younger daughter, Acacia, the girl who rescued abandoned kittens and orphaned fish as generously as she offered love and shelter to fellow wanderers, was found dead in a bath tub in an apartment Robin had helped her rent with the proceeds from selling his night club. In conversation after conversation, he worried how I would present her in the book I was writing.

"She was a sweet girl," he said, telling me again the story of Home Again, how Acacia had sung to the gay men in the hospice as they were dying of unspeakable cancers, men she'd grown up knowing during her weekends and summers visiting her father. What was I to do? Take back the story of the bull dykes who skulked after her, of the blotches of black paint left behind when she vacated her father's apartment? I had no desire to add to his misery. Maybe she'd seen too much death, he said, in one conversation; in another, he said how ironic it was that he got to hold the hands of so many friends who'd passed through his life, comforted them in their last days, yet his own daughter had died alone with no hand to hold. I wished for a minute that we were both back there on Octavia, Robin and I, and that there were time to stop whatever moments of fate and choice and happenstance would lead to this young woman's death, that Mister Tambourine Man could take her and Robin far from the twisted reach of crazy sorrow.

A long-handled shovel is a wonderful tool – spade, fulcrum, scoop, hammer, vice. I needed all its virtues as I spent the months back from San Francisco rehabilitating a corner of my Vermont yard that had been used as a communal dump long before I bought the property. I'd begun the project years previously and returned to it each spring upon my arrival in Vermont, exhuming what others had deposited there while my brain unearthed its own rubble, seeking to understand all that had transpired in the preceding months, in this case the move to Noe Valley, the transformation of the Laguna Sidewalk Café into a Zen tea house, the presidential primaries, the crash of the housing market, Wisdom Man's homelessness, Acacia's death. Life is so full of tragedy. It could demolish a person. I did not want to be demolished.

Ann had been right; I had not needed to move. The economy had put an end to Jul's TIC plans within a few months of my move. He rented my old apartment to three young women, converting my former living room into the third bedroom and jacking up the rent.

As I dug up the rusty remains of an ancient lawnmower, a bicycle, a stove pipe, dozens of brown beer bottles, clearing them out so I could make yet another garden, I had to admit Jul had been right: I was happy in Noe Valley. I had a new coffee shop, Bernie's, run by an independent woman who welcomed me as a regular within a few weeks of my arrival in the neighborhood. The coffee shop provided other interesting reprobates to hang out with. At Bernie's, it was old men, radicals of varying stripes from Trotskyites to Sandinistas, who provided morning entertainment. Together, we had spent the winter and spring agonizing over the Democrat's primary season, months and months after the Republicans had picked John McCain. Sarah Palin gave us great pleasure with her flawed geography, her twisted history. I was addicted to the news as never before, following the machinations of the electoral game as only an addict can. I missed my morning conversations with Ted and Wisdom Man and Jay and often wondered what riffs they would have come up with to satirize her broken sentences, her fragmented syntax. But I liked not stepping over bodies. I liked having a garden out back and a deck off my sunroom where I could sit at night and watch the stars and clouds stream by.

Finally, the agony of the primary season ended. America would pick the aged white warrior or the young community organizer who happened to be half African. Of course I was obsessed. I hoped Obama was for real. I hung on every word, hearing reason where there had been irrationality. But that hope I had, it was a fragile, almost desperate hope.

And so I dug, thrusting the spade into the soil, fitting it against boulder after boulder, prodding, putting my weight upon the tool, my hands deep into the earth and leaf mould, working out stones then digging deeper, unearthing glass and tin and more glass and tin. I dug. I exposed barbed wire, a washing machine hose, a burn barrel, a boot, a fork, a broken shovel. This was a scavenger's paradise, a place where someone like Jay or Stretch could find his fortune. People left their discards wherever they lived, whether on the streets of San Francisco or in this backyard dump. We would learn from our past or we would not. Susan, the Susan who had been a little in love with Mister Tambourine Man, took chunks of it away where they reappeared in her garden and her art, short stories told on black cloth from bits of metal and wood and road litter, a different form of art by distraction.

When I came upon an item too heavy to move, I nudged and jabbed, shoveled and tunneled. The thing was metal, oblong, unbudging. Finally, Chuck came to my rescue and together we pried and dug some more. That dump had contained everything *and* the kitchen sink. It took three days to grub it out. It had been deposited upside down, its high backsplash wedged amongst rocks and other debris. Disinterred, it got a second life as herb garden.

Digging is like walking. It's an exercise that provides the brain the opportunity to do its own burrowing. All the while, I thrust the shovel deep into the earth and turned over the loam of my brain. I found, lying fallow among the junk, this booty: I was my own Mister Tambourine Man, chasing answers to questions we'll be asking for the rest of time. I attended the Wisdom School all those months and years. It had met at the corner of Laguna and Page. My fellow students were Jay and Ted and Tom and Silent Guy. Wisdom Man had been our guide. The thoughts and ideas had bounced from the mauve house where he once lived to the Zen Center to the window overlooking our sidewalk classroom. There, amongst friends I would never have known had I not attached the Angela Davis pin to my backpack on the way to the airport all those years ago, had I not stepped into that small café in the Castro before looking at the apartment on Octavia, had I never met and argued with a stranger named Jul, my education in San Francisco would have been far less enlightening, my journey less magical. It would continue in the fall when I returned, new chapters unfolding on other streets. The struggle between progressive politics and super-capitalism, between the haves and the have-nots, between the old world and the new, whatever it would be, would continue.

In October, I would help Alexandra carve her Halloween pumpkin. Ann and Alexandra were family forever, whether we lived in the same building or not. Gordon would be our private prince, rescuing us from dead batteries and lost keys, from crises small and large, whether I lived on Octavia Boulevard or across the city in a neighborhood where I rarely saw a homeless person. I did not know if I would see Stretch again, but I hoped I would.

And in November, Jul and I and everyone else in America would find out how much gender and race mattered in America. I was hoping Jul was right and I was wrong, that hard work and determination would win the day. I was hoping, also, not to be fooled again, but it was a slim and fragile hope.

Postscript

Jul has a private club now. He installed it on the top floor of his home in the Outer Mission. The lounge has a beautiful bar that, of course, he built himself. His collection of art deco lamps shine above. He's studying the bartending trade. He throws soirees to which he invites people he met at Burning Man, or on the Internet. One month it might be a gathering to celebrate a local DJ; another, a performance by local classical music students. He invited some of these acquaintances and some of the major characters from this book for an early reading. Everyone knew I was describing Jul in the opening chapter. Ann and Liya laughed when I read about Gordon and his chlorine-bleached undies. Leif wanted to edit his chapter; he didn't like the word "channeling." Jul supplied me with several hundred pages of "clarifications." I told them to write their own stories; this was mine.

After the election, I took Obama on his challenge, put my action where my anguish was and began doing volunteer work with the homeless. I served up food at a homeless shelter. I helped the homeless write for their free newspaper, the Street Sheet. And I signed up to count homeless people during the next homeless count, the census that determines each city's share of federal funding for homeless care and housing. On Jan. 27, 2009, volunteers from around the country in many major cities took to the streets to count the number of people living on the streets, in cars, encampments, boxes and shelters. More than four hundred people had volunteered in San Francisco. After a brief training, my team tramped up and down a less-than-ten-block slice of the city that from one street to another encapsulated some of San Francisco's most opulent hotels and restaurants, smart boutiques and art galleries, and also its sleaziest single-residence hotels, humble ethnic restaurants, and darkened, crumbling buildings covered with graffiti.

We didn't know whether to count the black transvestite who hassled the throngs of fancy people on their way to dinner or the theater. Our instructions had been vague. We weren't to ask anyone if he or she were homeless; we had to decide for ourselves. Sometimes it was obvious, possessions stuffed inside a plastic bag, a shelter created in an alcove of a Muni station. Sometimes, as with the transvestite, how did you know? She looked destitute, emaciated, ill, but she was moving through the crowd, trolling the street, not hunkered down in a doorway or lugging a battered suitcase.

A block further, an even thinner woman, skeletal really, no teeth, hair a clump of snarl, clutched a thin black coat around her caved-in frame as she begged money for dinner. "I'm starving," she repeated plaintively as people rushed by. "Please," she said again. "Starving."

In less than two hours spent canvassing eight blocks, we counted eighty-two homeless people or people we thought were homeless. We found them huddled in small groups, shivering in wheelchairs, passed out on the sidewalk, wrapped in blankets, selling dumpster trash, pawing through trash barrels, singing, playing the saxophone and stuffed into a sleeping bag. Again and again, we saw the transvestite. Two businessmen engaged in conversation as they smoked outside Kuleto's, an upscale Italian restaurant in wood and glass where the wine flows generously and the veal chop costs $37, ignored her. "All I need is four quarters. I've got the dollar," she said, over and over, a pitiful mantra.

Where I had lived on Octavia, most of the homeless were white; here, they were eight-to-one black and their appearance and health were so markedly worse than the homeless I'd encountered daily in my Octavia neighborhood that I thought several might be dying, especially the toothless woman pleading for food money.

Later, after we'd turned in our report to the city officials, our group silenced by the weight of what we'd witnessed, I headed back to Market Street. I retraced my steps past the upscale Hilton San Francisco with its ornate lobby outfitted with two-ton chandeliers, penthouse suites and its rooftop Starlight Lounge with a million-dollar view of San Francisco. Chauffeurs deposited guests or their expensive luggage and purchases into limousines with darkened windows. People hovered on the sidewalk, wrapped in long wool coats, in furs, against the frigid night air. "Such a gracious city," one woman said as a doorman helped her with her packages. All the while, the wraiths of the neighborhood cruised for soft sells, anyone with a handful of change.

I was watching all this when I heard a man in a handsome leather jacket over smart trousers tell his equally well-dressed companion that he was going to Killington the following week. Killington is a ski area located near my Vermont home. In response to my question about his connection to Killington, the man said he'd "just purchased a get-away home there, deep in the woods. A four-bedroom cottage in the mountains." He was talking to me but looking at the woman, using his cabin in Vermont and the money he was about to spend on her in the chic cocktail lounge they were about to enter as enticements.

As if on cue, the skinny woman with no teeth hobbled our way. "Please," she said, still clutching her stomach, "Please, can't you spare something? I'm awful hungry." The man with a second home in Killington and his companion gave her a look of scorn as they ducked into a cocktail lounge packed with spenders.

And later, on the J-train home, I let my eyes explore the body of the woman sitting next to me on the Muni. She was big. She smelled of drink. Her face and hands, the only parts of her body not swathed in clothing, were covered in sores. She cleaned her filthy fingernails with a Swiss Army knife and juggled an avocado. She got off at my stop and headed in the opposite direction. I started to follow, to see where in upscale Noe Valley she would bed down for the night. If I'd passed her during the official homeless count, she would have earned a checkmark. I was hungry, tired. My own rooms, filled with the things that give comfort – books, food, plants, music, art, Daniel – awaited. And so I turned back toward home when she crossed 24th Street, headed downhill and ducked into a little grove of trees where perhaps tomorrow or the next day I might begin to hear her story.

A Thousand Kisses Deep

I cannot thank my husband, Chuck Clarino, enough for his patience and support as I wrote and rewrote this tale, for our years now, the steps we've walked together, books read, love made, support unending, a thousand kisses deep. Nor Deb Thompson, who line edited the text when the book was several hundred pages longer. Deb saved me from many embarrassments, and, thanks to her, copious uses of the word fabulous have been excised from this book. I am grateful to and for Angela Hart, my wonderful former student, gifted beyond compare, diligent, quirky, smart; she read the book again and again, asked questions I would never have thought of, brought a fresh young eye to the text. Tom and Jackie Lueder, thank you so much for your careful reading and your enthusiasm about this book. A special thank-you to Debbi Wraga at Northshire Bookstore, whose support, professionalism and patience went far beyond my expectations. I am also grateful to and for Rebecca Kmiec, who designed the front cover, understood what it was I was trying to do with this book, and helped in so many ways from publicity to commiseration. I remain indebted to the members of my various writing groups, especially Jo Keroes, Beverly Voloshin, Ellen Peel, Judy Breen and Elise Wormuth, who encouraged me to put myself in this tale, and the attendees at the Green Mountain Writers Conference, you know who you are, those of you who have heard version after version of some chapters, who helped me to shape this story. And of course, thank you Jul for being just who you are, so engaging, so contrary. Couldn't have done it without you.

In her first weeks in San Francisco, YVONNE DALEY found herself walking around with her mouth open and her mind near blown. Every day in her inner-city neighborhood presented new dramas and conundrums -- comedies, tragedies, genius and absurdities unfolding on the sidewalk, in her apartment building, the café and classroom, the concert hall and along the protest route. After spending most of her adult life in Vermont and despite having written extensively for some of the nation's leading publications, Daley sometimes felt as if she'd parachuted into a foreign land, at times magical and inspiring; at other times pitiful and heartbreaking. Here in *Octavia Boulevard*, we not only get a record of life in an iconic American city at a crucial time in history, but also commentary on deinstitutionalization, the clash between progressive politics and capitalism, the non-nuclear family, drugs, sex and marriage, the bicoastal life, the counterculture and, best of all, love and friendship.

Yvonne Daley lives in Rutland, Vermont, where she is director of the Green Mountain Writers Conference, and San Francisco, where she is a professor of Journalism at San Francisco State University.